IN PERIL

First published in the UK in 1990 by
Spellmount Ltd, Publishers
12 Dene Way, Speldhurst
Tunbridge Wells, Kent TN3 0NX
ISBN 0-946771-51-0

©Robert Hughes 1990

British Library Cataloguing in Publication Data
Hughes, Robert
  In perilous seas. – (Into battle series)
  1.   World War 2.   Naval operations by Great Britain.
  Royal Navy – Biographies
  I.   Title   II.   Series
  940.54'5941'0924

ISBN 0-946771-51-0

Typesetting by Vitaset, Paddock Wood, Kent
Printed in Great Britain by The Ipswich Book Co Ltd
Ipswich, Suffolk

IN PERILOUS SEAS

'Here is my journey's end, here is my butt
And very sea-mark of my utmost sail'

(Othello Act V Sc ii)

Robert Hughes

SPELLMOUNT LTD
Tunbridge Wells

In the Spellmount Military list:

The Territorial Battalions – A pictorial history
The Yeomanry Regiments – A pictorial history
Over the Rhine – The Last Days of War in Europe
History of the Cambridge University OTC
Yeoman Service
The Fighting Troops of the Austro-Hungarian Army
Intelligence Officer in the Peninsula
The Scottish Regiments – A pictorial history
The Royal Marines – A pictorial history
The Royal Tank Regiment – A pictorial history
The Irish Regiments – A pictorial history
British Sieges of the Peninsular War
Victoria's Victories
Heaven and Hell – German paratroop war diary
Rorke's Drift
Came the Dawn – Fifty years an Army Officer
Kitchener's Army – A pictorial history
On the Word of Command – a pictorial history of the Regimental Sergeant Major
Marlborough – As Military Commander
The Fall of France

In the Military Machine list:

Napoleon's Military Machine
Falklands Military Machine
Wellington's Military Machine

In the Nautical list:

Sea of Memories
Evolution of Engineering in the Royal Navy Vol I 1827-1939
In Perilous Seas

In the Aviation list:

Diary of a Bomb Aimer
Operation 'Bograt' – From France to Burma
A Medal for Life – Capt Leefe Robinson VC

CONTENTS

1 The desperate years

The West Country express sighed to a stop one October evening in 1940 and exhausted a pent-up gout of steam high up into the girdered roof of Lime Street Station, Liverpool. The sailor, who had been my mentor on matters naval during the journey, swung open the carriage door and leapt lightly on to the platform. I followed him in my civilian clothes with my small suitcase and breathed the standard air of all major railway termini of those days – a mixture of coal-gas, exhaust steam, rotting fish and human sweat.

He jerked his head towards the exit and we joined the crowd of servicemen, predominantly sailors, and civilians streaming outwards past the lantern-jawed chin-strapped and belted Naval patrol, gazing balefully at anything in navy blue. The sailor grimaced at me and urged me outside into the black-out.

Almost immediately there was a blue flash, as the conductor arm of a passing tram missed contact with the overhead wire. I winced involuntarily, thinking of bombs, for even then Liverpool had been bombed quite frequently. The sailor laughed.

'It's not a bomb mate, anyway not yet! Too early in the evening for a raid!' He pointed to the huge stone lions guarding St George's Hall. 'The lions of Lime Street! They're supposed to roar when a virgin goes past, but the buggers haven't said "Meeow" yet!' He snickered, 'Come on, let's find some Big Eats!'

Down stone-setted streets and past huge stores we swung in the darkness until we stopped before a blacked-out entrance made of plywood bearing the words, Services Club. Inside there was a hubbub of shouting, masticating jaws, clatter of cutlery and ringing of crockery as a mass of servicemen, again mostly sailors, got down to the mysterious ritual of Big Eats. The sailor pushed his way into the crowd at the food counter and I followed shyly, conscious of my brown Harris tweed jacket, but clutching my call-up papers in my hand as proof of my bona-fides, to receive a meal at a Services Club.

From behind the ladies officiating at the counter, huge fried eggs ogled us oilily from ranks of frying pans and sausages rudely extruded their contents with self-satisfied plops, while chips spattered spitefully in their baths. We each grabbed a plateful of these delicacies, then fought our way to vacant seats, tripping over gas mask straps, surmounting kitbags, ditty boxes and the ubiquitous green canvas and leather-cornered naval suitcases, muttering the appropriate apologies, as a head collided with a forkful of fried egg at the wrong moment. We got down to Big Eats, and the sailor gave me directions as to how to reach Gladstone House, the Toc H Mark in Rodney Street where I had arranged to spend the night before the fateful morrow when I joined the Royal Navy at *HMS Wellesley*, at a mysterious address given in my papers as Caryl Street, Liverpool 8.

The meal ended, we took leave of each other, he to his destroyer in the Gladstone Dock, and I to a new future, but more confident now that I had experienced even a little taste of the comradeship of the sea. The streets and buildings loomed in the black-out – Renshaw, Adelphi, Shaftesbury and then the shadowy Georgian of Rodney Street, the Harley Street of Liverpool, the brass plates of the consultants and specialists gleaming faintly in the black-out. Then came a brass plate with a touch of the sea – Moss Hutchinson Line – whose ships I had seen in my home seaport town of Port Talbot in South Wales.

Soon came the bulk of the steps of Gladstone House, the former Liverpool city house of William Ewart Gladstone, Prime Minister of Great Britain. I climbed them with reverence and made my way inside. A sailor crossing the hall stopped in mid-stride, smiled, and asked if he could help. He ushered me into a large lounge, each easy chair occupied by sailors, either reading or chatting in unmistakeably cultured voices. They all wore gold badges of the crossed flags of the naval visual signallers or the winged lightning of radio operators, with the addition of the gold initials of the Royal Naval Volunteer Reserve or the Royal Naval Volunteer Wireless Reserves. This combination became an extreme rarity as the war progressed when everyone was a conscript.

I could see that I was in the company of an élite, and the scraps of conversation confirmed this.

'What sort of ship did you get last convoy?' enquired a voice.

'Very swish indeed,' came the reply, in a public school accent from the leather depths of a chair. 'Norwegian cargo liner – Wilhelmsen Line – all mod cons and a cabin of my own!'

'What's old Admiral X like as a Commodore?' asked someone else, 'I hear he's a decent old buffer?'

'I hear old Smithy's ship copped it on a Sierra Leone convoy and they had to pay her off on the breast stroke!' laughed another chair. By this time the first sailor had joined me and volunteered a laughing explanation of some of the conversation.

'He means that they all had to swim for it! You see we're all on the staffs of various Convoy Commodores who are retired Admirals and whatnot

8

and we always embark on one of the best ships in the convoy, and do all the signalling, radio work, coding and decoding etc. We have all just arrived with convoys from America, Gibraltar, Sierra Leone, and we always put up here while awaiting the next convoy job. It's a good place.'

'I'm supposed to be joining the Navy as a Coder,' I volunteered meekly, in the face of all this expertise and experience.

'Never heard of such a rating!' He raised his voice to address the chairs, 'Chap here says he's joining the Andrew as a Coder. Anyone know anything about such bods?' There were grunts of incredulity and I had a feeling that I might as well take the next train back to Somerset.

'Might come in useful and take some of the work off our hands' said a judicial voice. 'Anyway, isn't it about time we went downstairs and made a bit of toast?'

So we descended to the spotless kitchen to begin a routine I came to love in my many visits to this place – the surreptitious making of toast under the huge burnished steel covers of the Aga cooker hotplates. After a short tour of the building to visit the dining room with its oak refectory tables, the Chavasse room with its grand piano on which I played for a few minutes when alone, I made my way to the dormitories and turned in.

Before I fell asleep, a ship's siren gave a lonely moan far down in the city, as she nosed her way out of one of the docks and into the Mersey. For some reason the name Ellerman Papayanni came into my mind, the name of a shipping line I had read long long ago in some shipping journal, and other Liverpool shipping lines floated through my mind – Brocklebank, Blue Funnel, Blue Star, Royal Mail, Cunard, White Star, Larrinaga and Canadian Pacific. Drowsily, I realised that by this time tomorrow, I would no longer be Robert Hughes, assistant master at a school in Taunton, but Robert Hughes, Ordinary Coder, Royal Navy, D/JX229673. The siren moaned and I must have fallen asleep for when I awoke daylight was filtering through the black-out curtains.

The next morning, suitcase in hand, I wandered through Liverpool's vast dockland, searching for *HMS Wellesley*. Bland Chinese smiled apologetically and shook their heads to my enquiries, white teeth flashed in dark faces and shoulders shrugged in regret. Slatternly women taunted my expensive clothes until I finally had my route pointed out by a pinch-faced, mufflered dock labourer outside a building which announced itself as the area clinic for the treatment of venereal disease.

'It's the old Royal Southern Hospital you want, wack!' he said, and pointed out streets and turnings. Smoke drifted in the upper air, and there was a strange smell of damp, burning porridge which my guide informed me came from a grain warehouse still burning after the last air-raid. The Royal Southern Hospital was a huge Victorian square building with towers at each of its four corners. Between two of the towers a White

Ensign fluttered and there were sentry boxes manned by tough-looking sailors around the walls. From the balcony of the very modern block of council flats opposite a raucous female voice bellowed at my hesitation in entering the door.

'Get in there, wack, and get them bloody bell-bottomed trousers on!' This sally was greeted by a sycophantic cackle from the other harpies leaning over the balcony, and as I fled through the door, I heard one of the sentries bawl, 'Why, for Christ's sake, don't you silly bitches shurrup and get some work done!' I heaved a sigh, and put behind me for the duration the polite conventions of school and college, and offered myself up to an indoctrination into a new way of life.

Once inside there was a baffling routine of signatures, forms and directions, during which time I went from office to office, along spotless corridors, standing aside to allow passage for hurrying squads of sailors, all bent on some mysterious task, and savouring from huge steaming cauldrons in the kitchens, the aromas of meals to come. Finally, I was shown into a large canteen filled with bewildered men in civilian clothes, drinking cups of tea and chewing at tough looking buns or smoking.

I got into conversation with a bespectacled man from Grimsby who must have been in the Navy half an hour longer than I had, but had profitted by the experience and seemed a mine of information. He told me that most of the Coders were being recruited from former white-collar workers, hence the studious expressions and spectacles; that *Wellesley* had only just been established in this building, having moved from some country house in Gloucestershire; that the place had formerly been used to train gunners for merchant ships; and that finally some petty officer was coming to put us into the picture soon!

Sure enough, there was an immense bellow, matured over the years on many a parade ground, and an elderly, sturdy petty officer mounted a platform. To my innocent eye, he was like a god, a god in clean, pressed blue serge, gaitered and glittering with gold badges, the crossed guns of a gunner's mate and the chevrons and anchors of a long-serving petty-officer. His white collar and shirt were immaculate and his tie knot a sartorial gem. However, he looked rather old to me, because some grey was visible under his severely-angled peaked cap.

'Pay attention!' he ordered, and like vestal virgin sailors we listened to the Oracle. 'You're all here now, and from now on you are members of Rupert Class and I'm your Petty Officer.' I was not impressed with our new name, which reminded me of Rupert the Bear in the *Daily Express*, but I continued to attend to the Oracle. 'You'll all call me Sir while you're here, right?' He paused for our reply. 'Well, comealongthen, comealong then,' he cajoled, running the words together, but accentuating the last one on a rising note. 'Whatja call me, comealongthen?'

'Sir!' we bellowed in unison, our first disciplinary lesson learnt.

'I'm a Petty Officer, see!' he grated, pointing to his golden sleeve, 'and this here crossed guns badge means that I'm a Gunner's Mate, the most feared and respected rate in the whole Navy, right?'

'Yessir!' we chorussed.

'See this cap badge?' he enquired, pointing. 'Foul anchor they calls it and that's a POs badge. Now a Chief Petty officer see, he's a little different; he's got a badge like this but there's all little tea leaves round it, like. He doesn't wear his rate badges on his sleeves like me, he wears 'em on his coat lapels. You wait until you see your Chief Petty Officer Telegraphist, who's going to tell you all about this here coding stuff, then you'll notice the difference. Besides, he's got three gold anchor buttons on each sleeve as well. Midshipmen or snotties used to wear them three buttons years ago to stop the snivelling little bastards wiping their snotty noses on their lovely doeskin sleeves. But now Chiefs have 'em. Get me, then?' We got him, and he continued.

'Now, to get on with this rank stuff, this here matloe at my right is a Leading Seaman.' A wizened little monkey of a man with grizzled hair, humourous eyes and a mouth twitching to repress a smile, joined him on the platform. His sailor cap sat straight on his head, slightly tilted forward, his uniform was tailored to fit tightly, his bell-bottomed trousers were neatly creased latitudinally like an opened concertina. His silk scarf framed the V-shape of his jumper, flat and neat, and the tapes which secured it tied in a neat bow, the ends hanging below the regulation length and fashionably cut into graceful swallow tails. His collar clung tightly to his jumper, washed and ironed to a pale uniform blue. The PO pointed to the anchor on his right arm.

'This here's the badge of a Leading Seaman, one rank below me and still a hell of a way above you lot. You are now Ordinary Coders, same as Ordinary Seamen, and you'll stay like that for nine months, providing you pass your examinations. In fact, you lot are the lowest form of naval life in the Communications Department of His Majesty's Navy! Get me?' We got him.

'Yessir!' we snapped.

'Now on his sleeve this Leading Seaman has got three stripes, which means at least 22 years of service in the Royal Navy.' His face softened. 'Some calls it 22 years of undetected crime, don't they Leading Seaman?' He grinned and we smiled politely but with restraint.

'There are some that calls Leading Seamen such names as Hookey, and if they have Long Service and Good Conduct stripes, they calls them Stripey, but if there are any stroppy young bastards among you that gets familiar-like with my friend here and calls him Stripey or Hookey, his bloody feet won't touch the ground while I doubles him to the Quarter

Deck in front of the Officer of the Watch. Because . . . ' and he paused dramatically, 'You lot are the lowest form of life on the Lower Deck, right?' We dutifully agreed with him in full voice.

'With regard to officers . . . ' he became pontifical. 'The Commanding Officer here is a Commander with three gold rings on his sleeve and on the peak of his cap he has golden leaves, commonly called scrambled egg. Then there's Lieutenant- Commanders with two and a half gold rings, Lieutenants with two, Sub-Lieutenants with one, Warrant Officers with one very thin one, and Midshipmen have white patches on their coat lapels. Them lot are like you, the lowest form of officer life in the Navy.

'Officers have straight stripes if they're Active Service or full time; wavy stripes if they come from the Royal Naval Volunteer Reserve, Rockies or Wavy Navy we sometimes call them, and lastly those with sort of interlaced bands like rope: they come from the Merchant Navy, the big shipping lines and they belong to the Royal Naval Reserve.' He paused and waxed confidential. 'The officers have a saying: The RNVR are gentlemen but not sailors, the RNR are sailors but not gentlemen, and the RN are neither sailors nor gentlemen!' He grinned momentarily but reminiscently, and continued in a bellow, 'But whatever they are, whatever has gold on it, you salute it from now on, right?'

We acknowledged the rightness of his instructions, and he cleared his throat.

'Now, me and my colleague, the Leading Seaman here, will teach you all about your uniforms, the customs of the Navy and how to tie a few knots to save your bleeding lives. We'll see if you can swim, teach you to pack your hammock, to sling it, and many other things, but above all we'll teach you a bit of discipline with marching and rifle drill on our little parade ground.' He paused to relish these grim prospects for us, and cocked an ear as if to listen to some heavenly voice. As if at a pre-arranged signal, there was a hum of static from some hidden loudspeaker and a piercing whistle assailed us, followed by a nasal voice in a sing-song cadence.

'D'ye hear that?' it said. 'D'ye hear that? Rupert Class muster at the Clothing Store! Rupert Class muster at the Clothing Store!' The PO galvanised into action.

'Let's get fell in then!' He pointed to a tall thin man in spectacles, 'You there, Lofty, that long string of frozen piss standing over there by the counter. Come and stand here!' Lofty obeyed and sprang to the indicated spot. 'Now you, Tiny!' He pointed to a gangling six-foot youth. 'Get fell in behind him.' Tiny shuffled to Lofty's side. 'Not there, you stupid matloe! Get behind Lofty's arse, but don't take any liberties with the poor bastard. Now you other matloes, get fell in on their right in two open files!' There was a mad scramble, above which the POs voice rose in an anguished moan. 'Don't you know what a bleeding file is?'

'A tool or a piece of office equipment,' I murmured to my neighbour and smiled. I found myself confronted by the ruddy face of the Petty Officer.

'You seem pleased with yourself, young feller,' he said. 'You enjoying yourself?'

'Yes, sir!' I answered politely. 'I find it most interesting.'

'Cor,' said the PO. 'We're getting some queer types in the Navy. He actually enjoys this!' He gave a fleeting smile and resumed his task. 'Now then, right turn's towards the door, left turn's towards the counter, and there's no more tea, so right turn it's going to be. Rupert Class, right turn!' We executed this manoeuvre to his satisfaction. 'Now you've all played soldiers, so when I says quick march, you steps out with your left foot and away we go. Rupert Class, by the right, quick march!'

Down corridors and down stairs we shambled with a Hip Har, Hip Har, rhythmically snarled out by the PO and interlarded with injunctions to swing those sanguinary arms, and have a bit of pride in ourselves. We entered a large warehouse, ringed with counters, backed by the shelves of some giant outfitter who only dealt in articles of navy blue, and came to a shuddering, colliding halt.

'Christ!' moaned the PO with real feeling, and then went into a long harangue about the issue of uniform. Out of chaos order emerged and in no time we found ourselves with a kitbag full of mysterious garments and a wooden type-face bearing our names which had been miraculously prepared for us. Bearing this arm-tearing load we repaired to the dormitory which had been assigned to us, dumping the lot on the first cot we could see. I was fortunate in securing the lower of the two in my part of the room, and I sank down exhausted on the unyielding springs of the bed. At least it seemed we would not sleep in hammocks yet! My partner on one side turned out to be an accountant, very sleek and smart in a well-cut Glen Urquhart check suit.

'Get out of those civvies, pack 'em in your own suitcases or whatever you've got, address the luggage label you'll find on your bed to your home address, tie it on the case, and say goodbye to those civvies for the duration. Come along then, chop, chop! Get into your uniforms and let's see what pusser matloes we've got! Pusser means smart, boys, so come along then, chop, chop!' Exhausted with his efforts he sank down on a bed next to the Leading Seaman and awaited developments.

'What do you think of this lot?' asked the accountant, struggling into his bell-bottoms. 'The language is fearsome, isn't it?'

'Bits of French, Chinese, original Anglo-Saxon, and the profanity is amazing,' I answered, beginning to itch all over at the roughness of the blue woollen jersey.

'Come here, shortarse!' ordered the PO, pointing to a studious youth, toying with the tapes of a blue and white navy collar, 'And I'll show you how to put that on. Gather round, and what's left over go with the Leading Seaman.' His hands moved swiftly, threading and tying, and he talked as he worked. 'Funny uniform this, but very tiddley – that means smart, see. Supposed to have been introduced by William the Fourth, the Sailor King, so the story goes. He saw this wench riding in the park in London Town, with a little saucy hat and a blue jumper with an open neck and a fancy striped collar. Just right for my matloes, says the king, and so he gets his jewing firm, that's to say his tailoring firm, to make this uniform and so it gets adopted all over the Navy, see? Up till then, each Admiral dressed his sailors according to his fancy, and very smart some of them were, and very sloppy were some others, too. They'd always had bell-bottom pants, of course, because they're easy to roll up when you're scrubbing decks. I'll show you how to fold them some time, to get those concertina creases in 'em.'

We struggled, threaded and tied, and then came the claustrophobic donning of the skin tight jumper. I was imprisoned in navy blue serge, tugging, pulling and almost panting, when two strong hands gripped hold of the bottom of the jumper and tugged with such force that my knees bent and my head popped out into full daylight, to be confronted by the PO's grinning face.

'D'ye find that most interesting?' he asked with a sly wink and grin.

The morning flew by as we learned how to fold the black silk square and secure it with the tapes the regulation two fingers below the knot. The Leading Seaman's scissors darted continually as he cut us tiddley swallow tails, while the PO sat on a bed as we admired the way he fitted the black cap ties with the gold letters *HMS Wellesley* around the caps. For one lucky new entrant he skilfully inserted a silver threepenny piece in the finished bow, and embellished it with swallow tails. This art I determined to master at the earliest, for I had, by now, vowed to become a real 'Tiddley Matloe', with the addition of a navy blue raincoat and kid gloves which seemed 'de rigeur' with the real sailors I'd seen around.

Dinner came and went and we drew hammocks and bedding, while the PO, to our immense admiration, plaited the nettles or cords which fanned out from the hammocks, into a tight little triangle of what seemed like crochet work, and finished off the large slinging rope or clew, with a tight back splice. We learned to lash the hammocks into all sorts of queerly shaped sausages of canvas, using our first hitch, the Marlin hitch, to accomplish the task. We tried to sling hammocks with single or double sheet bends, and sprawled on the floor, or deck as we now had to call it, when our bends turned into ineffective slip knots. My short period with the Scouts stood me in good stead, along with a seaside upbringing, and I

14

.weathered the test, though I learned abiding wisdom from the PO.

'You looks at a knot or a bend or an 'itch and you works out what jams what, see, and if nothing jams, you ain't got a knot nor a splice nor an 'itch. All you got is a snowball 'itch which melts away and lands you on your fat arse in the 'oggin, which is what we calls the sea, or on the deck, which is what you lot used to call the floor, see?' I saw, if nobody else did.

After tea we began the messy business of marking all our clothes in specified places in white paint with the type with which we had been provided. Then came supper, after which I lay on my cot and opened the book we had been given – BR67 *Manual of Seamanship, 1937, Volume One*. Not for Sale. From that moment a new profession began for me – the craft of the sailor. I had always wanted to be a sailor and this was my chance. The fact that we were at war at that moment, was superfluous. In a few short hours the Royal Navy had captured and enthralled me, and in a way I had achieved one of the sea-marks of my life. There would be many to come. Lost in a dream of tar and traditions, of sunny places and stormy seas, I was not aware that the PO had entered the dormitory.

'Rounds will be in ten minutes, so tidy up your beds, stow away any rubbish. When you hear the bugle, stand up to attention wherever you are and wait until the officer goes past. The bugle call is called the Alert, and then after the officer has passed, it will sound another call – the Carry On. Then you can stand at ease. So wait for it.'

We scurried around the beds, tidying up here and there, then came the martial tramp of feet and a bugle blared an insistent, arrogant call. Into the room marched the bugler, followed by a tall, elegant RNVR Lieutenant and a Petty Officer. We stood transfixed as ordered and the little cavalcade strode past and entered the toilets at the far end of the room. They came out, the bugler grinning, the officer smiling broadly, and the PO with a face like thunder. Down the room they strode and as they left, the bugler sounded the relaxed call of Carry On, on a rising cadence. All eyes turned to the toilets, from which emerged McGowan, our wild Irishman.

'Begorrah,' he shouted. 'I goes in there for a quiet crap, nice and comfortable, when in comes this bloody bugler who nearly blows me off me seat, and then this officer man comes in and, remembering what the PO says, I stands up from me labours, stands to attention and me bloody bell-bottoms falls down!'

There was a roar of laughter and McGowan had established himself as the humourist of Rupert Class. Carter, the accountant, leaned across from his bed and remarked,

'Notice how our life here seems to be dictated by bugle calls, that boatswains' whistle, or call thing, and that raucous sailor's voice? What does it all mean? I'm tone deaf!' We chatted desultorily until the loudspeaker began to crackle, and then came a bugle call which I would

15

remember all my life, the haunting Sunset call of the Royal Navy. As the notes died away, the voice came on again, no longer raucous, but soothing, 'Pipe down! Pipe down!' it said. The bugle sounded again, two notes repeated twice, the second note long drawn and sweet.

'Lights out!' said the voice, and the dormitory was plunged in darkness, save for the dim blue pilot lights at intervals. I snuggled down in my rough blankets and composed myself for sleep.

I awoke with a start, to find the PO stamping up and down the dormitory banging on anything which would make a noise, resplendent this early in a snowy polo-necked sweater under his uniform jacket, and bawling out a ribald reveille.

'Come along then, come along then! Rise and sh-ine for the morneeing's fine. Pull up socks, hands off cocks!' I shook with laughter at this vulgar start to the day and alerted myself for more. 'Charley's waiting for you lot!' he intoned and immediately a bugle sounded and the PO began to sing to it.

'Charley, Charley, show a leg Charley; Charley, Charley, show a leg do. Chuck off those blankets, lash up your 'ammick; Lash up your 'ammick and stow it away. Charley, Charley, show a leg Charley; Charley, Charley, show a leg do!' The bugle faded. 'Come along then. Up you get you lazy matloes!' With one swift arm motion, to emphasise the point, he yanked at one bed and brought the tardy occupant, mattress, blankets and all crashing to the floor. He stamped his feet together in a gargantuan leap to attention, and 69 beds were vacated simultaneously.

The morning passed in a blur of bugle calls, parade ground drill and profanity, broken only by a break called Stand Easy, which gave time for a much-needed pipeful of tobacco and a swill of debilitated canteen tea, before we resumed our work.

'Up spirits!' said the disembodied voice from the tannoy.

'Stand fast the Holy Ghost!' roared the PO in the middle of his lecture on naval routine. 'That means rum ration for the Ship's Company, but not for you lot yet – you're too young for rum! Me little tot'll be waiting for me in the mess before dinner. Lovely!' He smacked his lips in anticipation and we gazed at him in envy. 'Petty Officers has it neat because we can be trusted, see. All below has it watered down to keep 'em sober – what they call a two-water tot! Now pay attention.'

After dinner we stood stripped to the waist in a long line outside the Sick Bay, clutching our loosened bell-bottoms, while the PO explained.

'This here routine is called a Short Arm Inspection and it is to find out whether any of you are lousy, or has such things as crabs and what not. When the doctor comes up to you, you lets go those bell-bottoms, to fall to the ground, and you throw up your arms, like Christ crucified, while the doc looks to see what you're blessed with! Got it?' We got it, but only vaguely. The doctor was coming up on my left, bell-bottoms were dropping and it was my turn, so I let go and threw my arms heavenward.

'Any complaints?' drawled the doctor with infinite boredom.

'Oh, no, Sir!' I replied, brightly. 'I like it in the Royal Navy.'

'What I mean, is,' said the doctor, pityingly, 'do you have anything wrong with you?'

'Oh, ambiguity!' I answered brightly, 'no, I'm quite fit, thank you, Sir!'

'Dear God,' he implored, 'what did you do in civilian life?'

'I'm a schoolmaster, Sir!'

'I should have known it! Ambiguity,' he muttered and passed on.

2 First command

A week passed and we grew wiser in the ways of the Navy each day. We could march and drill in fours, for the Navy still retained this older, though smarter form of drill. Each morning as we marched up the road outside, with the Royal Marine Band playing *The Midshipmaid*, four abreast, the two long lines that emerged from the fours, as the PO bawled, 'Rupert Class . . . Into Lines . . . Ri——ght Turn!' grew straighter and smarter with practice, and all heads snapped smartly to the right, as we passed the Commander, at the salute for Divisions. We could handle a rifle tolerably well in the drill and I had emerged as a bit of an expert at the field training or square-bashing, as I had had the advantage of having helped to form a Company of the Local Defence Volunteers, the early Home Guard, in Taunton the previous spring and summer, and knew most of the drill already.

Petty Officer Tucker, for now we knew his name, also fired my interest in gunnery, for as a former mathematician, the problems associated with it intrigued me. He took me under his wing, and christened me Doc, a name which stayed with me. Coding was another vaguely mathematical matter, and I entered into this with verve. Morse and semaphore did not come quite so easily to any of us and flags were worse, but with the aid of mnemonics, proper or vulgar, we began to assimilate.

One afternoon, we were again outside the Sick Bay, arms bared for vaccination and inoculation against typhus and tetanus, a much feared jab in the days when inoculations were a rarity. Slowly the file moved forward to the dreaded needle, and suddenly a few places ahead of me, a tall figure slowly folded up at the knees and fell in a dead faint to the floor. He was hustled away by the sick berth attendant, and the smell of surgical spirit wrinkled my nostils. It was my turn and the needle went in and stayed for numbing seconds.

'Everyone change to PT kit, chop, chop!' bawled PO Tucker, and in no time we were trotting through the drizzling streets, up towards the huge Vestey Tower of the Cathedral, driven mercilessly by the PO and a couple of PT instructors. Finally we stopped in front of a wall near the Cathedral, our stomachs queasy and our swollen arms beginning to pound. Rigidly we stood at attention until quite suddenly two men fell forward on to the wet stones, were picked up and hustled to the wall. A man vomitted and others followed suit and went to the wall. Large gaps appeared in our lines and PO Tucker marched slowly up and down in front of the remnants. He stopped in front of me, and smiled grimly.

'Feeling lousy, Doc?' I nodded. 'Well, pack it in like the others, eh?'

'Not bloody likely!' I growled, having quickly adopted the Shavian epithet.

'Good lad!' he said, and called out, 'all right, fall out the rest and have a couple of drags, those that feel up to it!'

I walked to the wall and squatted in the South Wales miners' crouch against it, my whole body howling with pain. I took out my pipe, filled and lit it in a gesture of defiance, though I did not need its solace.

'What in hell you smoking there?' enquired the PO, 'donkey clippings and camel shit mixture?' I managed a wan smile. Some time later we reformed and jogged back to *Wellesley* to a half-eaten supper and a night of tossing and turning feverishly in our beds as the inoculation took its hold on us.

At the end of the second week, I was in trouble. I was completely in disagreement with Naval PT which consisted of a daily morning run through the streets and then a session of Swedish drill on the parade ground when we bent knees and threw up lead-weighted arms, while the child's prayer ran through my mind, 'Here before Thee Lord, I stand; Throwing up my either hand; Cold as paddocks though they be: Offering up a prayer to Thee.'

In 1933 the Ministry of Education had issued a new syllabus of PT, casting aside these formal Swedish exercises in favour of a more informal, graceful set of movements, and on these cold Merseyside winter mornings I was in complete accord with their views. Some braver soul had managed to dodge the evil, and alone, I decided to join them. I therefore hid in the hammocks, acquiring what I found out to be a flea in the process, and got away with it, or so it seemed, until the tannoy blared out a list of names, mine amongst them, enjoining us to report to the quarter deck at the double!

Arriving there, I found myself, hale and hearty amongst a bunch of crocks with plasters, sticks, arm-slings and pulsating boils. A fierce looking PT Instructor in snowy vest, bursting with muscle, read out our names in an aggrieved tone, ending by saying,

'In that they did miss PT instruction this morning for no good reason!' The officer walked along the line listening to stories of sprained ankles, septic pimples and housemaid's knees, while I waited like a lamb for slaughter.

'And your excuse, Hughes?' asked the officer, eyeing me quizzically.

'I have none, sir!' I shrugged and went on, 'I just don't agree with Naval PT!'

'You intrigue me,' he said, 'please enlarge on your views!' So I told him all about the 1933 PT syllabus. 'Very interesting,' he mused, and I felt he must have been a lawyer, 'and in civilian life, quite a justifiable plea.' His voice and manner hardened to a steely quality, 'But you are not a civilian anymore, Hughes, you're a naval rating, and you must learn to obey!' He paused, and I could see myself running up and down the parade ground with a rifle over my head and a pack on my back. 'Now, get to hell out of here and think about what I've said!'

I saluted and fled, two lessons learnt. One, that of obedience, and second, that the Navy seemed unable to cope with the unvarnished truth! Excuses they were used to and could deal with, but the truth caught them on the wrong foot. I decided to cultivate truth.

I passed my swimming test by the skin of my teeth, swimming the regulation distance quite easily, but nearly sinking to the bottom of the baths under the weight of a saturated suit of duck canvas, already used by dozens before me. I trod water frantically, and was definitely sinking when the PTI called 'Time'!

We fired our rifles on the rifle range, and once again my LDV training, and my youthful catapult and air-gun practice stood me in good stead. We were given regular evening leave now, with afternoons off on Saturdays, and weekend leave which was only of use to those living nearby. I therefore explored Liverpool, discovering many joys in this great city. There were the weekend concerts of the Philharmonic Orchestra, free on Sundays to service people, the Walker Art Gallery, interesting shops, but above all, for me, the docks, and the ride on the Elevated Railway.

I saw ships I had never seen before, passenger liners with famous names, specialised cargo liners with heavy lifting gear like those of the Clan and Harrison Lines, Blue Funnel liners with their Chinese crews, Brocklebank liners with their Indian crews and other ships from all over the world. The only drawback was that they had lost their pre-war smartness of coloured funnels and spotless white superstructures, and were all a uniform grey, but they had not lost their characteristic specialities, and the tall funnel of a Blue Funnel ship was still easily recognisable in grey.

The naval uniform was an open sesame to all the docks, and I peered into warehouses full of currants and raisins from the Mediterranean, palm nuts from West Africa, rubber from Malaya and armaments from America. Then in the Gladstone Dock were the ships of the Liverpool Destroyer Flotillas – Vs and Ws of the First World War, destroyers of the Thirties, and large numbers of sloops of around about a 1,000 tons, bearing names of seaside resorts of Britain. Now and again the new corvettes were to be seen, showing their trawler ancestry and as special attractions the huge Gladstone Dock held a major war vessel such as the aircraft carrier *Indomitable* newly commissioned, or a Colony class cruiser, newly built across the Mersey in Birkenhead.

As the short winter afternoons drew to a close I would return to the Pier Head for a civilised tea in the Kardomah, Ridgways, Reeces or Lyons if it was pay day, or the Services Clubs if I was verging on bankruptcy. Then the evening would be spent at Gladstone House, reading or playing the piano, or if the air-raid sirens sounded, crouching in the shelters. Odd bombs fell here and there, one on a beauty preparations shop in Bold Street, the Bond Street of Liverpool. On our way back to *Wellesley* we picked our way along the sweetest scented street in Europe, a river of Chanel, Lancome and Lentheric mingling their fragrances in the gutter!

'Commander Brock wants to see you, Doc!' said PO Tucker one afternoon, 'so fall out, smarten yourself up, and double off!'

I knocked on the Commanding Officer's door, and went in at his call, mystified, and sat down in front of him as directed. He came to the point immediately and devastatingly.

'I'm going to put your name up for a commission. We've been keeping an eye on you and a couple of others. D'you want to have a go?'

Thoughts of a commission had never entered my head, my brush with authority over the PT had not inspired me to any promotional ambitions, and there were other bits of foolishness as well. I found the work extremely easy and a little boring, but the seamanship side interested me deeply. There had been sly digs about officer material from my shipmates which I had ignored. And above all, I'd always heard of the expenses of an officer's life – the uniform, the mess-bills, etc. I became evasive.

'Well, Sir,' I began, 'I'm very happy as I am, and I've heard it's awfully expensive being an officer!' The Commander leaned forward.

'Dammit, man, do you mean to sit there, a man of your education and ability, and moan about expense? This war is going to last a hell of a long time, and if at the end of it you return to schoolmastering as a bloody Able Seaman, what will they think of you, eh? Now I'm offering you a commission in the Special Branch RNVR, and you'll be commissioned in a fortnight!'

'Do you mean a Green Striper, Sir?' I asked.

'Well, what's wrong with a Green Striper then?' he demanded.

'Well, it's a sort of office job but anyway, Sir, I'll have a go!'

'Right, up you get to the doctor's and we'll run a test on you!'

At the doctor's there were various eye tests and strange colour vision tests. There were four other Rupert Classmates there including the suave accountant.

'Hughes, report back to the Commander!' said the doctor. 'The other four back to instruction.'

Once again I sat before the Commander.

'There'll be no green stripe for you!' he said, smiling, and looking down at some notes. 'Perfect vision, and above all, perfect colour vision. The other four have all failed, but will go into Special Branch nevertheless. You will have a chance to go into the Executive Branch, the ruling class, and specialise in Gunnery, Navigation, Torpedoes, Communications, the lot! But it'll mean a sacrifice for you. You'll revert to Ordinary Seaman and I'll transfer you to *HMS Ganges*, the Seaman Training Establishment at Shotley. I doubt if it will be before Christmas, so you'll continue here and you'll pass that examination, and if you're wise you'll do well for the experience. So once again, there's your choice. Special Branch Commission in a fortnight: Executive Commission in about a year perhaps. What'll it be?'

'Executive Branch, sir! I'll revert to Ordinary Seaman, as you say, Sir!'

'Good man! Now off you go, and the best of luck!'

The days that followed were dream days as I tried to envisage a future which had been a boyhood dream – to be an officer in the Royal Navy, and in the Executive Branch too. The other four chosen ones had left, and the buzz or rumour had got around that I was in for even bigger things. I dropped out of the mainstream of the class from the social point of view, being regarded as someone apart, but I entered the examination room as one of them. When the results were announced I had come out first in the class by a long way, having dropped only five marks over the whole range of subjects.

'Hughes, RFC,' called the Chief Petty Officer Telegraphist, '395 marks out of 400 – the highest marks so far recorded. And what a bloody waste to revert to Ordinary Seaman. You'll be the highest qualified OD in the *Ganges*! Next is . . .'

At that moment I didn't feel very proud of myself. I was an academic prig. But I sewed my gold Coder's badges of crossed flags with a letter C underneath on to my best uniform, and similar red badges on to my working uniform, for after all I had not yet reverted to Ordinary Seaman. So, resplendent, I went home to South Wales for Christmas leave.

McGowan was telling the tale of his Christmas leave when we returned in early January, brandishing a pair of gold good conduct chevrons in his hand.

'As soon as I gets on the boat for Belfast I sews these on me jumper, and the first boozer I goes into a fellow calls out to the barman, "Draw a pint for the Corporal Sailor!" Begorrah, it was like that all the time, and even me mother was pleased at the way her son was getting on in the Navy!'

A messenger touched me on the arm.

'Commander wants you, at the double!' I hurried away. The Commander was brisk.

'Congratulations on your examination marks. Now, here's your first command. You take nine other men from various classes who are also reverting to Ordinary Seamen, across to *HMS Ganges* near Ipswich, leaving tomorrow morning, 0900. Here's the list, travel warrants etc. You're the senior rating and only qualified Coder among them, so get them across safely, and the best of luck to you!' He stood up and shook hands. I saluted smartly.

'Thank you Sir! . . . And thank you for my first command,' I added shyly.

3 The lowest form of life

'D'ye hear that?' snarled the Tannoy after breakfast the next morning, 'Draft for *Ganges* muster at the Quarter Deck!'

I heaved the heavy kit-bag over my shoulder, tucked the ungainly hammock under my arm, grinned self-consciously at the send-off party in the dormitory,

'Well, er, I'd better be off, I suppose? All the best, lads!'

'And the same to yourself, Sorr!' grinned McGowan. I turned away quickly and hurried down the corridors to the Quarter Deck where my first command waited. A supercilious voice was already eroding my authority.

'Who's in charge here, d'you think?' enquired a tall, pale young man who looked as if he had just changed from cricket blazer and white flannels at a minor public school after the last team photograph. 'I think, I'm about the most senior type around here, wouldn't you think?' Catching sight of me, he gave me a cursory glance and grudgingly included me in the vote of confidence in him. 'How about you, what?' he asked. 'You agree, eh?'

'No!' I spat, 'I happen to be in charge!' I straightened out my right arm and pointed to the crossed gold flags, 'Anybody got any of these around here?'

'Oh!' said the fair-haired youth, and there was a titter of laughter from the rest.

'Alright, come on then, let's get fell-in into two lines with a blank file!' There was a quick scurry, and a front line of five, and a rear line of four with a blank space left, took shape smartly. Names were called, instructions issued, the squad was brought to attention and I marched to the Officer of the Watch and saluted.

He was none other than the legal man turned sailor and he recognised me.

'Draft for the *Ganges* mustered and correct, Sir!' I snapped. He eyed me humorously, well aware of the nature of the draft.

'Aha, the PT expert!' he purred. 'Well it seems that crime does pay, even in the Royal Navy, eh?' His face broke into a smile. 'All right. Carry on please?' He paused, 'And all the best!' I saluted and returned to the two rigid lines.

'Right,' I said softly, 'we're moving off, so let's do it smartly!' The commands cracked out and we clattered away to the waiting truck for Lime Street Station and were soon bumping along the cold stone setts of Dockland. The train was waiting and we tumbled in.

'Manchester got badly bombed last night, so I hear,' volunteered a square-jawed Welshman who looked every inch a sailor with his ruddy complexion, but who was one of the other two schoolmasters besides myself.

'Very convenient,' I grumbled. 'It so happens that we change stations there, so I hope they're intact. This is a hell of a cross country journey at the best of times!'

When we entered Manchester there was a heavy pall of smoke swirling in the drizzling sky. As we squealed to a stop in London Road Station and tossed our bags on to the platform there was the acrid smell of burning wood and a thin dusting of shattered brick and plaster everywhere. Miraculously the naval truck assigned to us was waiting and we were soon threading our way slowly through unfamiliar back streets, over snaking firehoses and past smouldering buildings. The war was beginning to lick at us.

The cross-country train swallowed us and the day dragged on in a blur of chatter, station tea, Cornish pasties, hand-rolled cigarettes and speculation, until we reached Lincoln where we changed trains.

Our train glided into the platform, a sinuous streamlined essay in silver steel, one of the latest Silver Link series of streamlined trains of the pre-war London and North Eastern Railway. There was a whistle of admiration.

'Thought they'd put away these shiny things in store for the duration! And they've got a bar, too!' said the voice of experience.

We entrained extremely rapidly and indeed there was a bar and it was quite well-stocked for war-time. Ipswich arrived much too soon, but we clambered into the ubiquitous naval truck in a most expansive mood. We left the outskirts of Ipswich and entered the cold sea-swept Suffolk countryside. Over the hedges, the sails of a spritsail Thames barge ghosted along on the way upriver to Ipswich, and the whisky laughter petered out.

'Bloody cold!' shivered someone. 'They tell me that they have you out at crack of dawn pulling whacking great cutters all over the river!'

'This must be it,' pointed one of the schoolmasters, 'I can always tell a block of classrooms.' Some modern two-storey buildings moved past the canvas flaps of the truck.

'I can see a ruddy great mast on this side!' reported the port look-out from the other canvas flap.

'*Ganges*, here we come!' bellowed someone.

'Oi,' I commanded, coarsely. 'Knock it off, we're nearly there, so let's smarten up!' The truck slowed to enter some heavy gates with guard houses on either side and a regulating petty officer, an equivalent of a policeman, materialised at the tailboard.

'Out!' he barked succinctly. 'And get fell in – there!' A finger stabbed, and we obeyed. I reported the draft to the Petty Officer.

'Yes,' he acknowledged, 'the CW candidates from *Wellesley*. You'll all be in 43 Mess. There's no room in the proper CW Mess which is 35, down the Long Covered Way!' All this was meaningless to me, but the mystic letters CW were becoming more and more important, and at this early stage we did not know that they signified matters pertaining to officers generally and would soon become part of our administrative lives. No one seemed to know exactly what they stood for, other than perhaps Commissions and Warrants, which fitted well.

'Everything's done at the double here,' said the Regulating PO, whose popular name throughout the Navy was The Crusher, to distinguish him from his immediate superior, The Jaunty, or more officially the Master-at-Arms, the most senior rating of all, entitled to wear a sword on ceremonial occasions. 'So get those bags and hammocks up, and get ready to move out, following that rating there!' A rather downtrodden looking rating who must have suffered under The Crusher, trotted up, belted and gaitered and looking faintly horsey.

'Move!' bawled The Crusher and we galloped away like a string of pack-horses, down endless alleys, across a gravelled quarterdeck, the huge mast getting nearer and nearer, with its ratlines, rigging, futtock shrouds and stays. We trotted under a great expanse of safety net which surrounded the base of the mast. High above the mast looked down haughtily, challenging us to scale it.

'Christ!' breathed a voice. 'What a height! We'll never climb that thing!'

'Ah, well,' said another, 'if you fall off, you land in the safety net!'

'Them that falls off the mast and lands in the net,' intoned our horse-faced guide, 'always bounces right out of it, and lands on the 'ard concrete and we scrapes 'em orf wiv shovels!' Remarks languished.

We passed a huge wooden figurehead of some bygone ship, the head, arms and trunk of a white robed Indian rajah, surmounted with a golden crown and festooned with wooden pearls the size of cricket balls. He had, to me, a regal and quite benign look.

'Snooty old bastard,' said our guide, dismissively, 'figure'ead of some old warship. Anyway, 'ere we are.' He pointed to a two-storey mess block, '43's the downstairs bit. Wait 'ere, and I'll get the PO!'

'Let's fall in ready,' I advised and we lined up, bags and hammocks neatly stacked. Down the steps of the Mess block came another immaculate Gunner's Mate – small, quick, sharp-jawed, piercing of eye and much younger than our fatherly Petty Officer Tucker of *Wellesley*. He danced to a halt and I saluted smartly and reported our presence. He looked me up and down.

'And what have we here, then?' he asked the world at large, pointing at my right arm. 'A real tiddley matloe with a lovely gold badge on his arm and a pale blue collar, eh? What in hell are you supposed to be, eh?'

'I'm a Coder, sir,' I stuttered, my ego beginning to deflate.

'Indeed you are not, my lad,' purred the PO, like a bishop chiding a deacon. 'We're all Ordinary Seamen here and that bloody badge will have to come off!' Behind me, there were polite titters from the non-badge men and I drooped visibly. The PO relented and I saw a ray of hope. 'Well, keep it on until I've seen the Divisional Officer, but I've never seen an Ordinary Seaman wearing a Signalman's badge before.' He paused and tugged his uniform straight. 'I'm Petty Officer Hunt and the Chief and I run 43 Mess. You'll see much more of me than the Chief. Now, let's have your names, eh?' We gave him our names, length of service, etc, and he smiled.

'Well, I'm glad to have some people with a little experience to make up our numbers. The others have only just come over from the New Entrants Block which is that dark painted place across the Parade Ground. Unfortunately the class leaders have already been chosen and I'm afraid you'll have to knuckle down to them, though they may be junior to you.' I felt his glance on me and took the hint. 'Anyway, you're all supposed to be candidates for commissions and I expect you to use your loaves. You'll find a few other CW candidates in there, but the rest are all ordinary lads, and I won't stand for any of you lot coming the old acid over them, see? To me you're all bloody ODs, the lowest form of life in the Navy.' Inwardly, we sighed at the oft-repeated incantation, but he went on, 'You may have got your university degrees, and been to good schools but in the ways and craft of the Navy, you are nothing but babes in arms.'

'What are you all then?' he bawled heavenwards. Wiser now in the ways of Petty Officers we gave him our answer.

'Babes in arms, Sir!' we chorussed. He stiffened suddenly and his boots clattered a quadruple rhythm on the ground.

'Double-up, double-up, double-up, then!' he yowled. 'Get those bags and hammocks stowed, and find yourselves beds inside!'

We banged our way through the entrance, past smaller rooms and emerged into a long room, with scrubbed mess tables and benches in the foreground, glittering with highly polished mess tins. Beyond there was a long vista of highly polished floors with beds down either side. Warm air engulfed us cosily, and there was a clean smell of soap and polish in the air. From the beds the members of 43 Mess regarded us with interest and amusement.

'Class Leader!' called PO Hunt, and an extremely handsome sailor doubled forward and stood at attention with an air of quiet confidence. I immediately felt that we would not question his leadership.

'Sir?' he enquired, in a carefully modulated, quiet voice.

'See that these men get beds and detail some of the duty watch to get them their supper.' He turned to us, 'And a couple of you go with them to the galley so that you'll know where it is for the future. After they've eaten, Richards, you bring them up to date on our routine here. That's all!'

He stamped away and we hurried to choose our beds, stomachs rumbling at the thought of a meal. Richards, the class leader, guided us quietly around and sat with us as we wolfed down a meal of surprisingly good fish cakes, chipped potatoes, bread, butter and strong naval cocoa or kai. We began to relax as Richards explained the routine, the scheme of instruction, the games, the swimming, the drill.

'I don't think they've changed the routine or the syllabus since the boys left here when war broke out,' he explained. 'Of course, you know that this was the Navy's chief Boys' Training Establishment and the going's pretty rough, and especially so for us CW candidates. There's a complete CW Mess here as well, but we're a mixed lot, and I think all the better for it too and we tan the balls off 35 Mess at rugby. Some of the ordinary lads are real characters. Take that little chap over there . . . rejoices in the names of Clifford Robert Falcon.'

'Almost the same as mine except for the Falcon. Mine's Francis!' I blurted.

'Hey, Beaky?' called Richards, 'Come over here and meet a fellow with almost the same Christian names as yours!' A little man with a face like Punch minced his way over to us with mock femininity.

'Ooooh!' he lisped, 'Where's this lovely man then?' He put a dainty finger under his chin and looked coy. Richards pointed to me.

'Oh, what a beautiful sailor. And look at his lovely gold badge,' he drooled.

'Cut it out, Beaky,' implored Richards. 'You're giving quite the wrong impression.' Beaky's face discomposed itself, and he burst out with a deep masculine laugh and sat down beside me.

'Is that right about the names, mate?' he asked in a typical Cockney accent. I nodded, explained and so made my first friend in *Ganges*.

The day's journey, the cosy warmth of the mess, and a small sense of achievement had me asleep within seconds after ten o'clock, yet it seemed only minutes before we were aroused by a bugle call which we blearily identified as our friend Charley or Reveille.

'Dew Mawr (Great God)!' growled Jones, one of the schoolmasters. 'It's only half-past five in the morning! What the hell's going on?' PO Hunt soon enlightened us.

'Comealongthen!' he caterwauled. 'Get dressed, get your kai and be ready for roll-call in the drill shed at oh-six-double-oh!'

Someone had already been to the galley for great steaming fannies or pots of cocoa into which we dipped our thick earthenware cups and drank the fatty mixture which was a meal in itself. In a short time we were doubling across the vast parade ground in the darkness to the cavernous drill shed used in bad weather, where we formed up in classes to be counted. There was a great deal of shouting, clanking to attention and reporting, and we were back on our way across the parade ground.

'Pointless bloody exercise, seems to me,' I breathed to Beaky. 'Do they expect us to run away?'

'Bet a few of the little homesick boys used to bugger off in the night before the war though,' he answered sagely.

The early rising was explained when the amount of work to be done emerged. Beds were made, floors polished to mirror-like surfaces, breakfast was fetched, eaten, and cleared away, boots polished, gaiters adjusted and there was just time for a pipe before PO Hunt burst on us.

'Get ready for Divisions in five minutes!' he barked.

So began the daily divisions, a massed assembly of everyone in the vast establishment who aligned themselves for the final inspection by a drill which I only ever saw at *Ganges*, called Dressing by the Drum. From a rough line-up of Divisions on a single command from an officer, a drum rolled briefly followed by a staccato tap, heard all over the ground. At the tap the divisional markers snapped on to their marked positions. The drum rolled briefly again, paused and tapped, and every man lined up on the markers. The final roll allowed you to adjust the line and as it ceased each line had to be perfectly straight. Then the Divisional Officer's inspection began. As he passed me, he noted my red working clothes badges on my sleeve.

'Get those off!' he spat, and I sighed inwardly, as I slid down a snake in my promotional game of snakes and ladders.

No day was the same in *Ganges* – there was seamanship to be learned, a much wider range of knots and splices to be mastered, practical skills such as steering by compass, pulling at an oar to be acquired, a Guards' precision in rifle drill and field drill to be attained. We moved from classroom to parade ground to gun battery to riverside with bewildering speed.

After Divisions there was a spell on the parade ground and then we headed for a classroom, passing an outgoing class en route. They seemed an unusually rugged and rangy lot, not overawed by naval discipline. As one passed me, his jaws moved in a huge grimace and a cud of tobacco changed place in his mouth, to be followed by a brown jet of spittle which splashed noisily on the ground.

'Hi-ya, guys!' he drawled.

'We got Americans here?' I asked Richards. 'From the Wild West?'

'No, Newfoundland!' he laughed, 'Real sailors from the Grand Banks schooners, I hear.'

'Captain Courageous stuff, eh?' I added, remembering Kipling's novel of the Newfoundland Grand Banks fishermen. 'Doubt if they need any seamanship.'

'Ugh!' he pointed to the floor of the classroom, where they must have sat for their instruction. It was surrounded by slowly drying gobs of tobacco juice which they had surreptitiously ejected during the lesson. We sat down carefully to await our Chief, a much older, tall and weather-beaten white-haired man who took us through the intricacies of such knots as Midshipman's and Blackwall hitches, and the subtle differences between a West Country Whipping around a rope, a Sailmakers or an American. His gnarled hands moved deftly and my thoughts drifted to sailors on South Devon beaches, sitting on the pebbles in the sun at my pre-war favourite drinking and fishing place at Beer.

At dinner time, PO Hunt took the ex-*Wellesley*s aside for a confidential chat.

'This lot don't know it yet,' he whispered, 'and you don't breathe a word either, but they're having their inoculations after dinner and you'll be their nursemaids while they get over it.'

'Do you mean to say, Sir,' I asked, 'that they'll have the afternoon off on their beds? We went for a five mile run through Liverpool streets at *Wellesley*. Cor!'

'I don't care a bugger what they did in Scouseland,' he retorted. 'This is the way we do it, and you lot will do it too. Right?'

'Yes, Sir,' I agreed, his point taken. The tannoy spoke the dread words and 43 Mess quailed, fell in silently, and returned within minutes, nonchalantly, but only momentarily.

'Christ, look at my arm!' wailed Beaky. 'Somebody's pumped it up!'

Sailors began crawling to their beds. There was weeping, wailing and gnashing of teeth, and even the imperturbable Richards and Rupert Curtis, another leader, were ready to give a quiver to the traditional stiff upper lip. The afternoon passed and few wanted supper and we hale ones could well have died from a surfeit of bangers and chips.

'I wanna drink,' a voice would cry from the semi-darkness after supper, and one of us would put down a paperback and fill a mug.

'Mama's coming dearie,' Jones would call.

'I wanna be sick,' a voice would wail.

'Florence Nightingale, the Lady with the Potty, will be with you,' I would lisp. 'Oh, you poor dear boys of Scutari. Spew into this!' Gradually they fell into a fitful sleep and the Mess was quiet. PO Hunt came in.

'All right, you lads. You've finished your nursing. Why not visit the canteen for a drink?'

The three schoolmasters, Jones, Hutchings and I needed no second bidding and were soon marching down the darkened alleys to the canteen. A vast gust of sound assailed us as we entered the smoke-swirled hall and fought our way to the bar. As we neared it a huge man turned away bearing aloft two great enamelled jugs of beer, some of which slopped over towards us, narrowly missing our uniforms.

'Sorry, guys!' drawled another of the rugged, tobacco-chewing Newfoundlanders. 'Saves time buying it by the jug.'

We bought our drinks and moved to a table, not overly impressed by the comfort, or the quality of the beer.

'Let's walk to the jetty?' suggested Hutchings, and we drank up and left. Down at the jetty, the River Orwell flowed dark and mysterious, joined by its companion the River Stour, as they entered the North Sea, and the port of Harwich was faintly discernible on the opposite Essex shore. The half moon threw a fitful light over the waters when, out of the shadows a shape moved and a destroyer glided into the North Sea, the hum of turbines and fans coming to us faintly. She was followed by another. A signal lamp winked mysteriously and they disappeared eastwards on their warlike missions.

'Two months from now, perhaps,' mused Jones, in the darkness, 'and we could be doing that!' There were murmurs of assent as we moved away back to the Mess, guided by the dim shape of the brooding and ever-present Mast.

My former command's afternoons were fully occupied with field and rifle drill, as we were not considered skilled enough, coming from a communications establishment, but the Drill Petty Officer considered us well versed and consequently wasting our time. He suggested a visit to the baths, which we accepted with alacrity.

'*Ganges*' swimming baths was reputed to be the largest and most lavish of its kind in East Anglia, and we were suitably impressed. The Drill PO, intent on a quiet smoke and a chat with a colleague, passed us on to a Physical Training Instructor, a type I was beginning to detest, with torso like Charles Atlas, encased in snowy, blue-edged, white singlet, with crossed Indian Club badge, tight blue trousers and pipe-clayed canvas shoes, always dancing around on dainty feet, like a featherweight boxer.

'Done your swimming test?' he enquired, haughtily.

'Yes, Sir,' we replied.

'Well, you can do the bugger again then.' He gloated, 'Strip off and get in.' Away went our thoughts of aquatic horseplay and we surveyed the line

of water-logged duck suits waiting to put their clammy touch on our warm
bodies.

·· 'One length ordinary swimming, change into duck suits, and two
minutes tread water,' he ordered. A length accomplished we shivered our
way into the duck suits and trod water. 'All failed!' leered the PTI, 'but I
tell you what – swim ten lengths and I'll pass you all. Ta-ta!' Off he trotted
to join the Drill PO in a cigarette while we passed our tests with horseplay.

That night there was an air-raid and we spent the first of many
uncomfortable hours in the low-lying, waterlogged air-raid shelters,
passing the time by speculating on the possibility of tunnelling a passage
into the neighbouring shelters from which came the high voices and
occasional giggles of the *Ganges* Wrens. Meanwhile, out at sea the
German minelaying aircraft searched for the swept channels into which to
drop their magnetic mines.

The following morning we assembled at the riverside jetty for our first
attempt at what I had always thought was rowing, but which the Navy
insisted on calling 'Pulling'. The Chief had already mentioned the
rudiments of a boat's anatomy and words rolled off his tongue which we
had never heard before, such as garboard strakes, and clinker built,
pintles and poppets. As some seemed to verge on coarseness, much ribald
comment was made on the caution to be used in not getting certain parts of
the male anatomy caught in the rowlocks. The *Seamanship Manual* was
full of innuendo also, in such phrases as 'crutches as the substitutes for
rowlocks' and 'poppets are vertical pieces'. There was much speculation as
to the use of 'the hog piece' but we Welsh were reassured to know that
there was at least a 'tabernacle' in the boat.

The east wind was blowing keenly in from the sea, penetrating our thick
blue serge, and the boats moved uneasily below in the swell.

'Down chinstraps!' called PO Hunt. 'Down into the boats with you.'

I never became enamoured of a 32 foot pulling cutter from the time I
stepped into its huge wooden interior and stepped along the thwarts to my
indicated position on the bow thwart. It seemed that bow oarsmen should
be be smallish fellows, and there seemed to be some compensation
granted to them in that their oar was always just a little shorter than the
usual oars, which to me, with small hands, seemed like juvenile telegraph
poles. However, attached to the office were such duties as pushing the
bows off with a boat hook, grabbing for the shore on your return, and
performing a somewhat tricky operation with ropes when hoisting, known
as Passing the Lifelines. On first hearing the phrase I thought it meant
chucking out one of those cork lifebelts found at the seaside, inscribed
Borough of Torquay, and not forgetting to hold on to the rope.
Alternatively, I had a vague recollection of having heard the phrase used
by the Salvation Army on street corners, in a hymn called *Throw out the*

lifeline, someone is needing it now. The Chief, however, put an end to these misconceptions by showing us what it really meant, and I hoped profoundly that I should never have to perform it.

We spent the whole morning moving erratically across the river, tossing oars to vertical positions, resting on them, pulling them, cursing them, feathering them and then thankfully, at the end of the morning, shipping them and stowing them on the thwarts, and climbing out of the boat, arm-weary and palm-blistered. Beaky Nash summed up our feelings as we clumped up the steps, by singing a parody on the popular words of *Colonel Bogey's March,*

'Rowlock and the same to you!' he sang, and we joined in the chorus, sincerely.

There were many more such sessions and we gradually improved as we learned the functions of the various leverages which when correctly applied, eased the labour and improved the swing, until we began to take pride in the way the boat picked up speed, in the clean swirl as our oars were feathered out of the water, and the rhythm of the team. Competitiveness emerged and many were the short races which were organised out on the river, with the POs laying the odd bob on their crews with their opposite numbers.

At an early stage we were introduced to the Heavy Gun Battery, just as a soldier comes first to his rifle. The Battery overlooked the river, housed in a long building fronted with huge, hinged windows which could be thrown back in summer and closed in winter. The flooring was spotless holystoned teak, which we had cleaned in our turn, and on this at intervals, were mounted a varied assortment of guns, from the small 12-pounders, to the heavy six-inch guns. All were superannuated, and I felt a slight awe for these polished, whitepainted six-inch muzzled steel monsters which could well have been mounted in some long-scrapped cruiser or in the six-inch batteries of one of Jackie Fisher's first Dreadnoughts. They had probably gazed out at faraway coral islands, glittering icebergs and been washed by each of the seven seas.

Like everything else in the Navy they had a language all their own and a pronunciation which bore no relation to the letters of the word, and a lecture went something like this:–

'So that no water gets down the muzzles,' explained the Gunner's Mate, 'they screw in a sort of cork, like this, see?' He held up a thing like a giant bath plug. 'They call this a tomkin, spelt t-a-m-p-i-o-n. If we was to leave this thing in the muzzle and then fire the gun there would be a damn great explosion and shit and guts all over the place. So, the first command is – "Out, tomkin!"' I giggled as I had visions of a young tom-cat being kicked out of the house at midnight, to rampage on the rooftops.

'Right, being you think it so funny, you go and screw this thing in the

33

muzzle!' I departed with alacrity, then returned to the disciples.

'This Ordinary Seaman has now performed the action what is taken when the command "In, tomkin" is given, that is, when a ship goes to sea, or when the guns is finished with.' Again I could see the returning tom-cat, responding to the doorstep call of, 'In, tomkin' teetering and befuddled with fornication and smelling to high heaven, but I restrained the giggle.

'This here is called a dewmerrick,' said the Gunner's Mate, pointing to a complicated brass instrument. 'And it is used for calculating aim-off to allow for your speed and the enemy's speed.'

'How do you spell it, Sir?' enquired the usual studious note-taker.

'D-u-m-a-r-e-s-q,' dictated the Gunner's Mate, 'quite simple – dewmerrick, right? Now, the cordite is contained in a bag made of a light material called shalloon . . . '

'How do you spell it, Chief?' enquired the student.

'Christ knows!' snapped the Chief, 'but that's how you say it – shalloon!'

'D'ye know what a shalloon is?' I enquired of Beaky, in a whisper, 'it's a balloon inflated with farts!' He choked with laughter but escaped the POs sharp glance towards us. It wasn't until many years later that I looked up this word and found that it was derived from the French town of Chalons, where it was manufactured as a dress material. The Master-at-Arms' nickname of Jaunty had a similar French origin, being a derivation of 'gentilhomme', while our word 'matloe' was pure French.

Other words were slipping into our vocabulary, such as the Hindustani 'dhobi' for washing, the Polynesian 'kai' for food applied to cocoa, and the Chinese pidgin 'chop-chop' for hurrying or hastening. One phrase always defeated me as it was applied to so many situations, and this was, giving something a 'stroke of the old shamdooey', which could apply over a range of activities from a light hammer tap, through a wipe-over with a rag, to sexual activity. Not only was our vocabulary changing but there was a general coarsening of our attitude in many ways.

The mechanics of the gun seemed to hinge around a simple handle called the breech mechanism lever, which opened the breech of the gun to allow the shell and the cordite bag to be put in. It was always shortened to BM Lever, and in every operation BM Lever always had a key role; he was always called upon to open and to close, to be on hand for misfires and other misdemeanours, and Mr BM Lever became ingrained in our souls. Many a hotel register proves that it must have been visited by Lt and Mrs BM Lever off on a dirty weekend, and he has signed many a chit and receipted many a delivery note to my knowledge, ranging from Seafire naval aircraft to coils of steel wire rope! He lay a close third to Lts Donald Duck, and M Mouse, nearly always members of the Royal Naval Volunteer Reserve.

Six-inch Gun Drill was violent physical exercise with the shell weighing the equivalent to a sack of coal to be manhandled to the breech for Mr Lever's attentions, then to be rammed home with a heavy steel-shod ram, followed by a weighty bag of cordite. Gun muzzles had to be sponged out, elevating and training levers spun at dizzy speed, but the easiest jobs were range-taker and communciation number, the former fiddling with some brass pointers at the side of the gun, the latter draped with a telephone headset for relaying mythical orders.

The curtain would be rung up with us all at our stations around the gun, waiting for the Gunner's Mate.

'Target bearing Red Four Five, 8,000 yards, moving left etc, etc. Load, load, load!' Handles would spin, boots clatter, breech blocks would clang shut, after shell, charge and ramrod had done their act.

'Open Fire!' This was the anti-climax, for in the silence would come an ineffectual little click from the firing pistol. Then hell would be resumed again as the gun was reloaded and another target indicated.

'Change Rounds!' would bawl the PO and everyone would move to another position on the guns. In this way you gained an all-round experience of every function of the crew, and counted how many more rounds it would take until you could have a quiet fiddle with the range-setter, or a breather with the headphones. So it would go on all afternoon.

'Change Rounds!' bawled the PO for what seemed the hundredth time, and in the lull, Hutchings, threw his hands in the air and declaimed,

'Once more unto the breach, dear friends, once more;
Or close the wall up with our English dead!'

'Still!' roared the Gunner's Mate. 'What the bloody hell's come over you then? Shellshock?'

'Shakespeare, Sir. Henry V, Act 3, Scene 1, at the siege of Harfleur I believe . . .' There was a silence which I could not allow to pass.

'Sink me the ship, Master Gunner – sink her, split her in twain!
Fall into the hands of God, not into the hands of Spain!'

'Shakespeare, again, I suppose?' he enquired, acidly.

'No, Sir, Tennyson, actually – Sir Richard Grenville and *The Revenge.*'

'Oh, God,' implored the Gunner's Mate, 'why did I have to have these bloody CW candidates chucked at me. And I suppose there'll be more to come?' He held his head in his hands, then inclined his head and stiffened his jaw, until his tie almost popped out. 'Change Rounds!' he screamed. 'You brainy bastards!'

After what seemed like weeks of imprisonment we were given weekend leave, and as there was a special coach for Birmingham, Jim Lucas, another new friend invited me to Edgbaston for the weekend.

Saint Augustine's Vicarage was a far cry from 43 Mess, with its elegant rooms, its silver, good food and the lovely grand piano in the drawing room. The area had only recently been bombed, and some distance away a huge oblong landmine was still hanging from the branches of a large garden tree, its parachute cords entangled in the branches. Saturday was the usual suburban day of shopping, visits to friends, dinner and a short visit to an elegant pub. Sunday was naturally a day of services at Saint Augustine's, where I was able to timidly attempt to play the famous organ. After lunch I sat doodling at the grand piano, when Mrs Lucas entered and slipped a thick volume on to the music rest.

'Have a quick look at that, while I tune my violin, and we'll run through it!' I turned to the title page – *Beethoven – Violin Concerto. Solo Violin, orchestral accompaniment arranged for piano* and shuddered. The violin tunings ceased and Mrs Lucas spoke over my shoulder.

'Away we go then!' And so all that afternoon we played away, with many an admonition to me for sloppy tempo, wrong notes and weak introductions, but we were making music, and the coarseness of our life slid away, leaving me clean and content. The early start on Monday morning, the snow-covered fields and the prospect of our rather bleak existence was not encouraging and the motor coach was silent for much of the journey, but improved for me when we stopped at Cambridge and managed a short walk along the Backs.

Our time at *Ganges* was coming to a close, there was talk of examinations and tests, and we had yet to climb The Mast. Sundays seemed to be a mast climbing day for those who wanted some practice, but for the Newfoundlanders it seemed like home from home. They swarmed over it like monkeys, directing streams of tobacco juice on anyone unwary enough to come within their range.

On most days instruction finished at dusk at this time of the year, leaving scant time for a practice ascent, but on one or two Sundays when the Newfoundlanders were dry-mouthed we had climbed to the feared futtock shrouds. This was the end of the first stage where the rope rigging and ratlines for the feet narrowed to a point under a wide platform or truck. A new set of shrouds was then rigged from the mast outwards to the edge of the truck, and as soon as you set foot on these shrouds you were climbing outward and backward at 45° for a short, though hair-raising distance, until your groping hands found the edge of the truck and you hauled yourself up on to it.

Then began another steeper, narrower set of shrouds which led you to the last goal, the main-truck, a platform about six feet long and a foot wide, across which you edged yourself and began the descent in reverse order. Of course it was possible to avoid the futtock shrouds completely by climbing onwards through a hole in the truck flooring or deck, contemptuously called the Lubber's Hole. No self-respecting seaman would use this method, and indeed, he was deterred from doing so by a Petty Officer stationed there with a rope's end, cunningly knotted, which he was eager to use on any Lubber craven enough to use the Hole!

The Newfoundlanders used to swarm up both sets of rigging to the main truck, then climb up a flimsy-looking ladder which led to the ultimate top, the famous button, from which sprouted a lightning conductor, necessary for such a lofty structure, reputed to be well over 150 feet high and equivalent to some of the loftier church spires. It was quite usual to see one of them grasping the lightning conductor lightly, whilst performing a tap dance on the button top which could not have been much larger than a coffee table.

One foolhardy soul, seeking to outdo all others, hung head downward with his legs wrapped tightly around the lightning conductor which bent dangerously under his weight. How often had we seen film comedians like Harold Lloyd and Buster Keaton in similar situations, but only a few feet from the stuc·. floor in reality; this was for real and for 150 feet of fall if your nerve went, with only the dubious safety net to catch you! We held our breath while he strove to regain the button, his hands gripping the conductor, but his body jack-knifed so tightly that he could not gain leverage to lift himself past the horizontal. After several attempts to do so, he jerked his legs apart, releasing their grip on the mast, and with a shoulder-jarring jerk, he now hung from the steel rod by his outstretched arms, his feet frantically seeking the rope ladder. There was a massed exhalation of breath, as his feet found the ladder and he climbed slowly down. From a regulating Petty Officer far below, came a stentorian bellow, which tarnished any gilt on his performance.

'Come down at the double, you stupid bastard! Report to the Officer of the Day!'

One Monday, just as we sat down for lunch, PO Hunt remarked casually,

'Eat up lads. You're going to climb The Mast this afternoon!'

Appetites palled immediately and the clock hands flew around to the dreaded appointment. We went up in pairs and the first set of rigging was comparatively easy, but as I came up under the shrouds, I was genuinely afraid. PO Hunt sat on the truck blocking the entrance to the Lubber's Hole, idly swinging a knotted rope's end. As we came to face him amidst the tracery of rope and rigging, he posed us a question.

'Across the arsehole if you go through the Lubber's Hole! Across the buttocks or across the futtocks?' He crashed the rope on the deck to indicate the force to be received, so I chose the futtock shrouds, partly out of respect for my tender parts, but mostly out of pride. Once embarked on the climb which felt like being a fly on a ceiling, I was detached from reality and a determination took hold of me to survive. Soon the edge of the truck was to hand, and the final ascent and crossing of the main truck, apart from the dizzy height, was comparatively easy.

In a few short seconds I had learned that climbing was a divorce of surroundings, and a marriage of your self with that piece of rope immediately to hand, however high you might be. Little did I realise that I would do such a climb three times a day and more, in gales, ice and snow, entering and leaving a lofty gunnery Director high up the mast of a cruiser, together with many other ascents, both necessary and foolhardy, over the coming years.

As Feburary drew to its close, the weather grew worse and snow blizzards cut across the parade ground. Beaky Nash and I fought our way across on our morning visit to the lavatories or Heads, a routine which horrified me in its lack of privacy. The closets had no doors and there was always a queue before Divisions. Woe betide the sailor with constipation, or one who was used to a leisurely visit with morning paper and pipe. The waiting crowd was always restive and ribald.

'Hurry up there. Break that one off then and keep it for after dinner!'

'That was a quick one, mate. Got the squitters then?'

'When I was cleaning this Head last week, they found a turd a foot long. Without a word of a lie, I tell you! The Captain of the Heads had it varnished and mounted on a teak base with a brass plate. It's in the museum now!'

'Come along then,' moaned the anxious one, 'you're all piss and wind in there!'

As Beaky and I waited our turn, he pointed to the white painted board screwed to the wall, a feature of every toilet block in the establishment. 'Cleaned by Drake' it announced in bold black letters, meaning that it was the responsibility of Drake Division.

'That's what I like about the Navy,' said Beaky, 'even the most famous admirals have had to start right at the bottom. Sir Francis Drake must have cleaned this one out. There's a couple more scattered about which have been cleaned by Nelson, and Rodney. D'ye think Nelson lost his arm down one of these toilets?'

As we neared the head of the queue, the delay today was obvious, a huge coke brazier was glowing in the alley to keep the water from freezing.

'Oh, boy!' smiled Beaky, 'what luxury – toilets with central heating. Hey, come on, Doc, there's two blokes leaving!' Ensconced in adjacent booths, opposite the brazier, I could hear Beaky cooing happily and breaking wind noisily.

'Lovely tone, today!' He broke into ribald verse about a wind-breaking competition in some mythical part of England which always ended with a commercial. 'Zam-Buk for torn arseholes!' he shouted.

'Come on, Beaky,' whined the Greek chorus. 'Cut it out and snap it orf!'

A few days later, 43 Mess split up for ever and we went our separate ways to the great barracks of Chatham, Portsmouth and Plymouth. Beaky, being a Londoner went to Chatham, and as a West Countryman, I was drafted to Plymouth. My little command was now scattered to the winds, and new friends had to be made as we sorted ourselves out for the long cross-country train journey to Plymouth which managed to include both Cambridge and Oxford in the itinerary! We shunted into the barracks from Keyham, a GWR pannier tank engine pushing us slowly into the heart of the barracks into the arms of another Gunner's Mate.

'All out!' he screamed. 'Dump your stuff and follow me up to Jago's for supper.'

We had all heard of the dreaded Jago's, a system of mess catering invented by a legendary Warrant Officer Cook or Steward, called Jago. Everyone ate together in a vast dining hall in relays, and the rush to eat, as your turn came, was a fearsome thing. Rumour had it that every day sailors were maimed for life or trampled to death in the rush, but tonight all was quiet and we sat down in front of a meal the centrepiece of which consisted of two anaemic-looking sausages, attended by soggy chips and a haemorrhage of tinned tomatoes.

'Christ,' said someone, 'train smash with two coaches!' Anything with tinned tomatoes being referred to as a railway disaster.

The meal being ended, the Gunner's Mate took the stage.

'You sleep in the Heavy Gun Battery, tonight, so follow me!' With bags and hammocks, we staggered between great buildings to the usual Gun Battery, and left to our own devices we unrolled our hammocks on the spotless teak deck and immediately fell asleep. The sun through the great Battery windows awakened me, together with the Gunner's Mate's chant:

'Rise and shine for the morning's fine! Come along to Jago's then!' The staircase to Jago's was crammed with humanity, like maggots in a dead sheep, and I could hardly breath. Suddenly there was a surge forward and I was lifted up the stairs and translated like Enoch, into the upper regions. I fell into the first place and a plate of bacon and fried eggs was slapped down in front of me, and like everyone else I got stuck in. After breakfast we mustered in the Battery and jogged off to some unknown destination which turned out to be the Swimming Baths.

'Who's passed their swimming test?' enquired the PO. We all shouted an affirmative which fell on deaf ears.

'Well, you'll all pass the bastard again! Get stripped off!'

So for the third time, I passed my test, but this was followed by a more fortunate situation. An elderly Chief entered the baths, puffing and blowing, with a list in his hands.

'Found you at last,' he wheezed. 'Answer your names, if you're here.' He read out a short list, with my name amongst them, and as we fell out it was obvious that we were all CW candidates. 'Get your bags and hammocks,' he commanded, 'you're all going into Exmouth block for further instruction!'

So began a short halcyon period in Plymouth. The winter sun was strengthening now that it was March, shining on the whiteness of the great barrack blocks, touching them with a patina of a great naval tradition. Over the blocks the sun shone on the masts and yards of the cruiser *Exeter* still undergoing repairs after the River Plate battle, and aboard which was a school friend of mine, an Engineer Lieutenant, but as remote from me now as a God.

We were spared the terrors of Jago's, possessing a galley of our own. We passed pleasant sun-filled mornings and afternoons, under the guidance of elderly, fatherly Warrant Officers who were Boatswains, Shipwrights and Gunners. There was time for quiet, unhurried study and I learned more and more of the mysteries of anchor and cable work, fiddling with the miniature anchors, chains, slips, stoppers and capstans on the beautiful scale model fo'c'sles and sterns of battleships and cruisers made by the famous firm of Basset-Lowke. We dropped and weighed anchors, picked up moorings, moored to buoys, unfouled anchors and a host of other evolutions under the gentle instructions of men who must have performed these tasks in harbours all over the world, on the Yangstse, in mangrove lined creeks in Malaya and mist shrouded Scottish lochs.

We spliced rope, both hemp and wire, learning the secrets of the rogue yarns by whose colour you could tell from what ropewalk the rope had come; we learned to tie a thief knot, a cunning knot which was to all intents and purposes a reef knot, but the ends emerged at the top and bottom, instead of only at the top. Old sailors used this knot to tie their kitbags and knew immediately if their bag had been tampered with and retied, because it was usually retied with a traditional reef knot.

We graduated to fine knotwork – the variations of the Turk's Head, the Stopper, the Wall, but the legendary Matthew Walker defied us. I used to dream of this Matthew Walker, as a rather roguish, fair-haired sailor always doodling with ropes' ends in some snowy sailed frigate, ingratiating himself with his Captain by decorating everything with Turk's Heads and whippings and then one day finally producing his masterpiece to offer to his Captain.

'And what have you tied, today, Matthew?' the Captain would say.

'Indeed, Sir, 'tis a cunning knot,' would answer Walker. 'Eminentiy suited it be, Sir, for securing standing parts of ropes and making beckets for buckets!'

'So it is, Matthew. Alter all the beckets on my buckets and we will call this knot after you!' That is how I felt he must have passed into posterity, and as far as I know he must have taken the secret of his knot to the grave, because I never tied it, despite the sinuous drawings in the *Seamanship Manual*.

One fine morning in March, 1941, we marched proudly past King George VI and Queen Elizabeth in her powder blue coat, long lines of us moving across the parade ground past the saluting base. That night we felt a little proud of ourselves as we sought our hammocks in Exmouth Block. We had hardly snuggled down for an early night when the air raid sirens began to moan and our speculative life ceased and the massive air blitz on Plymouth began.

4 The Plymouth blitz and the first ship

The first few hours of the Plymouth blitz have always possessed a dream-like quality for me; a nightmare dream which you think you can dismiss like all nightmares, but this dream can never be dismissed because it really happened. In the first few hours time ceased to exist and we crouched in the air-raid shelter like soldiers waiting to go over the top in the First World War, from some dug-out on the Western front – steel-helmeted, gas-masks slung to the front and crouching at the ready. The ground shook with the ceaseless explosions of bombs. In the lulls could be heard the rising and falling note of the unsynchronised engines of the German bombers which would be immediately joined by the crash of the anti-aircraft guns from shore batteries and ships in the harbour. Then would follow the whine of the falling bombs and the ear-blasting explosion. Plaster hissed sand-like down the walls at every explosion, and then the smoke began to filter down into the shelter. A Petty Officer clattered down the steps.

'You, you, you . . . eight, nine ten. Alright, that's enough, follow me.' Away they went into the inferno above and we waited our turn. Another grim figure appeared in the entrance.

'Ten men . . . you, you, you . . . that's enough!' I came up into the open air to see a sky like a surrealist fantasy, crossed by the white beams of searchlights, reddened by the reflection of a hundred fires, untidily washed by huge drifts of black smoke and starred incessantly by the glow of bursting anti-aircraft shells. We hoisted ourselves into the waiting naval truck and caught the shovels, pick-axes and crow bars thrown up to us. The truck jerked away and into the streets of Devonport which seemed undamaged. Ahead of us the heart of Plymouth was bleeding red into the sky and the truck sped towards it. Fresh debris appeared on either side of us, fitfully lit by flames and we began to jar on fire hoses and bits of fallen masonry, finally coming to a halt at a wall of shattered brick and wood beams blocking the road.

'Clear a way through it!' came the peremptory command from the darkness, and shovels and picks clattered on the ground and we followed them down.

'Get your ear-plugs in!' advised someone, and we groped for the little rubber cones lying forgotten in our gas mask cases, and inserted them. The hellish noise dimmed a little and we dug on and through, apprehensive now that the plugs would conceal the whine of a falling bomb.

'Don't worry, lightning never strikes in the same place twice!' shouted someone, and almost immediately a bomb fell close by, glowing briefly red, and then the blast caught and whirled us around like rag-dolls. We picked ourselves up and resumed digging.

The way being cleared for communications, we moved onwards nearer the centre, coming to a huge fountain which gushed up for 50 feet, then crashed down to mix with the debris into a filthy pus-like mud. In the main streets, well-known department stores like Dingles, were ablaze from top to bottom, as were the city offices near the Parish Church of Saint Andrew's. The little winding streets that led to the Hoe had ceased to exist and were only dimly visible as giant screes of rubble, pierced everywhere by the flames of ignited gas mains. Spent incendiary bomb cylinders were littered on the ground where they had burned out harmlessly, but others had done their deadly work.

The huge fountain was bleeding the city centre to death, like a severed jugular vein, and the fire-hoses were reduced to a dribbling spittle of water. There seemed nothing left but to let the city burn itself out. High facades of buildings gave at the knees like toppling heavyweight boxers and collapsed into the roadways to be cleared by the hundreds of sailors.

'Where are all the civvies?' enquired a voice.

'Under this bloody lot?' growled another figure, pointing at the ruins.

'D'you think the Jerries knew the King and Queen were here?'

'Wonder where they are?'

'Christ knows! Watch out here comes another bloody wave of bombers!'

In this night and in succeeding nights, over 1,000 people died in the city, with 4,000 injured and an immense damage to property. This made Plymouth proportionately the worst-hit city in Great Britain, much more sorely wounded than London or Coventry, but being a Service town, this revelation to the enemy would be a tactical mistake, so age-old Plymouth suffered her agony in silence as a fighting service city and not a city of civilians!

So the night wore on, shovelling, levering, smashing, in the Dantean death throes of the old city. Our ears ached with the reverberations of bombs, our throats and lungs were parched by smoke and dust and our uniforms, filthied by the endless number of times we had thrown ourselves down as bombs fell nearby and slates clattered on our steel helmets. Sometime in the night we were relieved by another squad and returned to the barracks where we immediately fell asleep.

On awakening, we slapped the brick dust and plaster from our uniforms and examined our cuts and bruises hidden under a red muddy cake, and returned to Exmouth Block for breakfast. Smoke still drifted in the sky and there was an eerie quiet, but the sun shone strongly, picking out the white buildings and bathing them in a patina of tradition that always moved me. After breakfast, Chief Petty Officer Ford, an elderly Welshman from Welshpool, assembled us and gave us our orders.

'You're going to be a special squad,' he informed us, 'so get your overalls on, tin hats, gas-masks, oilskins and fall in here in five minutes!'

When we returned a large truck was drawn up by the Block. We embarked and started on a journey around the various stores where we loaded on tools of every kind used in demolition or construction work. Ropes, blocks, tackles and then a large wooden contraption known in the Navy as a sheerlegs, being simply two poles lashed together at the top with which you could improvise a kind of crane, using blocks, tackles and pulleys, and so perform a large number of lifting or pulling operations.

'Careful with this, and stow it safely!' warned the Chief, handing up a large strong box. 'It's explosives! And for God's sake don't drop this one!' handing up a smaller box. 'It's full of detonators and they're as delicate as eggshells!'

'What are we supposed to be doing with all this gear, Chief?'

'You're going to recover safes, documents, money and all sorts of stuff from bombed buildings. Somebody get some red rag and tie it on the end of those sheerlegs. They're sticking out a mile over the tailboard.' Thus emblazoned with a huge red rag we rolled away into the city centre. Apart from sailors the city was deserted.

'Where's all the civvies?' came the unanswered query. 'Are they all dead?'

Soon we located our first task, from a list in the Chief's possession . . . ground floor office, one large Chubb safe. A pick-axe clanged on heavy metal in the rubble and the first safe was found. The sheerlegs were anchored securely in the rubble, the tackles rigged, strops passed around the safe, and soon it lay on the pavement.

'Tip it over on its face,' said the Chief, 'and let's rip out the back. They're always weak at the back, usually only sheet iron, because they let them into walls and the back is often protected by concrete and brick work, so get the cold chisels and sledges out of the truck.'

Cunningly applied cold chisels and crowbars soon had the safe looking like an opened sardine tin, and the contents were handed out and the inventory commenced.

'Two whacking great ledgers, Chief . . . bundles of share certificates and bonds . . . Holy Moses, bundles and bundles of fivers, Chief.'

'Count the buggers then!' growled the Chief, 'where's that bloody civilian? . . . Oh, there you are, Sir . . . sorry! Check with us please, Sir?'

Everything being in order, we moved away to a large store, an indeterminate mound of smouldering rubble, breathing a hot breath over us. This safe was lodged in the basement down to which we dug all morning. With another sailor, I was lowered down into a white-tiled alleyway which seemed fairly clear. Cautiously we edged along it, the tiles still hot to the touch, like the side of a baker's oven, and the plaster spilling over us in little cascades. At a turn in the alley I stopped aghast and pointed.

'Look!' Crouched in the angle of the wall was a calcinated human figure, like those in Pompeii, with an exterior like rough cast cement. 'Chief,' I called, 'there's a body down here. Better come down.' He joined us in the oven-like space, crowbar in hand. Tentatively he thrust it forward at the figure and almost in an instant it dissolved into a pile of ashes with a soft sigh, like sand running through fingers.

'Oh, God!' I whispered, as I realised the loneliness of this man's end, a caretaker perhaps, caught far under the building as it caught fire, the smoke choking him and the flames eating down deep to produce the incandescence which had cremated him. In a night and a day, and as unexpectedly as this man's end, I had come face to face with my war! The Chief's gnarled hands gripped our shoulders firmly.

'All right, my boyos, you've had enough. Get back on top and send somebody else down!'

Finally we located the safe, a much bigger one, and opened it with another technique, that of knocking off the hinges and prising the front off!

'Hinges are always a weak point,' said the Chief sagely, and we wondered greatly as to where he had acquired his knowledge. There were whispers of a spell in Dartmoor, but we found out that he was quoting from instructions drawn up, we supposed, by some civil servant for just such an emergency, in a quiet office down some remote corridor of the Admiralty.

As light relief to the grimness of our discovery we found Lulu. Seeing a leg sticking out from under some girders, we feared the worst, but the first touch revealed that she was a plaster model, miraculously intact from her waved hair to her dainty painted toe nails.

'Poor little thing's starkers!' said a sympathetic voice, 'let's get some clothes on her. There's plenty hanging around the shops!' So we fitted up Lulu in expensive lingerie, pulled silk stockings on her shapely legs, gartered them and dressed her in the height of spring 1941 fashion.

'Can we have her, Chief, in the truck with us. Like our mascot?' Chief smiled, and gave in to us. So what with our red rag which conferred on us the cachet of probable bomb-disposal experts, and the figure of our glamorous Lulu peeping out from the back of the truck, we became a well-known unit in the desolation. It was the WVS ladies who bravely

45

penetrated the ruins to give us soup, drinks and sandwiches who suggested that Lulu's wardrobe could be changed ad infinitum from the unlimited stocks around us. So, whenever we spotted something attractive, Lulu had it, ranging from Marks and Spencers to Aquascutum and Burberry.

The next night was the same pattern of bomb, fire and excursions into the city, but we were being excused owing to the heavy and hazardous nature of the work. As the days passed, safe followed safe, some as easy as tin cans to open, others inaccessible and needing explosives to open them or to dislodge them from between heavy girders. One stood, like an Indian burial platform high above a mountain of rubble, still secured in the angles of four high girders, about 15 feet above us. Being rather small and agile, I had the job of shinning up the girders for a reconnaissance.

'The only way we'll get this one out, Chief,' I called from my insecure perch, 'is with a set of sky-hooks and a couple of clouds!'

'Leave it then!' said the Chief, making a note on his pad, for a heavier explosive charge than we carried. 'Right, move on to Lockyer Street – American Consul's office, and an accountant's office.'

In Lockyer Street we were delighted to see female figures poking about in the debris next door to our destination. Contact was soon made with the ladies whom we found to be nurses from the Prince of Wales's Hospital, trying to salvage their belongings from the wreck of their hostel. Gallant Jack, sprang to their rescue, mundane safes forgotten. Rummaging in the rubble and brickwork, we soon located flattened chests of drawers and wardrobes.

'Hold it there while I give it a little persuader with a sledge hammer!' A well-aimed blow would soon return a chest to a squareness sufficient to prise open the drawers.

'And what have we here, then?' shouted someone, waving a wispy undergarment.

'Put it down, you big ape. That's mine!' squealed a little nurse. So the salvage went on, the Chief holding up the real work in sympathy.

'Don't you think you could get your men to concentrate on the safes, Chief Petty Officer?' enquired the accountant, querulously.

'All in good time, Sir,' replied the Chief with a quiet dignity and a quizzical gaze.

Then suddenly, amidst the rare laughter and horseplay, there was a shattering explosion from the direction of the Hoe, in Albert Street.

'Down!' screamed a nurse at my side, with more presence of mind than I had, and she dragged me down beside her among the bricks, as a long sliver of slate, like a throwing knife, slammed into the rubble inches from our heads. We looked at each other wide eyed, as the reverberations died away among the houses and the dust cloud gathered.

'It's that's Army Bomb Disposal Squad up in Albert Street!' I shouted.

'Something's gone wrong!' As one man we rose from the wreckage and sprinted up Lockyer Strret and turned right into Albert Street. I was leading the squad with another sailor at my shoulder. Ahead of us there was a shapeless bundle on the pavement in a putty-coloured mackintosh. We slithered to a halt beside him and saw the blood oozing out from beneath him. I turned the body over to reveal a man's face, but the top of his head slipped off like the sliced top of a breakfast egg, and his brains trickled greyly on to the pavement. I knelt transfixed.

'Leave him!' said the sailor, 'he never knew what hit him – just passing the end of the street when the explosion occurred.'

A few yards ahead, the smoke was clearing to reveal a ghastly scene. From the bare branches of a tree, hung human fragments of viscera and limbs and the walls were splashed with blood. Everywhere were pieces of the bodywork of the exploded 15 hundredweight army truck, mingling with the shattered flesh. And lying in the gutter was the huge, bloated, finned shape of a 500 pound bomb.

'Let's get out of here, before that goes off!'

'There's nothing we can do here.'

Then from a smoke-filled alley staggered a khaki figure, head cradled in his arms and numb from shock. Friendly arms embraced him and set him down gently. Careful fingers explored his body, but he was absolutely unharmed. He opened his eyes, wonderingly.

'The Sarge sent me down the alley to collect up the tools while they put the bomb in the truck, and . . . that's all I remember.' He trailed off and his head fell forward into his arms. Suddenly he lifted his head. 'Where's the Sarge, and the others?' he asked, looking around, and beginning to take in his surroundings.

'Don't look, son!' said the Chief, kneeling down and shielding his gaze from the carnage. 'There's a good boy, you just be quiet.'

An ambulance bell sounded at the bottom of the street and we handed over to them. Taking a last look at the malevolent unexploded bomb we hurried away to Lockyer Street and our unfinished task. Later that afternoon, we were surveying a safe in a wine-merchant's shop, sitting smugly on two girders in the burnt out ruins.

'Shin up there, Doc, and have a look,' said Chief Ford. I shinned up the girders and crawled across one to the safe, glancing down to an adjoining part of the shop where some of the staff were sweeping and shovelling among the debris. I heard a metallic clang, and from my perch I glanced down. One of the staff was pointing excitedly at an object protruding from the ground – the unmistakable fins of a big bomb. As one man, the staff fled, colliding with our squad as they went.

'Hey, Chief?' I called, 'there's a bloody great bomb in the room next door!'

'Out!' roared the Chief, and I was alone on my perch.

'Wait for me!' I shouted plaintively and unnecessarily. 'Miserable buggers!'

I came down with the adrenalin flowing freely and joined the squad outside, as the Chief wet the end of his pencil to write. 'One unexploded bomb, probably 500 pounds . . .' he mumbled. 'What's the name of this street? Ah, to hell with it . . . I'm going to buy you lot a nice stiff brandy each. We've had a bellyful today!'

So in a little undamaged pub called the Golden Galleon we sipped brandy for the rest of the afternoon, pooling our meagre resources gladly to make a drinking kitty.

Our specialist work was coming to an end as order returned to the city and our work became slacker. In Sussex Gardens one afternoon we drifted towards a group of sailors digging in the basement area of a large Georgian type house.

'Here come the gentlemen!' growled a sailor, scrabbling in the dust and plaster below us in the basement. 'You get the nice jobs, not like us, digging out dead bodies . . . take a look at this poor feller!' We squatted at the edge of the excavation, just in time to see the sailor's trowel reveal a human hand, green and marble-like. Around the wrist was a watch.

'Half-past 12!' called the sailor, peering closely. 'That's when they got it. There's another 11 in here somewhere.' We stopped to lend a hand, as the shapeless bundles, sexless, and seeming like mummies dug from the sand were uncovered and hauled up. As the last body was moved, there was a small landslide and the entrance of the basement was revealed, intact and safe.

'They must have heard the bomb coming, rushed out into the area-way and the whole damned front of the house fell in on them. If only they'd have stayed put,' said one of the sailors.

Spring was beginning to touch the hedgerows of South Devon with tentative strokes of light green as we walked on our country rambles around Plympton, down to Totnes and up on Dartmoor, for there was nowhere for a sailor to go in the mounded ruins of the city. On leave days it was now the custom to get on to the outskirts of Plymouth and hitch a lift to some quiet country pub. Life in Exmouth Block was a quiet backwater in the bustle and hurry of the barracks, but it could not last. Towards the end of March 1941, the call to the sea came over the Barracks' tannoy.

'D'ye hear that, d'ye hear that?' said the voice with a soft Devon burr. 'The following ratings report to the Drafting Office.' There was a long string of names and numbers and then, 'Ordinary Seaman Robert FC Hughes, D/JX 229673.' Up to the Drafting Office I doubled to find out my new ship, sorting out the possibilities as I ran . . . cruiser, battleship, aircraft carrier, destroyer. A destroyer was my private fancy.

'Here's your draft chit,' said an offhand voice proffering a piece of paper with an impersonal hand, '*HMS Scarborough*; report over there!'

Over there, I found my new shipmates, Lomas, lean, dark and saturnine from Manchester, and Baldwin, well-covered, rosy-cheeked and rather shy, from Birkenhead, though his appearance would have suggested a more rural home. They were very pleased.

'She's up in Liverpool!' they informed me in chorus.

'Just across the water,' said Baldwin.

'Just up the Ship Canal,' gloated Lomas.

'Just my ruddy luck,' said I. 'Miles from my home, as usual. The Welsh and the Scots – Britain's usual exiles!'.

'What kind of ship is she?' they enquired. Scornful of their ignorance, I was most superior.

'She's a sloop of about 1,000 tons of the Hastings class, built about 1930-31, two four-inch guns, 17 knots speed and I think she has been a survey vessel.'

'Cor!' said Lomas. 'Listen to that – proper mine of information. Ah, well you did say you were a schoolmaster, so I'm going to call you Doc, like that Dr Arnold of Rugby, and that other Head of Billy Bunter's school.'

'It's all in a book I've got,' I said disparagingly, '*All the World's Fighting Fleets* by Talbot-Booth. It's a very fat, dumpy book, I carry around with me. I'll show it you, sometime.'

'So, it's Plymouth North Road Station tomorrow at 0900 sharp and northwards we go, eh?' said Baldwin. 'I suppose we'd better get packed up.'

All next day we travelled northwards, passing through Taunton and close to the buildings and playing fields of Taunton School, with fleeting glimpses of the houses of friends, and distant views of the Quantock Hills which I knew so well. All now a little world detached and far from the world of navy blue serge, rope, steel, guns, depth-charges and salt seas in which I now found myself.

Naval Headquarters at Liverpool dashed our hopes of a shipboard home, by informing us that *Scarborough* was not yet due in from sea. We were despatched instead to a sports pavilion in a recreation ground belonging to Silcocks' seeds, where we spent some aimless days tending winter-ravaged flower beds, running errands, but at least existing flourishingly on an abundance of bacon, sausages and eggs, cooked by an old sailor, washed down with strong tea sweetened with condensed milk.

One morning we were bundled peremptorily into a naval truck which deposited us, kit-bags, hammocks and all, at the side of a jetty in

Gladstone Dock, every yard of which seemed to be occupied by a bewildering variety of smaller warships – World War 1 'V and W' class destroyers, one or two destroyers of the Twenties, corvettes, sloops, a Dutch training ship, a French submarine-chaser, and even one of the ex-American 'four stackers', thin, under-nourishied looking ships with tall pole masts, covered bridges, and four funnels, pipe-like and upright, and far too many. In some parts of the dock, the ships were two and three deep alongside, in what we came to know as 'trots'.

'*Scarborough*?' said a passing sailor, snapping his fingers to our query. 'Outside ship of that trot of three up there. Bad luck!'

We hauled and pulled our bags and hammocks across the decks of an ex-American destroyer, and a 'V and W' and came to a puzzled halt on the holystoned, teak decks of *Scarborough*.

'No band, no welcome committee?' I enquired facetiously, and there was an acid silence, so I gazed aloft at the masts and saw that the climb to the crow's nest was not really all that far, which encouraged me. My reverie was interrupted by a snarl and a tall, dark, cadaverous looking Leading Seaman materialised from somewhere, eyes blazing wickedly from under a long lock of dark hair, dropping across his forehead.

'You the new draft from Guz?' he snapped, using the slang term for Plymouth.

'Yes,' I mumbled, self-appointed spokesman. 'My name's Hughes and this is Lomas and Baldwin.'

'Oh, the posh buggers,' he said, 'going to be officers, I hear?' I was once again reminded of how hollow was the promise given to us when we had volunteered, that only our officers would know that we were being considered for commissions. We were being categorised from the beginning, and to some extent put on the defensive.

'Well,' said the Leading Seaman, 'you lot are in my Mess which is Number One Mess. My name's Brock and I'm a right bastard and I'm going to chase you matloes from arsehole to breakfast time. For a start, get those jumpers off, and let's have a look at your underwear!' We protested facially, with looks of horror. 'Get 'em off! That's an order!' We obeyed and wriggled out of our jumpers, being revealed in our obviously unwashed singlets.

'Just as I thought,' he snarled. 'Bloody filthy! You posh buggers are all the same – lah-de-dah accents and dirty underwear. Get up the fo'c'sle, dump your kit-bags, find a hammock-slinging place and then get straight to the bathroom and start dhobying all those stinking clothes. I'll not have dirty matloes in my Mess!' He was dressed in a faded blue boiler suit of many washings and scrubbings, open at the neck to reveal a silver chain and a crucifix, and the top of a snowy white singlet. He grabbed at the collar of the boiler suit and tore it open to reveal the whiteness. 'You'll be like that!' he spat. 'Now get on with it!' He loped away with long strides.

'Christ!' breathed Lomas, 'what a start!'

'And I bet he's an RC and hates all Protestants!' I added nastily.

'Oh, I expect we'll survive,' said Baldwin, the gentle philosopher.

The fo'c'sle was a small compartment, the bulkheads flaring sharply outwards on either side to the contours of the bow, and narrowing quite rapidly forrard towards the sharp cutwater of the bow. This ended in a transverse bulkhead in which there was a watertight door to some store, and flanked on either side by two pipes, obviously the hawse pipes for the anchor chains which must be stored in the chain locker on the deck below.

We had entered by a steep companion ladder on the fo'c'sle maindeck, abaft of the elderly-looking four-inch gun. There were four mess tables, secured to the deck, fore and aft, and the two on the starboard side according to naval numbering would be One and Three Messes, and the others on the port side would be Two and Four. One Mess was therefore up in the narrowest part of the fo'c'sle and to this table we made our way.

Up against the bulkheads were wooden seats with lift-up lids for storage and behind these a line of lockers for mess cutlery, crockery, provisions etc. There were railed bins for hammocks and bags and into these we dumped our earthly possessions, first seeking out the dirty washing and the huge bar of yellow soap. One or two sailors drifted in and out, giving us a cursory glance, and a pitying look at belonging to One Mess. The bathroom was located and we found some buckets and a supply of hot water. We scrubbed away morosely and a little pile of wrung-out garments grew beside us. Brock strode in and sniffed.

'Where do we hang them out to dry, please, Leading Seaman Brock?' I enquired politely.

'Anywhere on the upper deck,' he replied, and then relented a little. 'Come on then – I'll show you.' Soon our efforts were fluttering bravely from the lines we had rigged on the fo'c'sle, whipped by the strong breeze from the Mersey. They looked quite brave and professional and my heart swelled.

Within the next few days while *Scarborough* went through the mysteries of a boiler-clean, carried out by gangs of stokers stationed ashore, we began to get the feel of the ship. She was a graceful little ship with a much higher freeboard than the destroyers around us and much less warlike-looking, because at the after end she still carried the rather high superstructure of the chartroom of her survey-ship days. This was a large room, full of mahogany tables on which the charts had been prepared, long drawers underneath, glass-fronted cabinets which must have held instruments and to me, a rather romantic room still smelling, I thought, of the spices of the

West Indian Islands where she had been stationed before the war.

Scarborough carried more boats than seemed normal, for, besides the port and starboard whalers at the break of the fo'c'sle, she had two boats stowed near the charthouse, one a large cabin type motorboat, probably used for inshore survey work. Under the charthouse was the Wardroom, a big pleasant room with quite large square, railway carriage type windows, looking out on the the quarter deck which was one deck lower than the main deck. She was a flush-decked vessel, the deck running unbroken from the fo'c'sle to the charthouse, then it dropped to the quarter deck. Every deck, to our dismay, was spotless scrubbed teak on which Brock soon put us to work with holystones, bricks of Bathstone which we used, one in each hand, and on our knees in holy fashion, to scour the decks daily.

Her armament seemed very flimsy, consisting of the four-inch gun, made in 1917, a four-barrelled .5 calibre machine-gun, abaft the mast, which always jammed so were told, and two ancient Lewis guns mounted on swivel mounts, below and on either side of the bridge. Near the wardroom on either side were two depth-charge throwers, and right at the stern were two depth-charge racks, along which depth-charges were rolled on rails and dropped over the stern. Amidships the funnel reared up from the engine room and was surrounded by engine room hatches and fan outlets breathing hot air and the hum of generators from below in the engine room.

Forrard of the funnel was the mast festooned with radio aerials and signal halyards, but not as yet with radar antennae, at this early stage of the war. Instead it bore the traditional early-warning system – the crow's nest.

The bridge was next in line forrard, a cramped boxy structure on top for navigation and a small signal deck below which also housed the Lewis guns. The navigation bridge contained a platform for the gyro and magnetic compasses, a high seat for the captain, positions for the port and starboard look-outs, and a bewildering array of instruments to us, at this stage, unknown.

Below decks the lay-out was quite simple. Two long passages ran the whole length of the ship. On the outward sides of each were bathrooms, stores, lavatories or Heads, cabins for officers, chief and petty officers' messes and the ship's office. Between the two passages was the space taken up by the engine room and boiler room, a small sick-bay and surgery and the canteen or shop. Underneath this deck was another deck mainly taken up by magazines, provision stores, and a refrigeration room referred to as the CO_2 room. Below this deck lay the mysterious bilges, the propeller tunnel and the compartment that contained the Asdic dome, our chief weapon for locating submarines, and in those days, the most advanced anti-submarine device in the world. This was our most important weapon, much more important than an array of guns in the war in the Atlantic, waged against an enemy constantly under water and largely immune from guns, except when forced to the surface.

Our food was provided by a small ships' system known as Canteen Messing. Under this system we were supplied with the basic foods such as bread, meat and vegetables, free, but on top of this each rating was given a sum of money on a daily basis from which we bought other necessaries, such as butter, jam, pickles. Should we have saved anything by good housekeeping, cunning menus, etc, each mess was re-imbursed by the amount of this saving and shared out by the members of the Mess.

To achieve this saving, our menus, devised by Brock, were quite simple – breakfast, a cup of tea and a fag or some bread and jam. Dinner, a huge, meaty meal, followed by tea – the inevitable cup of tea – and a fag. Then came the long-awaited supper, another huge meaty meal. If you wanted anything fancy such as fish paste, sardines, or other delicacies, then you bought them out of your own money from the canteen.

In the ensuing months we lived like alternate paupers and lords, accruing sizeable savings with which we bought butter, sugar, jam etc from the stores, and took them home on leave to our rationed families. By the second day, I had achieved the dubious honour of being Cook of the Mess for a day, a duty I came to dread as I had no culinary ambition.

'Right, Doc!' said Brock after breakfast, for my nickname had now been established for me by Lomas and Baldwin. 'You're Cook of the Mess today, God help us, and God help you too if you make a muck of it. Today I have decided to have a Pot Mess for dinner.' I raised my eyebrows, interrogatively.

'What mess?' I enquired politely.

'A bloody Pot Mess!' bawled Brock. 'It's a sort of meat and vegetable stew. So first of all take this chit to Tanky, the storekeeper and draw us some stewing beef, some tins of meat and vegetable rations, M and Vs we call 'em, some vegetables and flour and suet for the dumplings. Then get round the other messes and scrounge all their bones and boil the lot together to make some nice stock.

'While that's brewing up, get the vegetables ready. Then after that, get weaving on the dumplings, and put them in last of all, and if the buggers sink to the bottom you're for it! I want them floating on top, half in and half out of the gravy, see? For second course we'll have stewed apples and custard and then a nice jug of coffee, and don't forget to put salt at the bottom to keep down the grounds! Got all that?' I nodded dumbly and prayed to Mrs Beaton for help. 'Then off you go, at the double!' he rapped. 'And see that you get a real hot place on the galley stove.' he added.

I assembled my ingredients at the end of the mess table and gazed morosely at them. The cooks of the other three messes were busily at work and still I gazed, helplessley. I was joined by a soft-spoken Australian Able Seaman called Boyd.

'Come a-bloody-long then, Doc?' he said, interpolating the bloodies between syllables, in the Australian fashion. 'Leading Bloody Seaman Brock'll have your guts for a necktie, if you don't hurry up. Too bloody right, he will. Come on, then, I'll give you a hand.'

Under his tutelage I soon had a nice stock bubbling on a fairly advantageous place on the large oil-fired range in the galley. The galley was presided over by a corpulent Leading Cook, a misogynistic character in greasy white overalls, whom I was told it was politic to address as Chef, even though his ability to boil water was often in question. However, he controlled the galley, and it was he who allocated the best places on the stove, so it was best to rub him up the right way. His conversation was strictly limited to one phrase, which brought any conversation to an abrupt end.

'Nice day, Chef?' you would say, sycophantically.

'Ah, shit in the bastard!' he would reply tonelessly, gazing sightlessly into the steam rising from the pots.

Having made my stock, the now-prepared vegetables, meat and tins of M and Vs were ladled in, and soon I was sniffing at a most agreeable savoury odour rising from my huge pot. Loth to leave my masterpiece I sought out Aussie Boyd for his wisdom on dumplings. I was soon back in the galley with a tray full of dumplings which I launched into the maelstrom of my stew. For a few moments my little fleet bobbed about bravely, and then one by one they sank, like the Russian Fleet at Tsushima in 1904.

'Chef?' I moaned, in mental agony, 'all my dumplings have sunk to the bottom. Brock'll kill me!'

'Ah, shit in the bastard!' rasped the Chef, helpfully.

But Mrs Beaton was on my side, and like U-boats they surfaced later, light and feathery just as Brock burst into the galley expecting the worst. The stewed apples were just right, the custard nice and thick, and the coffee grounds stayed at the bottom of the pot.

'Not bad for a bloody schoolmaster!' pronounced Brock at the end of dinner, belching. 'Warm you up nicely for the afternoon watch as jetty sentry. So see if you can remember your rifle drill. We've a reputation to keep up!'

I sniffed philosophically at the meagre reward for my haute cuisine, and spent the rest of the afternoon playing the Lone Tin Soldier up and down the jetty, saluting officers, envying them their girl-friends, and watching the busy life of the Liverpool Destroyer Flotilla as they re-provisioned, reammunitioned with shell and depth-charge, noting the famous names of ship builders and repairers on the trucks that constantly passed by – Cammell Laird, Harland and Wolff, the intriguing Grayson, Rollo and Clover Docks, and the mysterious navigational names of Kelvin-Hughes and Sperry Gyro-compasses.

Many such hours would I pass in the coming months, and many dishes would I prepare as Cook of the Mess, rising to such savoury heights as grilled bacon and tomatoes covered with a richly bubbling roof of nicely grated cheese, supplemented by a tenderly fried egg and gently browned chips. And as the sentry coming off watch I would eat everything left over by those seeking the beerier delights of shore leave, for a sea appetite is a huge and wondrous thing.

Brock seemed to be a teacher who believed in throwing his pupils in at the deep-end for next morning he rubbed his hands when we fell in with the Watches after breakfast.

'Big promotion for you, Doc!' he grinned, 'you're Captain of the Heads!'

'What's that, please, Leading Seaman Brock?' I enquired.

'Shit-house cleaner!' he ground out, 'but I'm going easy on you – you can do the officers' Heads. They go through the same motions as us, you know, but you wouldn't think so, the way some of 'em fancy themselves. Go on then, get your bucket and mop, your scrubbers and some strongers – caustic soda to you, Doc!'

I scuttled away to the Cleaning Store and armed myself as befitted my exalted rank. Seeking advice I entered the Ratings' Heads to consult my opposite number. I found him sitting on a toilet seat, a cigarette dangling from his lips, lasciviously glaring at an American girlie magazine.

'Take a look at that!' he offered, reversing the magazine to reveal a shapely scantily clad female. 'How'd you like to give that a couple of strokes of the old shamdooey, or a stab with the old mutton dagger?' He gave a sexy grunt. His bucket lay idle, the caustic soda bubbling.

'When are you going to start?' I asked, waving my arm around.

'After Stand-Easy,' he said, decisively. 'Why start now when as soon as Stand-Easy comes they'll be pissing and farting all over me clean Heads. Plenty time!'

I acknowledged the wisdom of his tactics and after a few words of advice on procedure, I left for the Officers' Heads. I began at once and had just finished one toilet, quite creditably, when an officer entered and chose my chef d'oeuvre as his sanctuary. Being polite I immediately retired, but not before hearing a sound that confirmed Brock's statement on human behaviour. Plumbing sounds indicated a cessation of his activity, and he came out and I scuttled back in. Brock was again proved right and sadly I began to clean the toilet pan all over again. I could never quite bring myself to respect that officer again for spoiling my handiwork!

That evening Daily Orders announced that we would sail the following afternoon, and I had a last run ashore to Gladstone House, a good civilised meal, the inevitable toast at bedtime and a last quiet run through the piano pieces I had memorised – an odd selection of music, ranging from Debussy's *La Fille aux Cheveux de Lin* to Edward MacDowell's *To a Wild Rose* and part of the Bach Chorale *Mortify us by Thy Grace*. I fell asleep, not unduly worried that I would soon be on my first deep-sea voyage in a few hours' time.

Next morning, Brock had Lomas, Baldwin and myself at the foot of the mast, gazing up at the crow's nest.

'Get up there!' he pointed at Lomas and angled his finger upward. Lomas took a deep breath and started to climb the rigging, growing smaller and foreshortened as he climbed towards the barrel-shaped crow's nest. 'Climb above it and drop in!' shouted Brock, and suddenly Lomas was safely inside.

'Down!' bawled Brock, and pointed to me. 'You next, Doc.'

Lomas dropped lightly to the deck and I began my ascent, remembering that it was one strong hand for yourself, the other for the Admiralty, and soon I was inside the steel tub, gazing out over the warehouses to the choppy Mersey.

'Down!' came the thin voice of Brock from below, and I grabbed the rigging and hauled myself upwards and out on to the ratlines.

After dinner, the ship seethed with activity. The engines were started up for a short burst, loose fittings were lashed and stowed and Brock nudged me with his arm.

'Up to the bridge with me,' he said, 'you're starboard look-out.' We climbed up to the small navigating bridge and he pointed to the starboard look-out position and handed me a pair of long Admiralty binoculars.

'Get the strap and lanyard over your head and keep it there . . . 20 quid if you lose one of those overboard. Centre screw focussing, magnification 7 and a 50mm object glass which gives you a hell of a field of view which is more important than magnification at sea when your horizon is limited. You can see at night with these. These object glasses are just like a cat's eye which opens wide at night to take in the light. These little levers here flick light filters across the lens to help you look into the sun if you have to. You know all about reporting objects, green and red, the angles, etc, and forrard and abaft the beam, eh? Got your life belt on?' I nodded, proud of the fact that I was now stepping on to the threshold of a real sailor's life.

'Right. Have a fiddle about with the glasses to get used to them. Captain and Navigator'll be up soon.' He moved across for a word with the port look-out, a seasoned veteran by his one Good Conduct badge. Behind me, a few minutes later, I heard new voices and turned slightly to see the

Captain and Navigator climb on to the bridge.

Our Captain was Lt Adrian Northey, RN, a tall, burly man two or three years my senior, with a humourous twinkle in his eye. Behind him came the Navigator, Lt Boyd, with the gold interlaced stripes of the Royal Naval Reserves. He was fair-haired and fine featured and I pictured him as sailing before the war on a cruise liner, the heart-throb of all the lady passengers. My reverie was interrupted by the Captain's voice.

'And who are you?' he enquired in a soft voice.

'My name's Hughes, Sir. Ordinary Seaman.'

'Ah, one of the new CW Ratings, eh? You're the schoolmaster, and the other two are in banking and insurance. Their names are . . . ?'

'Baldwin and Lomas,' I supplemented.

'Ah, yes. Well, when we've settled down, I want a talk with you three.' He turned away to the Navigator. 'Right, Pilot. We'll single up to a headrope and back spring, and I'll come astern on the spring, get her head out as far as I can and then bring her round to line up on the lock gates. Carry on please.'

'Single up!' shouted the Navigator, and faintly the command was repeated from the deck below.

'Standby engines!'

'Slow astern. Port 20!'

'Cast off headrope. Hold on to the spring!'

Slowly the bows began to separate from the ships in the trot as our ship came alive. The turbines could be heard humming faintly, and the fans joined in the rhythm. A long triangle of open water began to appear on the port side as the bow swung out.

'Half ahead. Hard a-starboard!' The wire rope of the spring began to twang gently, and then the tension came off as the ship gathered way forward and the stern swung clear.

'Let go the spring!' The *Scarborough* began to turn in a tight circle, and we were soon at right angles to the trot with the bows still swinging towards the entrance lock.

'Starboard 20. Stop engines!' The swing lessened, giving time for the Captain to judge his next move to line up on the lock gates. 'Wheel amidships. Slow ahead!' Slowly we headed directly for the lock gates, which began to open for us. With my head in a whirl at the string of commands, we glided through the huge Gladstone locks with yards to spare on either side, scornful of the help of the dockyard men slipping past us on the lock side above. My first sea voyage had begun.

5 Western ocean 1941

'Buoy bearing Green Two-Oh!' I reported, quietly and decisively, but not too obtrusively, like a butler announcing dinner for about the twentieth time.

'Hughes,' said the Captain, in a kindly but slightly chiding voice, 'it is not really necessary to report every little thing while we are in the Mersey; we must keep our keen look-out for when we reach the open sea! Understand?'

'Aye, aye, Sir!' I replied and relapsed into silence, having been taught one lesson about relevant and irrelevant reporting.

Scarborough was steaming down the Mersey at about 15 knots, en route for the Minches, between the Hebrides and the Western Highlands, where our convoy would be assembling. So far, my sea-legs seemed in good shape, and there was so much to see and hear that my mind was fully occupied. The ship settled down to a quiet routine and there was now little activity on the upper deck, everything having been stowed or lashed down.

I had been put in the Blue Watch, in the charge of Brock, and we would have the dreaded Middle Watch in the coming night, so after the proper sea-watch look-outs took over as we passed the Bar Light ship at the Mersey entrance I went down to the Mess. Already some sailors had slung their hammocks, sea-boots and heavy jerseys littered the locker seats, the air was thick with cigarette and pipe smoke and there was a huge pot of tea, and a badly hacked loaf on the table for those who felt like tea. I felt like it and filled a mug and hacked a bread slice. After tea I slung my hammock and did a few odd personal jobs and waited for supper. The motion in the fo'c'sle was distinctly peculiar and when supper time came my appetite had waned, so I sought my hammock, where I soon fell asleep.

In what seemed minutes, Brock was banging away with his fist at the hammock, advising sea-boots and duffel coats, as the weather was cold. On the upper deck, the Blue Watch huddled behind the gun, ready to spring into action on the gun, or waiting for our turn at look-out, either in the crow's nest or on the bridge. Conversation was desultory, and besides Brock, the main person to whom attention was paid was a stocky, dark little Welshman from Cardiganshire, Taff Evans, a three badge Able Seaman. As a fellow Celt I was drawn to Taff and hung on his words, picking up many little tips and a wealth of descriptive naval slang. He was also the captain of the four-inch gun which he described for our information, informing me that I would be sight-setter and communication number to the bridge. I tried on the huge earphones, feeling like Jack Cornwell, VC, at Jutland, and turned the handles of the sight-setting machine for various ranges.

'Useless bloody gun, it is mun!' said Taff, 'made for the Japanese it was, in the last war.' Linking this fact with the jamming propensities of the .5 machine-gun, and the obvious age of the two Lewis machine-guns, I was not impressed with our capabilities in a surface action.

Arriving on the bridge for my turn at look-out, the sailor I was relieving thrust a dark square at me on which there seemed to be some chalked writing.

'Read that!' he commanded. I peered closely at the word and made it out.

'Balls!' I said, in quiet triumph.

'And the same to you,' he replied. 'You're alright. Here's the glasses.' Such, in those days was our primitive method of testing whether our eyes were adapted to night conditions, and many were the catch-phrases and obscenities chalked on that simple board, until the scientists arrived with their goggles and night-adaptation routines. The Middle Watch in the Irish Sea that night was meaningless to me, except for the flashing of lighthouses, the dark shapes of ships and the shore, the rising seas and the conviction that my stomach was going to rebel against the constant roll and pitch of the ship. The watch came to an end, and I sought my hammock with growing misery.

Marmite and toast for breakfast did not appeal to me, and I mooched around in abject misery, paying constant visits to the Heads. During the morning we chipped paintwork on the upper deck, then rounded off the watch with gun-drill on the four-inch, supervised by Mr Burton, the Warrant Gunner, disgustingly hale and hearty and wrapped in a sheepskin jerkin like a cowboy on a winter range. We changed rounds interminably, and my stomach grew progressively worse. During the day I took enough notice to identify the mountains on the port side, as the mountains of Mourne in Antrim, which according to some song I remembered always 'swayed down to the sea'. At the time, and in my state, I was quite willing to let them keep on swaying until they reached the bottom of the sea, taking me with them.

Some time in the afternoon we went to Action Stations for practice, and I found myself in the .5 inch magazine, sprawled on top of numerous cases of explosive material. As far as I was concerned, the whole lot could have blown up and I could not have cared less. Down in the Mess, the radio was blaring and the Andrews sisters were brassily harmonising and extolling the manly qualities of some very gay caballero. This was followed by a sad song about some Dutch refugees which went something like this; 'My sister and I recall the day, when we packed our bags and sailed away.' All this was too much for me, so I sought my little misericord, a large coil of heavy manilla rope, behind the warm funnel, and sank down into it like a battered seagull. I must have fallen asleep for I was awakened by a sea-boot in the ribs, which as my eye travelled upwards I identified as Brock's. He thrust a plate of bacon, eggs and chips at me and my stomach heaved.

'Eat!' he commanded. I made a noise of revulsion. 'Eat the bastard!' he shouted. I replied with another revolting noise. 'Well, bugger you then!' he said. 'I'm leaving it here.' He clambered down. The smell of food began to tickle my nostrils and I took a tentative bite at some bacon, swallowed, and it stayed down. In moments, I was wolfing it down. I realised that I had found my sea-legs and for the next four years I never lost them again.

From the bridge my first glimpse of an Atlantic convoy was an inspiring sight on that April morning of 1941. As we patrolled back and forth across the front of the convoy, it seemed as if the whole sea was full of ships. And what a variety there was – Cardiff tramps, elderly and nondescript, haughty Blue Funnel cargo liners with their tall, aristocratic funnels, Clan liners with their usual heavy lift derricks, tankers with names of sea-shells, others with names of Spanish saints, trim little fruit carrying ships of the Macandrews Line, the odd cargo-passenger ship of the Ellerman City Line, and a great many foreign ships, Norwegian Wilhelmsen cargo-liners, French and Belgian ships and the inevitable antiquated Greek tramp, with some Greek family name in Greek characters on her stern and bows, for in those days they were the numerous, though poor relations, of the merchant shipping world.

What was most striking was the precision of the columns, the good station-keeping and the overall air of dogged determination as they plodded across the Atlantic at eight knots, not much faster than a bicycle and easy prey for even the slowest U-boat. On each of the far wings of the convoy patrolled the elderly destroyers and other sloops and corvettes, while astern, came another destroyer, like a collie dog cajoling and snapping at the heels of this great sea-flock. Very faintly could be heard the beat of the triple-expansion steam engines and the uneven beat of the odd motorship. Everywhere there was the deep blue of the ocean, the sea and the sky.

A quick calculation based on the presence in this area of 50 ships with perhaps an average crew of 40, revealed to me that there could be over 2,000 men here with all their hopes, fears, ambitions and ailments. It was in effect a small floating town and the frequency with which the many signal lamps flickered and flashed during the day confirmed this. There would be requests for a diagnosis of an illness from one ship, reports of engine trouble from another, while over all, were the signals from the Commander of the escorting warships to and from the Convoy Commodore in one of the leading merchant ships for the manoeuvring and fighting of the convoy.

Flags would appear at all the mastheads, and as they were hauled down, at the signal to execute a turn, the column leaders would lurch around, their wakes curving, with the others following in succession, varying speed until the columns were once again correctly aligned. At intervals, an escort vessel on the outer screen would detach itself to investigate a submarine contact and then the thud of depth-charges would shake the hulls and white mountains of water would erupt. The shallow depth-charge patterns made the more spectacular sights, while the deep patterns would produce a huge circular pancake of disturbed water, visibly quivering at the edges.

Binoculars everywhere would be quartering the skies for the always-expected German Focke-Wulf reconnaissance aircraft. With their four engines, shark-like nose and huge tailfin, shaped, according to the recognition manual, like a Mack Sennett comedy policeman's helmet, they were easy to recognise. The only aircraft to appear on this convoy were an elderly two engined Whitley bomber of very limited range, and a huge Sunderland flying boat of much greater use. We viewed these patrolling aircraft with some envy, knowing that they would be back in Britain that night, with leave for the aircrew and a pint in some country pub in Pembrokeshire.

By 5 April we had plodded our way westward to a position about 300 miles south of Iceland, into the area of U-boat activity and out of range of our protective aircraft. In the afternoon a sudden change in the engine beat indicated some unusual situation and like lightning the word went around the ship that we had a definite submarine contact. Almost immediately the alarm rattlers for Action Stations sounded, and I descended to my small-arms magazine.

What followed was, for me, a confusion of tremendous explosions shaking the hull as our depth-charges exploded or, which for all I knew, could have been a torpedo crashing into us. Down the open hatch came the confused thump of sea-boots on the deck as Taff Evans and his gun crew trained the four-inch gun on each area of hugely disturbed water, waiting for the hull of a U-boat to break surface. The explosions suddenly stopped and a voice shouted,

'Stand by to open fire!' But there was no cracking report, and then the engines slowed almost to a stop.

'We've got a bloody U-boat!' a voice shouted exultantly down the hatch, 'us and the *Wolverine*. Picking up the survivors now!'

Shortly afterwards we returned to normal cruising stations and I was able to go up on deck to see *Wolverine* a V and W class destroyer of 1918 vintage, looking very smug and self-satisfied as she completed the task of picking up the survivors. Our joint victim had been U.76, and her Captain and 41 crew had been rescued.

'Trust the *Wolverine!*' said someone. 'She's always in at the kill. Anyway, what is a wolverine, Doc?'

'Darned if I know!' I confessed, 'other than that trappers in Canada trap it, and it's got lots of fur.'

'And those aboard'll have plenty of prize-money too. Anyway, half of it's ours.'

This was the only excitement of my first three weeks at sea and visually non-existent at that. At latitude 27 west, we turned back and picked up a homeward bound convoy for Liverpool. This was little different from the other, except for the deck cargoes of cocooned American aircraft, tanks, guns and trucks which lined the decks of many of the ships. One strange sight was a Great Lakes steamer, with engines aft, a long uncluttered deck with many hatches, and a round-faced bridge practically on the forecastle. These ships were being tried out on the Atlantic run, such was the shortage of vessels, but by the way she rolled and pitched to an alarming degree, their use seemed to me limited and dangerous.

To see the twin towers of the Liver Building, the classical lines of the Custom House, the Cunard Building and the other buildings which make Liverpool waterfront one of the most imposing in the world, was a heartening sight. In the coming months I would see it often and secretly pray to see it again each time it faded astern as we sailed away. We slid into the Gladstone Dock and took up a place at our usual jetty. There was short weekend leave for those who lived nearby, but for me it was a stay at Gladstone House.

The Liverpool Philharmonic Orchestra always had concerts on Saturdays and Sundays, free on this latter day to Service folk. On the Sunday afternoon, Kendall Taylor played Beethoven's *Emperor Concerto* and I listened, entranced by the delicacy of the subsidiary theme of the first movement with the counter rhythms weaving a magic web which covered the starkness of our existence at sea, the destruction, the discomfort and the tension.

Returning to Gladstone House, I sought the music room, something prompting me to thumb through the pile of tattered music there. To my amazement, there was a two-piano copy of the *Emperor Concerto*, which I had never seen there before. So in this magic hour, I was able to hesitantly weave the web for myself, growing more confident with each playing. I felt my soul being re-charged like an electric cell and I returned to *Scarborough* quite happy and prepared for our next voyage.

62

After passing the Bar Light Vessel, the buzz, or rumour ran round the ship that we were going to Gibraltar, and as the days passed we indeed moved southwards. The Captain no longer appeared on the bridge in his ski-cap with a huge bobble on top, Gieves's inflatable waistcoat, riding breeches and carpet slippers, but in whiter and more sunny wear. Portuguese men-of-war jellyfish began to spot the oily swell with pink, and looking over the side I saw a turtle paddle past in the pull of the Gulf Stream. Dolphins played ahead of us and scratched the parasites off their backs by scraping along our roughened hull.

'This is what we joined for!' beamed Taff Evans, overalls rolled down and flexing his chest in its snowy white singlet. A lone bird planed over the crests and down into the trough of the waves, a bird I later came to know as a fulmar petrel.

'What kind of bird is that, Taff?' I enquired of his vast sea knowledge.

'A shite-hawk!' he answered decisively. I stored the word away as the seaman's name for that particular bird.

'That one, Taff?' I asked, eager for learning, pointing to a shearwater.

'That's a shite-hawk too!' said Taff judicially. 'They're all bloody shite-hawks!' I resolved to purchase a book on sea birds with a more extensive vocabulary than Taff's!

In these quieter days, the Captain and officers were able to give us some attention, and Lt Boyd, the Navigator, taught us how to use a sextant and calculate a noon position. In the charthouse, we had excellent facilities and day by day we grew more skilful, gradually coming to within a mile or two of his own observations. The First Lieutenant, or Jimmy the One, Lt Hanron, lectured us on ship administration and organisation, and set us various tests which arose during normal working.

One day, the sea-boat was lowered and pulled across to a large merchant ship to transfer a sailor to us. This sailor's mind had become unhinged and he had tried to throw himself overboard. As we carried a doctor he could be put under sedation aboard us and landed in Gibraltar. The poor, wild-eyed creature in canvas strait jacket, was hoisted inboard, and the falls were hooked on and the sea-boat hoisted aboard. As she came to rest under the davits with both pulley blocks of the hoisting tackle close together in the tightest possible position, the Captain called down from the bridge.

'Ordinary Seaman Hughes, let me see you pass the life-lines!'

This is an important operation, when the whole weight of the boat is taken on two life-lines fore and aft, permanently secured to the davits. It is effected by passing the life-line under the chain hoisting slings of the boat and over the hooked top of the davit a number of times and then locking these turns with a hitch around the middle, rather like a wheatsheaf. This enables the hoisting ropes to be slackened off and tidily belayed around the cleats of the davit. The whole weight is then on the life-lines which you hold taut. If properly passed the boat should not slip down, but remain absolutely stable. I climbed into the bows in some trepidation, while Brock sucked his teeth in disgust at using a raw sailor for such a responsible operation.

'Watch me!' said Pedlar Palmer, a three-badge AB from the stern. 'You'll be alright.' Surreptitiously, I watched and copied Pedlar's every move until the passing had been completed and we signalled our readiness.

'Ease to the life-lines!' said the Petty Officer of the Watch. The life-lines squealed gently at the strain, but the boat did not move.

'Belay the falls!' came the order, and Pedlar and I scrambled down to the deck. From the bridge wing, as I looked up, the Captain waved an encouraging hand but said nothing. Such were the little tests which were apt to arrive without the slightest warning, from a seamanlike operation to a question on the bridge about a current best-seller or your identification of an aircraft.

A couple of days later, I found myself acting as schoolmaster to the deranged sailor, now installed in the sailmaker's locker, a tiny compartment on the upper deck. He had expressed a wish to learn Latin and so we did some elementary Latin sitting on ropes and bolts of canvas. An armed sentry stood on the deck with the blue seas surging past, to which the eyes of the sailor constantly moved. At any moment I expected him to rush me in the middle of a declension and try to throw himself overboard again!

Gibraltar was my first foreign port and will always have a special place in my memory. We wandered over the Rock, exploring the fortifications, hunting for the famous apes, and basking in the sunshine while drinking the notorious and very cheap orange wine. The town seemed to burst at the seams with soldiers, sailors and airmen. The drinking clubs were like human anthills of thirsty sailors, through and over which crawled Spanish waiters, expertly bearing aloft trays of brimming beer mugs, while from the stage a woman's jazz band from Madrid blasted forth jazz with a dazzling blond and busty vocalist like Mae West, as the star attraction.

We rose at five in the morning to wash decks, hosing ourselves down in the heat more than the decks and horsing around generally. In the afternoon there was sailing instruction with the officers in the 27 foot whaler, and another skill was learned. Too soon, we sailed away for an anti-submarine patrol off Cape Espartel on the African coast, to the dolphins and flying fish, but we saw nothing but the famous Force H of battlecruisers, carriers and destroyers returning from some mysterious patrol. We returned to Gibraltar and immeditely took over a large convoy of 45 vessels homeward-bound.

HMS Scarborough, author en route for crow's nest, 1941.

Members of No 1 Mess *HMS Scarborough*, Gibraltar, May 1941.

HMS Broke, 1941.

H MS Scylla. Tail of the Bank, Greenock, 1942.

Gunnery Director, *HMS Scylla*,
September 1942.

SS Mary Luckenbach blows up. PQ 18,
September 1942. Shot down German
plane burning at right.

Winston Churchill and Sir Stafford Cripps with the C In C Home Fleet,
Sir Bruce Fraser, October 1942. On return from PQ 18.

Author in Arctic Survival suit in
HMS Scylla, Murmansk 1943.

HMS Scylla. HM King George VI en route
for Scotland, March 1943.

HMS Scylla, Russia 1942. Open Fire!
After armament. *Foreground:* 40mm Quadruple Pompom (Chicago Piano).
Middle ground: 2/20mm Oerlikon guns. *Background:* After turrets 4/4.5 inch
HA/LA guns.

After sinking German blockade runner *Rhakotis*, Greenock, January 1943.

HMS Slinger. As Training Carrier in Clyde 1944.

Burial of a fatality after a kamikaze attack, *HMS Slinger*, 1945.

Forecastle Division *HMS Slinger*. Author in front as Divisional Officer.

RMS Queen Elizabeth passing *HMS Slinger* at speed, 1945.

Convoy JW 43 to Russia. View of Arctic Ice Edge 'glare' Bear Island. The ship is *SS Temple Bar* of Bristol, sunk later, February 1943.

1845 Squadron's farewell salute to *HMS Slinger*, March 1945.

After half of deck cargo for Philippines at Brisbane, June 1945.

Japanese Navy POW's unloading relief supplies Hong Kong, 1945.

Escorts were being stretched tight, for there was only *Scarborough* and two large ocean trawlers to protect this huge convoy, though we were joined for a couple of days by two very modern L class destroyers, *Lance* and *Legion* from Gibraltar to give us moral support. They did indeed look very efficient and well-armed, but their crews as they passed us looked like twentieth century pirates in the variety of sea-rigs they wore!

After the destroyers left us, it was our bad luck to be picked up by a Focke-Wulf Condor bomber. He was upon us from astern before we could take action, and dropped his string of bombs on the rear of the convoy, hitting the stern of one ship, but doing no serious damage. In the afternoon another Focke-Wulf came up astern and as it passed Taff opened fire with the four-inch. I was on the signal deck at the time, chatting with the signalman and almost as a reflex action I leaped to the twin Lewis guns on the starboard side, cocked them and opened fire, the big butts juddering into my shoulder. The huge bomber, passed along the starboard side, Taff's shells bursting alongside her, and my arcing tracer pointing at her, but woefully short. In seconds she had gone, to resume her stalking game and to wait for another opportunity.

'Report to the bridge!' said Brock, coming grimly on to the signal deck.

'Who told you to open fire?' demanded the Captain, sternly.

'Nobody, Sir!' I muttered miserably, 'the guns were just there doing nothing.'

'But you were hopelessly out of range.'

'I know that now, Sir, and I'm very sorry.' The Captain smiled. 'Ah, well – a natural reaction, I suppose, but next time, wait for an express order. Alright, Hughes, carry on!'

Having been sighted, bombed and shadowed we waited fearfully for a submarine attack on such an ill-defended convoy, but none came, and in a few days the Liver birds were greeting us again.

Another Gibraltar convoy awaited us, and we made a quick turn-round and an uneventful voyage to Gib, with the weather getting warmer. There were a couple of days in Gibraltar during which we improved our knowledge, from the delights of afternoon tea in the library, hilarious film shows in the local cinema where the population heaved banana skins and nuts at the villain whenever he appeared on the screen, to the evening stroll in the Alameda Gardens where it was rumoured the flowers were supplemented by other, homosexual pansies, who hissed at you invitingly from behind the palm trees.

On our last night, Italian aircraft made a half-hearted raid on the Rock, and we dashed shipward, more in danger from the falling shrapnel of the fearsome Rock anti-aircraft barrage than from Italian bombs. As we ran we met the Chef, jogging along in a horse-drawn gharry, and as lugubrious as ever. To our hail he answered, 'Ah, shit in the bastard!'

The homeward-bound convoy was as big as and as thinly escorted as the former one, and we plodded northward. Then suddenly out of the blue came the warning that the *Bismark* had broken out into the Atlantic. If she came upon our convoy we could see ourselves cast in the role of the *Jervis Bay* of 1940, sailing out with our pea-shooter to take on a battleship. As we intercepted the signals, we plotted the courses on a school atlas, noting how it was possible for our courses to converge, and there was a grim silence around the gun during the watches. Then the *Prinz Eugen* detached herself and Brock expressed all our fears.

'I hope to Christ she doesn't come upon us and take it out of us, for what the Fleet is doing to *Bismark*.' But news came of the great ship's end and we relaxed to sail safely to Liverpool. I sighed with relief as I signed in at Gladstone House for a quiet evening – air-raid on Gib and then all that tension over the *Bismark* – some civilized talk, a good meal and perhaps some music would heal the scar. Dinner had just finished in the downstairs dining room when the sirens wailed, and the Liverpool blitz began!

For hours we huddled under the house, peering out to see the sky growing red as the fires took hold and the now familiar smells and sounds of a great air-raid pervaded the shelter. Crouching with us was the vicar of St Luke's Church, Leece Street, just over the garden wall. He was constantly asking if we could see his church. Near dawn the All Clear sounded, and we stumbled out into the garden to a fearsome sight. Saint Luke's Church was burning like a portrayal of some medieval hell, huge flames licked skyward from its windows and the nave glowed and died and glowed again as if in great agony. Tears glistened on the cheeks of the vicar as he mumbled in the lightening garden.

'Oh, my church, my poor church!' Behind the church, the great Liverpool store of Lewis's and the smaller one of Blackler's were both infernos, but the great Vestey Tower of the Cathedral was intact, blood red in the glow of the sea of fire below in Renshaw Street, Bold Street, Lime Street and Church Street. My return to the ship took hours, detouring past fires and avalanches of fallen masonry. I met an old lady, covered with dust, wandering in the street, mumbling, her memory of the night's horror gone, and asking over and over again, 'Where am I?' An air-raid warden relieved me of my care.

At the ship, rescue squads were being organised and for the next few days it was Plymouth all over again. The most important task was removing ammunition from a large ship in Canada Dock which was on fire. The firemen were fighting a losing battle against the flames and there would be a shattering explosion unless the ammunition was removed. All day we slaved, one eye on the flames, the other on the task, while the whole immediate area was evacuated of all civilians, and the place was silent except for the whine of winches and the grunts of the sailors.

Suddenly the shout went up to abandon the work and we ran wildly back, almost feeling the expected shock waves gripping us from behind. A few minutes later, safely below decks, the ship blew up, and *Scarborough* tugged at her moorings with the blast, while for hundreds of yards to the north the houses and shops disintegrated.

One night Brock and I crouched under the bridge in the middle of another air-raid. From the direction of the famous Caradoc pub at the Gladstone Docks entrance came a mighty green flash and an explosion that bowled us over, along the deck. As we picked ourselves up, Brock said,

'That's the end of the Caradoc and the duty watch sailors of every ship here.' As it was the custom for every duty watch to send members off to the pub for a quick nip in turn, I agreed with his grim remark, yet next day, the Caradoc was still there, alone and unbowed at the end of what had been a long street of houses, but was now a heap of rubble. Never was a crew so anxious to get back to sea as we were, and we heaved a great communal sigh of relief as we passed outwards through the Locks for another spell in the Atlantic.

As our wake seethed away behind us, so did the days and weeks at sea, some clear and sunny with the dolphins playing ahead of us, others dull and sullen with an endless succession of grey, white-topped waves, surging towards us, and the lone fulmar petrel, planing endlessly in the troughs, a little roundel on its wings making it look like a miniature patrol aircraft.

On one such dull, spiritless day, we were picked up by the inevitable Focke-Wulf Condor aircraft. After circling the convoy to assess the opposition, it made a run-in for a bombing attack, but the lively fire of the escorts and merchant ships deterred it and it sheered away in search of easier prey, at the same time reporting our position to any U-boat in the vicinity.

Shortly after it had left, the Ocean Boarding Vessel *Malvernian*, a requisitioned small cargo liner of the Leyland Line who seemed to name some of its ships after old boys of famous schools such as Malvern, left the convoy to patrol in search of neutral and perhaps enemy merchant ships slipping through our Atlantic patrols. Should they sight such vessels, they would be stopped and boarded and an examination made of their papers and cargo, to ensure that they were not carrying war materials to Germany. It was a lonely and dangerous job, far from the convoy lanes and completely at the mercy of prowling German aircraft and U-boats. She peeled away from the starboard wing of the convoy and was soon hull down and then away over the horizon.

Although we were in latitude 46° north, which was roughly on a level with Bordeaux, and 20° west longitude, the weather on this first day of July was far from what was expected in these warmer areas. It was dull, drizzly, cold and then in the afternoon a fog came down. For this we were thankful as it limited the visibility of the Focke-Wulfs. So we sailed happily on, until we received a radio message from the *Malvernian*, reporting that she had been bombed by Focke-Wulfs, was on fire, and sinking and they were abandoning ship and taking to the lifeboats. *Scarborough* immediately turned north-eastwards towards the reported position, steaming slowly through the fog. Reaching the area, the foghorn began to sound a long mournful howl through the swirling mist and extra look-outs were posted in the eyes of the ship and along the rails, searching for the white shape of a ship's lifeboat. Then, miraculously, the boat was spotted by a look-out and we stopped engines to drift down upon her. Scrambling nets and ropes were made ready to take on the survivors, and then followed a grim scene which was my first experience of the misery and agony of survivors at sea in war. The boat was a forlorn and tragic scene, oars all awry, injured seamen huddled on the thwarts, with the mist in tendrills around them.

'Careful with this one!' called an officer, 'he's been badly scalded by escaping steam.' He pointed to a figure tied in a canvas stretcher, laid across the thwarts. The medical staff stood by and gentle hands guided the pitiful bundle upwards to our deck. As he came level with us he moaned feebily from a mouth which was only a gash in a scalded face from which grey skin hung in folds like cobwebs in an attic. Other visible parts of his body were in the same horrible state. Other survivors climbed aboard, bandaged roughly and bloodstained, while the uninjured ones waited their turn.

When the boat was empty I gazed down at it with horror. The thwarts were bloodstained and covered with mucus and vomit, and scattered everywhere, so incongruously, were packets of Turkish Delight and Crunchie bars, sweets that I can never savour again. Anything eatable from the canteen must have been thrown pell-mell into the boat and they would not have gained much nourishment from such fare. An attempt was made to haul the boat aboard, but being Merchant Service pattern she was heavy and unwieldy, and there was little space for her on our decks, so she was cast adrift and after a long burst from the .5 machine-guns, which sent splinters flying from her waterline and punctured her buoyancy tanks, she sank under the waves and we resumed our course to rejoin the convoy.

Shortly after being rescued the scalded sailor died and was quickly wrapped in canvas with the traditional cannonball at his feet to weight him on his journey down. All available hands were mustered on the quarter deck where the bundle rested on a plank on the depth-charge rails, covered with a Union Jack. We assembled there, as we were, bare-headed, in overalls, sweaters, singlets and the wind blowing our hair in our eyes, and I raised mine to the setting sun, for the fog had cleared away and the whole horizon was a blaze of reds, while the sea reflected the sky like the inner lights of a ruby. The Captain fumbled through the pages of his Prayer Book as he found the place, the sea-breeze riffling the pages, so that in the silence of our reverence we could hear the thin rustle of the rice-paper pages. The wind snatched away his words, and tugged at the Union Jack as the shortened service went on, and then died away for us to hear the Commital.

'We therefore commit his body to the deep, to be turned into corruption, looking for the resurrection of the body, when the sea shall give up her dead.'

Someone lifted the plank, the canvas bundle slid away, hit the surface, floated momentarily then sank from sight, and in the silence we could hear the White Ensign whipping sharply from the gaff above us as if in ritual farewell.

'I wonder if anyone will tell his mother or his wife?' I asked, 'because, though I never knew him, I for one, will always remember his passing.'

Later that evening it was announced that an auction would be made of the dead man's effects.

'But, Brock,' I protested in innocence, 'he didn't have any effects.'

'Well, we provide 'em, see?' replied Brock. 'Look, you put in that clasp knife of yours, and then bid for it back. You needn't put any money down – it'll be docked from your pay, see? Just give what you can afford.'

So at the sad little ceremony, I bought my clasp knife back and over £70 was raised, to be sent back to the dependents, a rough and deeply kind gesture, not necessarily to a shipmate, but to a past member of the brotherhood of the sea.

The convoy passed safely on its journey, and we came to Gibraltar. We seemed to bear a charmed life in this desperate period of 1941 when our merchant shipping losses were so high and there was even talk of the Admiralty moving to Canada on the messdecks, but the return convoy was uneventful. On arrival in Liverpool, the persistent buzz that we were going in for a refit became a reality. Throughout one summer morning and afternoon we warped the ship through the maze of docks from Gladstone to Clarence Dock, near the Pier Head, never entering the Mersey once, but using our engines and winches, and our muscles, and heaving on great manilla ropes looped over endless bollards as we passed through the docks. Finally, we entered the small dry-dock at Clarence Dock, a dark, primitive dock, surrounded by early Victorian warehouses, with the great Clarence Dock power station looming over us.

Our hearts were gay and we put up with the inconvenience of the dock toilets, the most barbarous I had yet seen, consisting of nothing more than a long waterfilled trough, the only comfort being a rough wood edging on which to rest the buttocks. On the wall someone had scrawled, 'It's no use standing on the seat! The crabs in this place can jump six feet!' crabs being sailors' slang for a tiny crablike louse which haunted the pubic hair, with great irritation, rejoicing in the name of *Pediculosis pubis*! Taff Evans was an authority on this particular type of toilet.

'Oh, aye mun,' he informed me. 'They've got them like that in Guz, only the water runs faster, and you can play the Scorched Arses and Danglers joke if you're smart and sitting at the very far end, see. You light a rolled up ball of newspaper, set fire to it, drop it in and let the current take it down under the arses of everybody. Christ, mun, then you see some fun! But it's rather crude, boyo, and the best way to do it is with a candle stuck to a flat piece of wood, and then it floats gently down, and besides, there's no messy smoke.'

During this time the officers were able to form themselves into a Ship Selection Board which interviewed Baldwin, Lomas and me in turn. For me this was a most pleasant affair which turned into an animated discussion of jazz versus classical music, during which I dilated on the beauty of Mozart's music. We all passed successfully and in August we applied to be rated Able Seamen. This was granted, and for some reason, I was given a month's seniority over the others.

'Fat lot of good that'll do you, Doc!' pronounced our kindly Coxswain, an elderly Chief Petty Officer, due for retirement. 'You've only done the bare six months required, so it can't be back-dated a month, can it? It's the Captain's way of giving you a little pat on the back, lad.'

My turn for leave came, and as it was expected that we might be called to the Admiralty Selection Board in Portsmouth during the leave, we were instructed to take our hammocks home with us, an unusual and very cumbersome procedure on railway platforms. I went to say goodbye to Brock and found him on the Upper Deck, as we had met six months before, in pale washed overalls and dazzling white singlet.

'I've come to say goodbye, Leading Seaman Brock,' I said with genuine regret.

'Next time I see you, if I ever do,' he growled, 'you'll be a bloody officer, and then what'll you do, eh? Expect me to salute you, Doc?'

'No!' I replied, firmly, 'I'll ask you to come to the nearest pub and have a drink with me for old times sake.'

'Thought you'd say that,' he smiled, and reached into his singlet to fumble for a moment, and come out with a little brown plastic crucifix. 'Here,' he mumbled. 'Take that as a little remembrance of old Brock. I'm a miserable old bastard and I've chased hell out of you lot, especially you, because I hate bloody schoolmasters, but you've never murmured, though I know you'd have liked to clout me many times. You're alright, Doc!'

I was close to tears as I took the little crucifix from his hand.

'Thank you Brock. I'll always remember you!' I mumbled. I never saw him again, but I carried his crucifix with me on all my subsequent voyages over the world and still have it.

Taff Evans, a stoker Petty Officer, and I arrived in style in Lime Street, in a truck sitting on a pile of frozen lamb carcases. Brushing the spots of fat off our best uniforms we made for the Legs of Man pub for a few fortifiers for the journey, and left an hour or so later with a sackful of assorted bottles of draught ale, to catch the South Wales train.

'Excuse me?' said the lady in the corner seat of the compartment, 'and pardon my question, but does one of you gentlemen have any onions about you? I can definitely smell onions!'

'Madam,' I said, with bucolic politeness. 'I do indeed have some onions with me, and as there is a shortage of them in England, allow me to present you one, straight from Spain and with the compliments of the Royal Navy.' Wherewith I rummaged in my various bags and produced a huge onion. By the time we reached Shrewsbury, the bottles were empty and we disposed of them in target practice at the signal posts in the area where I now live. Arriving home, I laid all my gifts out on a table, butter, oranges, Canary bananas, sugar, dripping, Moroccan ware.

'You're like a general store!' said my father, grinning at the array.

'Plenty of cigarettes for the wedding!' I announced, 'and some sherry.'

'I suppose you've had a rough time at sea?' asked my mother. 'I do wish you'd joined the RAF like some of your friends. So and so's an instructor officer already, only a few miles from here.'

'Well, he's bloody welcome,' I grunted.

'And you've become so coarse and uncouth,' she protested, 'I do believe you're a bit drunk too!'

A few days later, I returned temporarily to gentility as an usher at my sister's wedding, complete in morning suit and grey topper, and the first time I had had a collar and tie on for a year.

There was no summons to the Admiralty Selection Board during my leave, so I returned to *Scarborough* in the Clarence Dock, and together with Lomas and Baldwin we were discharged to the Liverpool Destroyer Depot at Linacre Lane, a vast echoing building which before the war had been the Vernon's Football Pools headquarters. It was a soulless, transitory place, inhabited by folk like ourselves, awaiting transfers, and by the Boiler Cleaning Squads of stokers who departed each day to scour the boilers of the ships in Gladstone Docks. For a few days we scrubbed decks and dodged work, and then came a stroke of luck.

While swabbing the decks, an Instructor Lieutenant slipped on the soapy surface, and we made the necessary apologies and enquiries as to whether he had suffered any injury. Struck perhaps by our conversation, he enquired what we were doing at the depot. On being told, he expressed horror that we should be engaged on such menial tasks instead of doing some worthy study such as navigation. We too, quite untruthfully, agreed with him, and expressed our sublime ignorance of navigation. The upshot was that we soon found ourselves members of his little private class in navigation, and naturally he found us very apt pupils in that, to a certain extent, he was teaching his grandmother to suck eggs, as he had never been to sea himself.

I suggested to Lomas that we could extend our study into the realms of communications, as I had formerly been a Coder and a schoolmaster, so I put the plan to our rather gullible mentor, adding a masterly touch, that the best place for me to begin my class would be at the Signal Tower at Gladstone Dock, if he could make the necessary arrangements. Make them he did, and the next day we joined the boiler cleaning party, en route for Gladstone Docks, with our folded newspapers under our arms, and plans for the acquisition of as much duty free tobacco and cigarettes as we could scrounge from the ships.

The Chief Yeoman of Signals, a downy old bird, could see that we were working a nice racket, and consigned us to an empty room, together with copies of the *Fleet Signal Book* with their heavy lead covers, designed to sink rapidly rather than fall into enemy hands if the need arose. After a bit of desultory instruction, I began to itch, and in a minute or two produced from my jumper a huge flea, which I placed on the open signal book.

'Hell's teeth!' yelled Lomas, 'that's a bloody great flea. Kill it!' I slammed the heavy covers shut, flattening the flea which we then examined carefully. On this itchy note I declared the class closed and we slipped out of the Tower and went to a local cinema. So began an idyllic existence. Breakfast, a leisurely bus-ride, a perusal of the newspapers, and then to the Beer Canteen where we helped the ladies of the WVS to clear up the glasses from the night before. This was always rewarded by a couple of pints which we took into the billiard room and drank while we played a few frames of snooker.

We then made a tour of the ships, picking up the odd packet of cigarettes or American pipe tobacco, tasted the American candies such as Hershey bars, and then returned for lunch. The afternoon consisted of a bit of Morse Code, or a touch of signal flags, and then a bus ride to another cinema or a tour of the Docks. For a fortnight we lived like this, truant sailors, but then Nemesis overtook us. The tannoy at Linacre Lane blared our names, requesting us to report to the First Lieutenant. The possibilities were two-fold: either that we were to attend the Selection Board or, that our truancy had been discovered. Lt Cdr Fremantle, the First Lieutenant, was actually apologetic to us, and most polite.

'Gentlemen,' he began, 'I hate to have to do this, knowing that you are expecting to go to Portsmouth for the Selection Board, but the fact is . . . .' and he paused. 'I'm afraid I shall have to send you to sea again!' Our mouths and eyes expressed soundless horror. 'I know how you feel,' he continued, 'but the destroyer *Broke* has had to send three Able Seamen ashore to hospital and she must sail as soon as possible. You will be taken down to join her in an hour's time, so double off and get your gear packed. And once again, I'm terribly sorry, and I wish you all the best of luck!'

We saluted and left the office, dumbstruck at the bad luck when seemingly so near to our goal.

'Ah, well,' said Baldwin, our philosopher, 'we've had a good little run ashore I suppose.'

I took my dumpy book from the kit-bag and found the section dealing with *HMS Broke*.

'Shakespeare Class,' I read to the attentive Baldwin and Lomas. 'Flotilla Leaders, 1,500 tons, 329 feet overall, five 4.7-inch guns, one 3-inch anti-aircraft gun, six torpedo tubes, 40,000 shaft horse-power giving 36 knots. Built by Thornycroft at Woolston, Southampton, between 1918 and 1925.'

'Took their bloody time over the job, didn't they?' said Lomas, acidly.

'Hold on,' I said, 'I've got a bit of additional information here. She was actually completed at Pembroke Dock, so she's half Welsh, and that suits me!'

'Well, she's a bit more offensively armed than the old *Scarborough*,' added Baldwin.

A cheerful, rotund, three badge Able Seaman strolled over to the mess table.

'You lads are the temporary reliefs to those sick blokes, eh?' We nodded. 'Hard luck on you then. I'm Dinger Bell and I'm the senior AB of the Mess, and I won't go hard on you, as long as you do the work. You're all ABs and you've put in a good amount of sea-time, so none of you is green. We're leaving harbour soon, and I'll want a couple of you on the port side fenders, and one on the fo'c'sle. Right?'

'Who's who aboard?' I asked.

'The Captain is Cdr Churchman, and the First Lieutenant is Lt Peter Scott; he was a painter in Civvy Street.'

'I know of him,' I blurted, 'he paints ducks, mallards and geese flying into the sunset and all that, and he lives in a lighthouse on the east coast. His father was Scott of the Antarctic.'

'Listen to him!' said Dinger. 'Proper bloody mine of information, ain't he?'

'Schoolmaster!' said Lomas, pityingly. 'He can't help it!'

'Anyway,' went on Dinger, 'Jimmy the One, being an artist, has got this ship painted all fancy colours. All pink and red she is, to confuse the Jerries at sunrise and sunset. Barmaid's Blush we calls it. You wait and see her in daylight. 'Orrible it is, really 'orrible.'

The Quartermaster's pipe trilled on the messdecks, 'Hands to stations for leaving harbour!' he bawled, and we scuttled out into the twilight.

Lomas and I held a huge hazel rod fender over the side, and it groaned as the *Broke*'s steel plates ground it against the quay, as the engines and rudder levered the ship off the dock wall. Oily water bubbled through the rods and suddenly the pressure was relieved.

'In fenders!' shouted a Petty Officer, and we began to heave the heavy bundle of rods inboard.

'I'll tell you one thing!' I breathed to Lomas, 'I'm doing as little as possible on this ship. I reckon we've had a rough deal.'

'Me too,' he agreed. So we sailed out into the Atlantic, as bloody-minded as any press-ganged man of Nelson's Navy.

Winter was stamping its imprint on the Atlantic and the seas were grey and sullen, and the sun rarely shone. We escorted an American-bound convoy without incident, and took her far out to longitude 27° west, where we began picking up the American radio programmes with their constant interruptions for commercials. Arty Shaw's clarinet would soar through the cadenzas of his *Concerto for Clarinet* to be spoiled by a nasal voice announcing that it was pree-cislee ten forty-five, Bulova-watch time.

The homeward-bound convoy had a light escort of American destroyers, for in October-November 1941 the United States had not yet entered the war, but was willing to provide a non-belligerent escort for the convoys, ostensibly to protect her own merchant ships. One such destroyer, the *Reuben James* had been sunk by a U-boat, but this had not so far goaded the United States into any state of aggression.

Coupled with our ill-luck at being sent back to sea, and the apparent futility of our efforts in the Atlantic to stave off the U-boat menace, my personal morale was low, and I wished fervently that the Americans would enter the war. The U-boat Wolf Packs were attacking the convoys with increased success and ferocity, and the Atlantic bore a grey, wolf-like look. While on watch one morning, I spotted among the grey-white wave tops something which seemed to have more substance than its liquid surroundings, and which, at this early hour, could well be the conning tower and periscope of a surfaced U-boat.

'Object bearing, Green Two-oh!' I reported, and all binoculars swung across.

'Got it!' snapped Cdr Churchman. 'Could be a U-boat . . . starboard 20, come up to maximum revolutions!' *Broke* swung to starboard and began to pick up speed.

'Standby depth-charges! Standby to ram!' At this command, my mind took an inconsequential turn, and I tried to remember what you did on ramming anything – did you lie down with your head facing forrard . . . or was it aft? Peering through the glasses, the object was taking more definite shape; there was certainly a vertical thing that could be a periscope, but there was also a suspicious whiteness about the mass below; surely U-boats were a grey colour?

'D'you know what I think?' grunted the Captain from beneath his binoculars, 'it's a ship's lifeboat. Check and see if there's anything in it, and beyond it!' There were all sorts of tales about the wiles of U-boats; how they hid their periscopes under bits of ocean jetsam such as packing cases, or hid behind lifeboats such as this. But as we bore down on it, there was nothing in it or beyond it, and in moments the sharp bow of *Broke* crashed into it at 30 knots, shattering it into matchwood.

'Well, Hughes!' smiled Peter Scott, 'there goes your U-boat!'

The weather worsened during the afternoon and by nightfull, heavy seas were running, so heavy that one huge sea, slamming inboard at the break of the forecastle, reduced the ladder leading to the forecastle deck into a Gordian knot of steel, with as much ease as if it had been made of plasticine. Conditions on the messdecks were terrible; a constant six inches of water sluiced back and forth as the ship rolled, bearing with it a flotsam of sea-boots, mess tins and woollen scarves. As I slung my hammock, I made doubly sure that I used a double sheet bend for safety, as I did not savour a collapse into our private ocean.

'No wonder fellers get TB!' moaned someone, 'living in conditions such as these!'

During the Middle Watch, depth-charges began to shake the ship, the sound coming from astern of the convoy. Suddenly there was a huge flash from that direction and a wall of flame built up to a great height and sank again.

'That's a tanker,' said someone on the bridge. The asdic dominated the bridge, the pinging note echoing metallically from the loudspeaker repeat, but there was no break in the monotony or the rhythm which would have indicated a submarine contact, so we forged steadily ahead with the convoy while the battle between submarines and escort went on astern of us. There was another flash and booming explosion from astern, and as I could not turn around because my look-out sector was ahead, I had to glean the situation from the voices of the officers and the signalmen.

'One of the escort's been tinfished, Sir!' reported a signalman, peering at the minute flashes of the shaded signal lamp from an escort ship. 'It's one of the Yanks, Sir!'

'This'll bring the Yanks into the war!' said the voice of Peter Scott. 'They can't go on losing ships like this.' In my mind's eye I could see the American destroyer, with its two raked and cowled funnels, covered bridge, and five-inch turreted guns heeling over and sinking in the heavy seas, and the bobbing heads of survivors in their high necked life-jackets.

'Survivors being picked up by . . .' The wind whipped away the rest of the sentence but the words held hope. The watch dragged on, and there was no more activity. Surprisingly, the days following were uneventful, and with the convoy safely out of the danger area of what was known as 'The Rose Garden' the area south west of Iceland, beyond the range of our reconnaissance aircraft, we put into Hvalfjord in south west Iceland to take on oil fuel. Safely anchored in the fiord, we began to swab and dry out the messdeck, and order and warmth was returned.

'Here you are, Doc!' said Dinger Bell, handing me a fish hook and a length of line. 'Get up topside and catch us some supper – these fiords are full of fish!' So we fished for our supper with great success and there was beautiful fresh fried fish and chips on the menu.

The following morning Peter Scott decided that the Barmaid's Blush needed a washing, so in the raw, dimly lit sub Arctic morning we went over the side with stages. In *Scarborough* we had mastered the art of rigging stages in the proper fashion so that we could lower ourselves from the stages, without having to come back on deck. This was done by dropping the stages overboard, then throwing down the loose end of the fall, grasping both pieces of rope in our hands and between our legs as we slid down to the stages below, and then belaying the loose end securely around the crosspieces at the ends of the stages. This impressed Peter Scott, who didn't seem to have seen this technique before. He drew the attention of the other sailors to it.

'Look at the way these ABs from *Scarborough* rig stages,' he pointed out. 'They're real seamen!' Little did he know that his real seamen had other techniques to exhibit, the present one being a very high proportion of caustic soda in what appeared to be our soapy water buckets. In no time, we had huge areas of plating restored to their virginal and blushing pink. The First Lieutenant was so impressed that he decreed that we had done our share and over, and that our morning's work was finished. We retired to the messdecks to enjoy an ill-earned cup of tea and a smoke.

The next day we left Iceland, with only a fleeting impression of a cold, dark land, of long enclosed fiords, and the dark, predatory shape of the Arctic skua, ceaselessly harrying the other sea-birds to disgorge their catch.

The weather on the return voyage was sunny, the sea blue and white, and at Liverpool the news was good – we had been summonded to Portsmouth for the Admiralty Selection Board.

6 Academic interlude

Things moved slowly in Portsmouth, and we were not impressed by some of the company we were being obliged to keep. The special mess set aside for candidates awaiting their board seemed to be dominated by a clique of sailors who had established themselves rather as Al Capone characters than as officer-material. They seemed to be able to get all the best food and dodge all the menial tasks, and their leader at the time was a rat-faced character whom I sincerely hoped would fail his interview. Indeed, in retrospect, I often wondered whether these characters were being purposely delayed for some reason or other.

On the other hand there were some extremely colourful characters, notably Australians and New Zealanders, who were reputed to have an underground hide-out in one of the shrubberies in the barracks, to which they retired each morning at 'Hands Fall-In' there to play cards, read paperbacks and otherwise while away the time while we cleaned lavatories and swabbed decks. Each morning there was a different officer on duty, and this cunning band always fell out with the other permanent working parties, such as the Gunner's Party, reporting themselves as 'First Lieutenant's Digging Party'. Their leader would report to the Officer,

'First Lieutenant's Digging Party carry on as usual, Sir?' And he, believing in the permanent existence of such an organisation, would nod assent.

Pompey Barracks was a crossroads of the Navy, and one day I was hailed by a Coder from *Broke*.

'Hi, Doc!' he laughed, 'keep out of Peter Scott's way in the future. He's sworn to have your guts for a necktie. After you'd left, all that part of the ship's side which you washed in Hvalfjord, flaked off in great patches. What did you use – strongers?' I grinned reminiscently, waved the matter away airily, and after a chat passed on.

On another occasion I came face to face with a huge sailor who at the Liverpool Destroyer Depot had threatened to half-kill me if he saw me again. This man had stolen my smart raincoat, kid gloves, my slim cigarette case and new Ronson lighter, reducing me to a very mediocre sailor, sartorially speaking. Everything had been recovered, through the good offices of the Asdic rating from *Scarborough* who, recognising the

77

articles being flashed around by this sailor in a Liverpool pub, rushed to me and we confronted the thief later.

To my surprise he gave everything back quite willingly, but Taff, the Asdic rating, being a career sailor and utterly contemptuous of a thief, insisted that we report the matter. As a result he was sentenced to three weeks detention, and while I was cell sentry, by an evil coincidence, he had made his threat to me through the bars! Now, as I saw him approach, I prepared myself for battle. As he neared me, recognition dawned in his eyes, and to my surprise he smiled.

'Hello, Doc!' he grinned, 'still looking smart, I see. Sorry about that business in Scouseland. I was a bloody fool, but I didn't think that pal of yours would insist on going all King's Regulations on the matter. I know you didn't!' I breathed easier, and after a moment's chat we parted.

The elderly Admiral, sitting in the centre of the group of officers at the long table at the Selection Board, placed his elbows on the table, the sleeves heavy with gold lace, slipped down and took his grey head in his hands. The questions on every aspect of seamanship had been coming thick and fast, but the Admiral had taken little part in the interrogation. He grunted suddenly, and I shifted in my chair in front of him.

'What's a swifter, boy!' he snapped.

'A swifter, Sir, is a piece of rope with a cut splice in it used for . . .'

'Alright boy, alright.' He waved away further explanation and my mouth must have puckered in surprise, because he went on, 'Don't look so downcast, boy!' he consoled, 'when a man tells me that a swifter has a cut splice in it, he damn well knows what he's talking about and I don't want to hear any more.' There was a whispered conclave, during which I heard a magic phrase, 'very good reports from sea' and then the Admiral spoke again.

'We're recommending you for training for a commission at *HMS King Alfred* and you'll leave shortly for Brighton. The best of luck to you. Carry on, please!' I saluted with verve and attack, one fence having been successfully negotiated, left the room and awaited Lomas and Baldwin's return from their ordeals. Baldwin was first back and successful. He had had a morbid fear that he was going to fail because they'd ask what his father did, and as he kept a very large pub, he felt this would go against him. I'd assured him that they were not interested in commissioning his father but only the son.

'Did the Admiral ask about your father!' I enquired.

'Yes, he did.' My face fell.

'Snobby old bugger,' I burst out, my Welsh freedom boiling up.

'No, he thought it was marvellous,' beamed Baldwin. 'Wish I kept one, he said.' Lomas joined us, beaming with success and we repaired to our

Mess where Ratface was surrounded by his cronies at the end of the table.

'It gives me great pleasure,' I said viciously to him, 'to be rid of the displeasure of your company. We're off to *King Alfred* tomorrow and I hope to God I don't see you there.' As it so turned out, I never did.

The next fortnight was spent at Mowden School, a former preparatory school in the Brighton suburbs, being billeted out in civilian lodgings where it was good to taste home cooking again, though the landlady seemed to be putting us on short rations. Single fish cake and a couple of bangers, were in sharp contrast to our heaped plates in *Scarborough* and *Broke*.

We seemed to do little but field drill on the small playing field, and some of our members had us performing the weirdest evolutions, such as forcing our way through a brick wall for the lack of a command either to about turn or at least to halt. Some of the climbing roses which graced the walls had never heard such obscenities as we ground our noses into their withering winter foliage. However, there was some good rugby to be played and some night leave, though there was a long list of dubious dives in Brighton which we were not allowed to grace with our presence, for we were now Cadet Ratings, almost verging on gentlemen, and instead of black silk tallies on our caps, we now sported dazzling white bands to signal our slightly improved status.

When we moved to Lancing College, up on the Downs behind Shoreham-by-Sea, there began for me, one of the most pleasant periods in the Navy. The monastic lay-out of the senior Woodard public school, with its upper and lower quadrangles, the beautiful lofty School Chapel – the cathedral of the South Downs – the rural surroundings, all bred an academic calm which was balm to me after more than six months in the Atlantic, and two air blitzes etched deeply in my memory.

I settled down gratefully to a return of surroundings I knew well. Old friends turned up from *Ganges* – Jones and Hutchings and others, and we soon reformed our groups. We lived again in dormitories and, luxury of luxuries, we were waited upon in Hall, by trim and attractive waitresses at every meal. There were music clubs to belong to, rugby teams to play for, and we ranged as far afield as Portsmouth, playing Army and Royal Air Force teams, drinking huge quantities of beer and singing the old familiar rugger songs.

There was a great deal of intense instruction, especially in navigation. The instructors were often officers who had been wounded in action and had been given these less rigorous appointments before returning to sea. Their experience was invaluable. One such character rejoiced in the name of Arsy Tarsy, and invariably every lecture contained the following warning,

'You must be certain, you see, to do things in the proper order,' he would say, languidly, 'or, otherwise, every damned thing will go Arsy Tarsy!'

Six weeks flew by, and then came the second fence – a qualifying examination before we passed on to *HMS King Alfred* proper at Hove. I was feeling fairly satisfied, as I had been assigned to Greynville B class which by a process of observation of the personnel of the A and C classes, had been judged to be the star class. By juggling around with the class letters, it was hoped that we would not get an inkling of our prospects of success. Our conclusions were that A class were the shaky ones, and C class the average ones.

Greynville B certainly contained some academic highfliers, including a professor, and some very striking personalities. I felt very humble in such august company and as I always looked younger than my actual age, there was a certain amount of ribbing on this account. Examination results confirmed our judgements and most of our class were in the high mark ranges. Confirming it too, was the sad disappointment of some faces from the other classes, with the unhappy observation,

'Sent back to sea, poor bastards!'

HMS King Alfred at Hove was a vastly different place from the comfortable King Alfred (L) at Lancing. The building stood, gaunt and modernistic on the sea-front at Hove, close by the Sussex Division of the Royal Naval Volunteer Reserve headquarters. Designed as an entertainment complex just before the war, of restaurants, concert halls and underground car park, it had been taken over by the Admiralty and hastily converted. It was inevitable that our sleeping quarters should be the underground car park. Vernon's Pools at Liverpool had possessed at least a memory of human occupation, but an underground car park made us feel like flesh covered internal combustion engines, especially as we marched up the ramps from underground, goaded by the stentorian voice of Chief Petty Officer Vango, the legendary terror of the establishment, barking out the rate of the march with a Huff-Haw, Huff-Haw two stroke beat.

'Today, I think I shall be a Rolls-Royce!' I commented as we swung along.

'Stop talking in the ranks!' bawled CPO Vango.

Hove was the place where it was rumoured they tried to break your spirit after the mollycoddling of Lancing, and for me it was a place which made no impact whatsoever, except that I grew to like the Forest Brown Ale they sold in the bar! We fed in a huge dining room, divided into a large and a small section by a red velvet rope, gracefully draped from small ornamental posts in the floor. In the smaller section, dined the newly commissioned officers and staff, the former ornate and awkward in their new uniforms. In the larger section we ate, as befitted our lowly station.

'All you have to do at KA,' said someone, 'is to get over that bloody rope!'

The examinations were held in January 1942, and during the Navigation paper, I made a bad mistake in not putting a directional arrow on a course I had run off with the parallel rulers. At the time I was being badgered, sotto voce, by a New Zealander on the same chart table, to tell him how to do a certain question. Foolishly I tried to help him after I had finished the paper, and wasted the time when I should have been able to detect my mistake.

On comparing notes afterwards, I was horrified to find that I was steering a northerly course, while everyone else was on a southerly one. 25 marks had gone by the board, and with them went any hopes of my becoming a navigator and being sent to the special navigation school. As there were rumours that low marks condemned you to such branches of the service as bomb disposal, minesweeping and landing craft, I began to make up the lost marks on the remaining papers. Finally I emerged as tenth on the list out of about 75, securing the top marks in gunnery in the process. The marks in this area of the list were so close that had I not been such a fool as to throw away 25 marks, I could have been top man by a clear margin. At the final Admiralty Selection Board the President was congratulatory.

'With marks like these, you have an excellent chance of getting whatever kind of ship you like,' he smiled, 'what had you in mind?'

'An escort vessel, Sir,' I replied with alacrity, 'such as a corvette, or sloop.'

'Don't see why not!' he said confidently, rising to shake hands. 'Best of luck, Hughes!'

By this time we had been put into civilian billets in the large houses on Hove front, so that evening we climbed the stairs to our rooms, bearing the parcels and cases containing our brand-new uniforms for which we had previously been measured at the naval tailors of our choice. Though putting on a shirt and a reefer jacket was a little less claustrophobic than the jumper of a year or more ago, a stiff white collar and tie was irksome to necks which had been long used to the freedom of the jersey neck and the square cut white jumper of the Tropics.

I gazed with pride at the single wavy gold stripe on my arm and at the gold wire of the cap badge. I took a last look at my sailor's paybook which had been endorsed and returned to me – promoted to Temporary Sub-Lieutenant RNVR, it stated, from 12 February 1942; Daily rate of pay 9/-.

We walked across the promenade to the entrance to *King Alfred* for our first meal in the Wardroom. As we entered the foyer, the Quartermaster saluted us smartly and I think we all blushed, because probably a few hours back it had been,

'Wotcher, cocks, double up then or you'll be late for breakfast – 'errings in termarter sauce, I 'ear!'

Some time that evening we were officially welcomed into the Afterguard of the Royal Navy by Capt Pelly, the Commanding Officer, with a terseness I always remember.

'Welcome, gentlemen!' he said, in the clipped, executive voice of the typical professional naval officer, 'into the finest club in the word,' and he paused momentarily. 'The Officers of the Royal Navy!'

As we sat down to dinner, I could see the red velvet rope separating us from the cadet ratings in their square rig and I had a real sense of change in that we had now accepted a responsibility as executive officers, however lowly, to execute policy, to set an example, and to preserve a long and tried tradition. Soup was being served, and one of the wags of the Division began a mock instructional course in table manners in the language of a Gunner's Mate.

'On the command, "Eat!" you takes the spoon in the right 'and, lifting it into an 'orizontal position, and positioning it at a convenient 'eight above the surface of the soup. You then brings it down in a gliding motion until it makes contact with the liquid, making certain that you moves the spoon forward against the lay, as in splicing a rope. 'Aving loaded the spoon you lifts it carefully upwards towards the mouth. On the command "Drink!" you draws in your breath, at the same time taking in the soup, and you does it without making an 'orrible slurping noise. Right! You then closes your chops like a breech block, and returns the spoon to the first position. All 'ands standby to drink soup!'

The wag's words were in a sense prophetic, because, towards the end of the war, newly commissioned officers were being sent to Greenwich for a week to learn the niceties of naval manners in the famous Painted Hall. This course was commonly known as 'The Knife and Fork Course'! In our more urgent days, we picked up the traditions as we went along in wardrooms, great and small. In my case from Chatham Barracks Guest Nights to pickles and corned beef in a holiday bungalow on the South Devon coast.

There was a fortnight left of the course, dealing mainly with Officers' duties, and we went on leave before our first appointments. I went to the seaside village of Rhosneigr in Anglesey, our so-called ancestral home, where my mother was staying with her sister.

'You certainly look smart!' she said, admiringly, 'but I preferred you in your bell-bottomed trousers. You looked young then; now you look so serious!'

'Oh, come off it!' I protested, 'you were just seeing your little boy of years ago, in those sailor suits I used to wear. Let's go for a quiet walk?' So we went for a walk in the country lanes, and suddenly, around the corner, swung a jaunty Jack Tar.

'What shall I do?' I whispered, in panic.

'Well, say "Good Afternoon" of course,' said mother, logically. Thus I got over the saluting complex by turning it into a greeting, sincerely given and sincerely received whenever possible.

I slit open the buff envelope of the registered letter bearing the Admiralty crest, and began to read.

'Confidential. By Command of the Commissioners for executing the Officer of the Lord High Admiral of the United Kingdom, to Sub-Lieutenant Robert FC Hughes RNVR. The Lords Commissioners of the Admiralty hereby appoint you Temporary Sub-Lieutenant RNVR of His Majesty's Ship *Pembroke* for training as HACO, and HACS, and direct you to report on board that ship at Chatham on . . .'

'Oh, bloody hell!' I burst out. 'It's not even a proper ship – it's a Gunnery School at Chatham, and I know enough to guess that HA stands for High Angle, and that means Anti-Aircraft Gunnery in the Navy. Blast it!'

'You are still extremely coarse,' said mother, severely. 'Do officers swear like this?'

'You've just heard one!' I replied, and groaned. 'Why did I have to come out top in gunnery, the subject I hate, and lose marks in navigation, the subject I love? Now I'll have to go to some great big battleship, bristling with anti-aircraft guns, instead of a nice little sloop or corvette, or perhaps a destroyer . . . I bet all the others have been appointed to proper ships!'

I arrived in Chatham in a bitter mood, and was shown to my room in the Wardroom Mess. The rooms were Victorian with spartan undertones, especially the bath, which had a red line drawn all around it, five inches above the bottom, indicating the amount of hot water you were allowed under wartime restrictions.

The Wardroom Mess was full of elderly officers, none of whom seemed less than a Lieutenant Commander, all of whom were professionals, and we wavy-striped subs were less than the dust, more especially as we belonged to the Gunnery Department, popularly known as All Gas and Gaiters, and whose motto was 'Bullshit Baffles Brains'. This motto was pictorially illustrated in the Gunnery School by a cartoon in the entrance, in which a jovial butcher is extolling the merits of a tray of brains to a naval officer, who smilingly is declining them by pointing to a steaming pile of ordure deposited on the roadside by a passing bull, the while, saying, 'No, thank you – bullshit baffles brains, you see!'

We were a very small class, some of whom I knew, but there was no one from my old B Class which filled me with misgivings in view of our theory of our superiority, and I began to wonder where I had gone wrong. It was nearly 30 years later that I found that we had been chosen for Gunnery School because of an observed aptitude for quickly absorbing technical detail which I never knew I possessed until then!

There was certainly plenty to absorb, as High Angle or Anti-aircraft gunnery in the Navy was a very poor relation to Low Angle Gunnery or Anti-ship gunnery. Enemy attacks on the Navy were invariably from aircraft and the whole technique was going through a great change, especially as radar was improving. It was fortunate that I had studied pure mathematics as one of my Higher School Certificate subjects for two years after matriculation. I needed my knowledge of the calculus and my smattering of solid geometry in the eternal problem of being able to throw a shell at least 15,000 feet into the air, at such a precise distance in front of an aircraft travelling a certain course at 250 knots, so that shell and aircraft would arrive at the same spot simultaneously with shattering and fatal results for the aircraft.

Gradually my interest was aroused and I gave myself up to the study of High Angle Gunnery, the intricacies of the early gunnery computers, the recognition of allied and enemy aircraft, and even dreamed of inventing a system of my own! Of course, as our type of gun, ranging downwards from the new 5.25-inch calibre, to the 12 pounders were dual purpose guns, we also had to learn the theory and practice of Low Angle or Anti-ship Gunnery.

There were so many factors about Naval Gunnery which were different from land artillery; the unstable platform of a ship at sea, changing weather conditions affecting the path of a shell through the air, the constantly moving targets, and above all, the great imponderable in those pre-radar days – the course being steered by the target aircraft or ship.

Radar was still being presented by a wildy oscillating green line of peaks and valleys, the highest peak being the target; the plan presentation or plot where the target is indicated by a dot moving on a circular screen of which you were the centre, was only then being developed. One of the most essential ingredients to be fed into the early computers was therefore the one most susceptible to human error – the enemy's course and speed, and this was where I realised I had to accept my first responsibility as an officer. On my decision rested the accuracy of our gunnery and it was all contained in one stately phrase – 'The Angle of Presentation of the Aircraft.' I used to muse imaginatively on this problem in fantasies such as this; 'Unter Leutnant Hughes, may I present myself to you? I am Baron von Junkers, the 88th of that line, a bomber of great repute and of great carrying capacity and speed, and unless you can calculate my course and speed I will drop the whole bomb load on your despicable little ship, schweinhund!'

There was another elusive imponderable in gunnery, something about the time lag between the firing pin hitting the base of the shell and its leaving the muzzle. As it was such a small and puzzling problem, it was called Dead Time. We had another definition of Dead Time. Our Dead Time was the time from the beginning of the first lecture on a Saturday morning until the end of the class, and the beginning of weekend leave. At this period everyone was mentally exhausted and prone to fall asleep, so, if you felt sleepy it was always wise to surreptitiously place one of the tobacco tin lid ashtrays on your head, so that as your sleepy head fell forward, the lid was dislodged with a tinny tinkle, waking you up, and returning you to the drone of the Gunnery Lieutenant's voice.

At weekends there were the wartime delights of London and the Windmill Theatre, walks in the Kentish countryside, and as we began to settle in, quiet dinners and stories about the China Station, the Mediterranean, and West Indies from the elderly officers whom we had at first feared, but who turned out to be only too happy to help and encourage us.

At the end of April there was the inevitable examination of which we never knew the results, and we took the train to Plymouth to some mysterious place called Heybrook Camp where we were going to put theory into practice and fire real guns.

A naval truck took us from Plymouth station through streets with acres of devastation everywhere, a little more tidy than I remembered it with the rubble banked up, but now, an even greater illustration of the extent of bombing. We moved eastwards through country lanes, mistily green with the new leaves and buds of spring, and turned down a valley leading to the sea. There was a clutter of chalets, a large villa on the clifftop, and the truck wound its way up to a couple of small bungalows set amidst gorse and broom bushes on the valley side. I began to recall that this was one of the early holiday camps before the war.

'These are the quarters for officers under instruction, Sir,' said a steward, taking our baggage. 'The Wardroom for the ship's company officers is in the big house on the clifftop.' We acknowledged the subtle distinction with grunts, and went in to dinner. For culinary mediocrity Heybrook Camp took some beating and our first dinner consisted of thin soup, corned beef, fried potatoes, and as an added luxury, a bottle of HP Sauce which had seen better times.

'We haven't come to a Prisoner-of-War Camp by mistake, d'you think?' asked someone.

'I suppose they'll have the cheek to charge us Messing Charges for this muck', I said in disgust.

The hospitality of the Wardroom Officers was on a par with the food, and as inspiring as the jaded HP Sauce. We were actually invited up to the villa for drinks once, a dispiriting occasion which luckily we did not have to repeat because I and another officer discovered Newton Ferrers. On the second evening, after another trough-like meal I suggested a walk along the cliffs.

We forgot our dismal surroundings in the beauty of the Mewstone Rock, popping up from the sea like a huge green meringue, the cries of the mating gulls building their nests, the sight of Wembury Church Tower rising up in its little valley which had inspired John Galsworthy to write a poem about it, and the sound of the sea which accompanied us along the miles, as we walked. Suddenly the path plunged downwards and a magical sight was revealed – a deep wooded inlet of the sea where the River Yealm had its mouth, and a further inlet going up to Noss Mayo, and everywhere little houses nestling on the hillside, and clustering round the water's edge. There were boats, some naval motor launches, shrouded peace-time yachts, and unmistakeably, a little ferry boat.

'Good God,' I breathed, 'what a beautiful little place.'

'Come on,' said my companion, 'what are we waiting for. There'll be a pub down there!' We pounded down the slope, shouting to the ferryman as we went. He was waiting for us below.

''Ere,' he said, in a soft Devon burr, 'where do ye gennelmun, come from then? Us doan't get many naval officers come over the cliffs from up there!' We told him that we were refugees from Heybrook, and enquired about a good pub.

'Thee'll want the Dolphin, then' he advised. 'Her's a good pub, s'now!' So we found nightly refuge in the Dolphin at Newton Ferrers.

'We don't see much of you fellows in the evenings' said one of our instructors. 'Where do you get to?'

'We just go for walks,' we answered, guardedly and smugly.

The guns at Heybrook were built into the cliffs, pointing straight out to sea. They were controlled by a Director tower, exactly similar to that in a warship, higher up the cliff. Encased in heavy concrete, a stage lower down was the Transmitting Station, or computer which processed all the data sent down to it from the control tower telescopes, and from the Control Officer's assessments of courses, speeds etc. Three types of instruction were going on simultaneously; instruction and practical firing and control for officers such as ourselves, actual firing for seaman gunners such as trainers, layers, rangefinders, and communication ratings, and actual operation of the computers by other gunnery ratings, and Royal Marines. In addition there was training in the operation of ammunition magazines, shell lifts and range-setting machines.

Situated as it was, right on the seashore, it was also semi-operational, and part of the anti-aircraft defences of Plymouth area. If there was an air-raid, all instruction ceased, and we became operational and fully offensive. Whoever was control officer at the time, also became control officer for the duration of the raid, and I had the experience of actually ordering the firing of a barrage of shells over a certain sector during a short alert. Heybrook Camp, therefore, despite its starkness was quite a comprehensive unit, and nowadays it rejoices in the name of *HMS Cambridge* the Navy's chief anti-aircraft firing establishment.

Our course came thankfully to an end, and we left the valley to go on leave and await our appointment to a ship. I made arrangements to spend a few days in Taunton to see my old landlady and my headmaster. My landlady was out, but from pre-war habit, I opened the pantry window and eased myself indoors. In the little sitting room my books were still as I had left them what seemed years before, and in the best parlour my piano was discreetly closed, and still lovingly polished. There was a click of the latch at the back door, and Mrs Cattle came in with the meagre wartime shopping.

'Hello,' I called from the kitchen, forgetting that nearly two years had gone past, and I wasn't just coming home from school. 'It's only me.'

'Lawd's sakes,' she gasped, 'you give me a shock, boy. What's that lovely uniform, then? Are you an officer or something?' She grabbed me to her ample bosom. 'You great maze toad,' she cried, 'you're still as mad as ever; but you do look lovely'.

'Here,' I said, rummaging in my case, 'I've brought you some presents – mostly food that you can't get, and I've also got some pipe tobacco for Mr Cattle. Tell me, what's for tea?' I continued, knowing her skill as a former cook at Norton Manor, one of the great Edwardian country houses.

'You wait and see,' she said, firmly. 'Now go ye over to Mr Hurd's the Headmaster, while I get the tea. Then afterwards you can tell me and Walt all about your doings.'

The Headmaster was as austere and yet kindly as always.

'I trust that you have adjusted yourself to your new life, Mr Hughes? Ah, yes. There are few of you young schoolmasters left here now. They've all joined something. Hobbs and Andrews are in the Army I believe, and your friend Frank Gillard's joined the BBC. I don't think you've chosen very well, you know. The Royal Navy's bearing the brunt of it so far. I expect you've had some rough times, eh?'

'Oh, yes, indeed. Rough at times.' I realised that I could tell nobody anything until the war was over whichever way it went, and whatever horrors I had, or would see, so I led him to talk of the school he loved so much, and which I had grown to love too in the five years I had served under him.

I returned to South Wales to wait for the registered letter, and full of private conjecture as to what kind of ship I would be appointed to, or

indeed the dreaded shore appointment that could be a possibility. I was
rapidly developing the sea-going sailor's contempt of shore-based sailors,
engendered by my few months ashore. Apart from the old hands who were
too old to go to sea, there seemed to be too many 'Jacks-in-Office',
supercilious to those below and obsequious to those above. In the years to
come I would often hear the phrase:

'Wish I could go to sea, old chap, but it takes ten shore-based types to
keep one of you types at sea, ha, ha! And you do have your perks, you
know – gin and whisky at tuppence, and cigarettes at sixpence for 20.
Incidentally, could you slip me a few packets before I go ashore? Thank
you I will have another pink gin – I see you make it with the proper stuff,
good old Plymouth gin!'

'Well, I could slip a few knock-out drops into your gin, and we could
shanghai you for a trip!' I would reply, waspishly.

'Heaven forbid, dear boy! Must dash now, or I'll miss the last boat for
the shore.'

In a few days the appointment arrived, couched in the same archaic
form, laced with unintelligible initials, but the nub of the matter was clear
– HMS Scylla for High Angle Control Systems duties, and reading
between the lines, I could see that she must be somewhere on the Clyde.
My Dumpy book was vaguely helpful – there she was among ten other
Greek mythological names – Scylla – Dido Class light cruiser – Building –
5,450 tons, possibly ten 5.25 inch guns (a new calibre), one aircraft.
Scylla's aircraft never materialised, but her successor, the Leander Class
frigate was equipped with a Wasp helicopter, 28 years later!

'How about that?' I enthused to my father, 'a brand new ship and not
too big either; kind of a rather large destroyer!' Carried away by my
enthusiasm, I promptly caught the first cold for nearly two years, and I
began the long journey northward to Glasgow on 13 May. As the carriage
wheels rattled over the rail-joints, the rhythm of a sea-shanty developed
and I began to hum unconsciously:

'Oh, it's over the bar on the thirteenth of May,
To me way-ay, blow the man down
The Galloper jumped and the gale came away
Oh, gimme some time to blow the man down!'

The superstitions attached to the date suddenly obtruded on my
thoughts, my nose began to run, and I huddled morosely in my corner. 'To
hell with it!' I thought. 'This could be a new era for you. You might meet a
nice Scottish lass and settle down, and give up beer-swilling, rugger, and
. . .' My thoughts trailed away, and I fell asleep.

At Naval Headquarters in the St Enoch Hotel, Glasgow, they were
brisk and to the point. Proceed to Greenock and I would find the ship at
the shipyard of Scott's. It was drizzling with rain at Greenock and the

stone setts of the street were slippery and treacherous to anyone with two heavy suitcases. I staggered through dockland to the accompaniment of the frenetic clatter of the pneumatic rivetters, the whine of power drills biting into steel and the lurid flashings of welding arcs from the shipyard on my left which turned out to be the world-famous firm of Scott's of Greenock, builders of Royal Navy ships for generations. It was heartening to know that *Scylla* bore that Rolls-Royce cachet of the shipbuilding world – Clyde built! There was a little old man at the yard gates who cocked his head at me inquisitively.

'Aye?' he enquired.

'*Scylla*?' I asked.

'Aye,' he said, 'you'll be meaning Job Number 2615.'

'I suppose so', I countered.

'Then ye'll no' be needing those bags. She's not been commissioned yet and everyone lives ashore. You're one of the early birds. Leave your bags here, lad, and gang over to the ship. Ye can see the tops of her masts over yon sheds.' His finger pointed to an imposing array of radar aerials. I stowed my bags in his little office and moved away.

'Hey,' he called after me, 'the word is Hockey Stick!' I turned back mystified. 'Hockey Stick!' he repeated. 'It's the password for today if ye're coming in at night.'

'Hockey Stick', I said, smiling, though impressed with the security arrangements.

'Aye!' he said, unsmiling.

7 Flexing the sinews of war

As I came round the corner of the shed, her bows flared out at me leading my eyes upward, past the anchors snug in the hawse pipes, on to the fo'c'sle, and then upward to the long twin barrels of guns, lurking behind steel walls, ever upward to the bridge, a round steel gunnery control tower, the final narrowing of the steel tripod mast, and then the complicated cluster of radar aerials that had been my landmark, or more correctly my sea-mark. She looked forbiddingly large and overpowering, but then I realised that she was in light trim and there were still the hundreds of tons of oil-fuel, ammunition, and stores to come aboard to settle her in the water and assume that low, predatory profile I would come to admire.

As I moved along the wharf, the two gracefully raked funnels came into view, cowled on top, and with a cross section like a flat, slim, expensive Turkish cigarette. On either side was a bewildering array of searchlights, ventilating shafts, 27ft whalers, trim white motor boats and among them a girdered electric crane, beaked like some steel bird, for hoisting the boats. Menacingly on two high mountings on each side, were the two multiple-barrelled 40mm pom-poms, their eight flared barrels angled up already. These were the famous Chicago Pianos, beloved of every wartime newsreel cameraman and seen on every cinema screen, the eight barrels pumping in and out, spitting a deadly close-range barrage at enemy aircraft. At various vantage points, the barrels of 20mm Oerlikon guns, added their menace to the armament array.

I was impressed as I moved down the ship's side, past the smaller tripod mainmast, near which was another type of armament, the port and starboard quadruple 21-inch torpedo tubes. There was a small break in the superstructure, and then it built up again to what must be the deckhouses of the Wardroom, the Officers' Galleys and the Captain's Quarters. Atop these were some smaller deckhouses, another round steel gunnery control tower, a cluster of four Oerlikon guns, and finally a huge gun turret from which rose the muzzles of two guns. Falling to deck level again, there was the final gun turret, the clear space of the quarter deck, and then the depth charge rails.

Overall I was vastly impressed, but then I paused. Surely there was something wrong – there were only four twin turrets, and Dido class cruisers had five twin turrets with 5.25 inch guns! There was something strange about the muzzles of those guns behind the steel walls which could only be solved by going aboard, and I had a perfect right to board her now, for had I not been appointed to this ship? I walked boldly up the gangway, but no bands played, no officers appeared, but a girl in paint-streaked overalls, her hair held up in a coloured turban stood aside for me and smiled. I made my way to the aftermost gun turret, which according to traditional naming would be Y turret, the one above it being X turret, while the two forward turrets which had first taken my eye would be A and B. It then dawned on me that there would undoubtedly be a detachment of Royal Marines aboard to man the after turrets as their traditional battle station. Royal Marines usually had a Band too, I supposed, so we'd have some music. I whistled *A Life on the Ocean Wave* and stopped it in mid-bar, as I found the mystery of the guns behind the steel walls. These guns were semi-automatic 4.5 inch calibre, and these weren't even turrets, they were open-ended mountings with fuse-setting machines and ammunition lifts behind them. It was a bit of a cheat, I felt to hide these little guns behind these high steel walls. Why, even Tribal Class destroyers had bigger 4.7 inch guns in proper turrets, and this was supposed to be a light cruiser! Like Queen Victoria, I was not amused, and my first impressions of menace and power were becoming badly tarnished. I walked all around the ship, but saw no naval personnel at all, so I returned to the gangway where I met a workman coming aboard.

'Where is everybody?' I asked.

'There's only engineers aboard,' he answered, and glancing at the plain gold Executive Branch lace on my sleeve, added, 'and you'll not be one, but I think the Gunnery Officer is in that office along the wharf there.'

'Thanks', I said, following the direction of his finger, and scrambling outboard. The office was drab, black corrugated iron, and I pushed open the door as my knock was answered by a voice inside. A tall, well-built RN Lieutenant with a pink, cherubic face, looked up from a large ledger.

'I'm Hughes, Sir,' I announced, 'Gunnery Control, come aboard to join, Sir.'

'Well, well,' he beamed, 'welcome aboard. I'm Rupert Wainwright, Gunnery Officer and you'll be one of my team, and I need a bit of help. There's another Control Officer coming along sometime to make up the team. Shift those damned gramophone records, sit down and have a look at the Gunnery Orders while I get on with these ammunition returns.'

I shifted the slithery discs and took the bulky file over to what light came from the grimy window. Sure enough, the guns were 4.5 inch and only four turrets. I read on, the vast majority of the information being double-Dutch to me at this early stage.

'Excuse me, Sir,' I ventured as Rupert Wainwright paused in his work 'why 4.5 inch guns?'

'We're an anti-aircraft cruiser,' he answered, 'just us and *Charybdis*. I felt the same too,' he went on, 'but, believe me, we're the last word in anti-aircraft gunnery. These 4.5s are the coming thing – they've a high rate of fire and they're most efficient. Besides that, we've the latest air and surface warning radar in the Navy!' My spirits rose perceptibly.

'I like this word 'Zareba' for those high steel walls around the guns,' I said, pointing to the specifications in the Orders. 'They're the thorn hedges they erect around villages in Africa to keep off wild beasts.'

'Is that what it means?' he asked. 'Where did you pick up that?'

'Geography's my subject, Sir.'

'Of course, you're the schoolmaster, aren't you?' He paused. 'You know, you must have done rather well to get this appointment, you being RNVR and this ship being the latest thing. I hope we can make her into a real fighting unit.' I warmed to him immediately, realising that he was summarising for me what he must have read in Form S 202, the confidential report which followed every officer around with his appointments. He looked at his watch.

'Better get our lunch. Scott's pay for our lunch at the Station Hotel and throw in a pint of beer as well. You see, until we commission and do our trials and the Captain accepts the ship, she really belongs to them. Come along then, meet some of the other officers, and we'll see about getting you some digs, because we all live ashore.' As we walked back to the Station he listed the personalities of the ship whom I would meet.

'Our Captain is Capt IAP MacIntyre, CBE, a former submariner. He had something to do with the raising of the submarine *Thetis* before the war, then the second-in-command is Cdr Ben Fisher, and the other executive officers besides ourselves are Lt Green, our Pilot, Lt THP Wilson, the Torpedo Officer, and Lt Terence Stopford – he's an Honourable, by the way. The Engine Room Department is almost complete and they've been here for months – Cdr Hill, Lt Cdr Blanchford, Lt Fripp and Sub Lt Clark. The Principal Medical Officer, Lt Cdr Coulter has just joined. Amongst the Warrant Officers there's Daddy Poore, Commissioned Gunner; Jackie Perks, Gunner; Mitchell the Torpedo Gunner, and there's the Shipwright.'

'I seem to be the only RNVR type', I said ruefully, in the face of all this professionalism.

'Indeed you are' he continued, 'but there's a lot more to come and they'll be reservists, but generally, I hear that the Old Man wants a crack ship in every way. He's a pretty senior Captain, and his appointment was a few years before the war, so he's no stranger to the rank.'

I whistled soundlessly and cut myself down to size, determined to acquire as much professionalism as I could, for what else could I do; I had exchanged one profession for another, and there was no doubt in my mind of my love for the sea, the ships and the craft of seamanship.

'Incidentally, which of those three names do you like to be?' asked Guns.

'None of them,' I laughed. 'I've been successively Sandy, Taffy and Doc!'

'I like none of those either. I think I'll call you Hughie.' Thus in a way was I baptised into *Scylla* – on a wet, misty day, and christened with a new name.

Everyone was assembled at the hotel bar, Company pint in fist, laughing and joking, and with the kind word of welcome for me on introduction. As the Doctor came forward there was instant and mutual recognition.

'I know this bird,' he drawled, à la Noel Coward, turning to the Commander, 'he's one of the wild gunnery characters from Chatham Gunnery School. He and some of his cronies were actually playing leap-frog in the sacred precincts of the Wardroom, only a couple of weeks ago! But he paid for it with a lovely thick head the following morning, didn't you, eh?' I nodded guiltily. 'Had to come to me for a corpse reviver, eh?' I nodded again, feeling a recurrence of that headache at this revelation of my Farewell Party at Chatham.

'Hughes,' said the Commander, with mock severity, 'I trust that you are going to behave yourself in *Scylla*.' Veiled, or not, I took the hint, and decided to act 'Pusser' and to play everything according to the rules until, of course, I felt competent enough to either break or bend a few of them.

The day, however, ended on a happier note, for at the Naval Officers' Club, where I took over the Doctor's room, I met a pretty, slim Wren Petty Officer who was in charge, and we immediately got off to a good start because we found that we were both Welsh. She came from the beautiful maritime county of Pembrokeshire, having joined the WRNS at her home in Milford Haven. I went to bed early that evening after the long journey and the sobering day, realising that some of my train-thoughts were coming true; I was committing myself to a new era in my life, and that within hours I had met a lassie, and a Welsh one of all things, in this faraway place. There was a blackbird singing in the twilight of the Club garden, as I drifted away to sleep.

In the succeeding days I increased my knowledge of *Scylla*, probing far down into the depths – to the Gunnery Transmitting Station where our computer was sited, surrounded by oil-fuel tanks, and sealed by a four-inch thick armoured door worked on a counterpoise, a claustrophobic place; to the engine and boiler rooms where the great 65,000 horsepower turbines were waiting to drive the four propellers; to the various magazines, racked with thousands of shells for the 4.5s and even greater thousands for the 20mm and 40mm guns. These vitals of the ship were protected by four-inch armoured plate steel, like a huge box in the middle of the ship. This was the armoured citadel area, and its entrances and exits below decks, and port and starboard were marked by a different type of watertight door – one that was so heavy that it was operated by a large hand-wheel in the centre of the door.

Forrard of the citadel were the messdecks, with a special section set apart for the Marines and therefore known as the Barracks, the Sick Bay and Operating Theatre, food stores, the crew's galley, the bakery, the canteen, and various offices. Aft of the citadel were the various officers' cabins, the Captain's and Commanders' and Wardroom on the Upper Deck as I had previously divined, the others on the deck below, together with the Ship's Main Office, and the Cypher Office where the most secret signals were ciphered and deciphered.

It was immediately evident that *Scylla* was fitted as a flagship as some of the cabins bore neat metal notices – Flag Lieutenant, Admiral's Secretary, etc. Mine bore the latter title, and I was told that I would vacate it if ever we became a flagship. Its importance was indicated by its possession of a telephone and a framed *Internal Telephone Directory* above it, otherwise it was a compact little place, complete with bunk, desk, book rack, easy chair, and a folding wash basin complete with h and c. I longed to get into my first little home in the Royal Navy, but one of the turbanned ladies was in possession, complete with rags and polish.

'Ye canna come in, noo,' she admonished. 'I've no' finished the french polishing!'

It was amazing to learn that though the war had entered its third year, the ship was being completed according to peace-time specifications, even down to the Wardroom cutlery which was stamped Mappin and Webb. I dreaded the thought of this beautiful ship being sunk or blown up after all the care and skill being expended on her now.

In addition to my main Gunnery Control duties, I learned that I would also be Assistant Forecastle Divisional Officer, Physical and Recreational Training Officer, Assistant Boats Officer, and best of all, an Assistant Watchkeeping Officer, if Gunnery duties allowed. I promptly bought Volume 2 of the *Admiralty Navigation Manual*, dealing with Nautical Astronomy. The list of duties seemed formidable at the time, but as the months passed I added to them Wardroom Wine Caterer, and as a former Coder, I was welcomed as a Spare Cypher Officer, as the procedure was exactly similar though more secret.

Other officers began arriving day by day – Lt Watson, RNVR, a watchkeeper and my superior in the Forecastle Division, Sub-Lt Maclean, Aircraft Recognition Officer as befitted our role, Sub-Lt Holifield, the

Fighter Direction Officer, a misnomer, as he rarely if ever directed fighters, being concerned with the intricacies of the Radar Plotting Table. Sub-Lt Law, a Cambridge science graduate, was the Radar Officer and the Senior Sub-Lieutenant, by virtue of being RN, was Forbes. Our lowly rank kept us together at table and in the Mess, and firm friendships were formed, and we spent a lot of time together ashore, until I plucked up enough courage to ask the Wren Petty Officer to have dinner with me in Gourock, and she accepted.

'You're a fast worker,' said Paymaster Commander Barry, after meeting us ashore one evening. 'I've been here for months and to my knowledge she's refused umpteen people, and you've been here a week or so. What's her Christian name?'

'Charlotte,' I answered shyly. The Pay's eyebrows rose at such evidence of familiarity.

At the time appointed for the crew to arrive from the special train, Maclean and I stood on a vantage point on the upper deck waiting. Faintly over the sheds came the sound of martial music and then around the corner came the Royal Marine Band, followed by the Marine detachment and then the sailors, in threes, flanked by the Chiefs, the Petty Officers, and Leading Seamen. They must have been tired after the long journey, for they made little attempt to march in time, hindered by bags and cases, and when a halt was called, they came to a ragged stop, punctuated by sleepy collisions. They were called to attention, and someone's hat fell off and he bent forward to retrieve it.

'What a sloppy collection!' said Maclean.

'Oh, have a heart!' I snapped. 'It's early days yet, and they're obviously tired!' Little did we know that within weeks this unprepossessing crew would begin to distinguish themselves as one of the finest fighting crews in the Royal Navy, men that I would be ever proud to have as shipmates.

We had been posting guide notices and directions all over the ship to help them orientate themselves, and the Commander's organisation was such that in no time the tannoy was piping the hands to tea, and sailors were strolling around the decks as if they had been aboard for months. This was the first evidence of the standard of discipline and reliance which was being engendered aboard.

On 25 May, 1942, the ship was commissioned with traditional ceremony, faultlessly organised by the Commander. It was a blue day, a day of sun, with a few scurrying clouds, but a far, eternal blue in the sky. Capt MacIntyre, tall, lean with an aquiline face, read the Commissioning Warrant, and the gleaming White Ensign was hoisted on the mainmast, and the masthead pennant broken to mark the beginning of our commission, a short pennant at this stage. The Captain then called us to prayer, and asked God's blessing on our ship in the Gaelic Blessing of

1589. At each invocation, the crew's united voice came deep and sincere, 'Bless our Ship!' Prayers, hymns and readings followed, and though the great Naval Prayer moved me as it ever did, there was another prayer which I heard for the first time – Drake's Prayer – which I have never forgotten.

'Lord God, when thou givest thy servants to endeavour any great matter, grant us so to know that it is not the beginning but the continuing of the same until it be thoroughly finished which yieldeth the true glory; through him, who, for the finishing of thy work, laid down his life: our Saviour Jesus Christ. Amen.'

This was a germ of spiritual experience at the time, a time when we had not reached the turning point of the war, when the Navy had suffered grievous losses in men and ships, and yet I felt a growth of a spiritual confidence that a nation and a great fighting service which could hold fast to its Christian beliefs in the face of dire adversity must win through to final victory. As the years passed, my spiritual trust increased, and a deeper love for this adopted Service grew, a Service which for all its rough way of life on the sea, its bawdiness and toughness, always came back to the basic Christian doctrine of 'Love thy Neighbour' or more parochially, thy shipmate.

As an officer, I was beginning to see that I was just as much a man at sea, in a strange element, as the Captain or the lowliest Ordinary Seaman, but that I was special in that a trust reposed in me to uphold the best traditions of the Service by my example.

As a student, and even later, I had held left wing views, and had seriously thought about joining the International Brigade in the Spanish Civil War, and fighting against Fascism on the side of socialism, but all these views had been modified since joining the Navy. Of course there was strict discipline and irksome regulations, but in the all important field of human relations, I had always seen justice, tempered with mercy. I had met petty-minded people, but I had also met many whom I respected and to whom I would give unquestioning loyalty.

My loyalty and respect for Capt MacIntyre began shortly after commissioning, one evening when I was Officer of the Watch, and had to report to the Captain that it was, 'Five minutes to Colours', when the Ensign would be hauled down at 9 o'clock, to the beautiful, haunting notes of the Sunset Call. On the way to his cabin, I had a word with the Quartermaster, a glance at my tie in the lobby mirror, a firm tuck of the telescope under my arm. I knocked at his cabin door, and entered at his call.

'Five minutes to Colours, Sir!' I said, snapping smartly to attention.

'Is that really true, Hughes?' he asked kindly, glancing meaningly at the brass clock on the cabin bulkhead.

'No, Sir!' I replied, leaning slightly forward for a better view of the clock. 'Three and a half minutes to Colours, Sir!'

'Though custom dictates that you repeat that phrase, it can never be strictly true, can it? I am only interested in truth. Tell me the truth, always, however hard it may be at times. I think we understand each other, don't we?'

'Yes, Sir, we do!' I answered, taking his point.

'Carry on then, please,' he smiled, and I turned about smartly, walking away down the alley thinking that the Old Man and I had a similar philosophy, mine being Keats' distillation in his *Ode to a Grecian Urn*.

'Truth is Beauty, Beauty Truth,
That is all we know, and all we need to know.'

Within a few days of commissioning we moved from the fitting-out basin at Scott's to the famous Tail of the Bank anchorage off Greenock, now, since the entry of the United States into the war, the transatlantic terminus of the *Queen Elizabeth*, *Queen Mary* and other great passenger liners, disgorging whole divisions of American troops into Britain. It was an uplifting experience to feel the deck come to life beneath one's feet, quivering slightly with the thrust of the turbines, and to see the wake of the four screws creaming aft. The anchor plummetted down for the first time while we awaited preparations for our sea and acceptance trials. We were invaded by specialist civilians of all kinds – engineers, electricians, armament engineers, riggers etc – and all the ship's catering was taken over by civilian cooks and waiters, for technically the ship was still not ours until the Captain was satisfied with her performance and accepted her from Scott's.

Preparations complete we sailed down the Clyde, through the boom at the Cloch Light and headed for the measured mile off the Isle of Arran. Here *Scylla* was put through high speed tests, cutting flat-out through the water at well over 33 knots, making a great U-turn, to repeat the process on a northward run. As we turned, the ship heeled over dramatically, the fans and turbines whining, the rigging singing and the spray driving inboard, making what we knew must be a brave and thrilling sight. The engines were tested cruelly, being reversed from full ahead to full astern at times, a shuddering trial for a high speed engine and guaranteed to shake out any looseness.

At the same time the rudder was subjected to similar cruelty, being whipped over from hard-a-port to hard-a-starboard, the surprisingly small steering wheel in the lower steering position, deep in the ship's heart, a blurring disc of polished brass, as the helmsman obeyed the order, while our wake bubbled and surged like a huge white python astern. The whole process reminded me of a thoroughbred horse being broken-in, and from the way she behaved we all knew that we had a thoroughbred indeed.

As a very junior officer, I was not aware of the finer points of her performance, but they must have been highly satisfactory because Capt MacIntyre accepted the ship by signing a simple document to the effect that he had received from Messrs Scott's – one ship!

As we now owned a ship, it was our next task to learn to use it properly and to turn it into a major warship. Each day therefore, we left the Clyde soon after dawn to proceed to the exercise and trials area where the Firth of Clyde is at its widest, with the conical shape of Ailsa Craig or Paddy's Milestone, rising from the horizon at the midway point. This was Cdr Fisher's era when he drove us like galley slaves through all the evolutions we were likely to go through – we prepared to tow other ships, we prepared to be towed, we lowered and hoisted boats, rigged collision mats, did all sorts of peculiar things to our anchors, streamed paravanes to cut mine moorings, in fact we did every evolution, which, until then had only been for me mere paragraphs and illustrations in seamanship manuals.

We went to Evening Quarters, a custom more honoured in the breach than in the observance, that of performing evolutions after tea. We sailed out at night to test the radar and the look-outs, in night encounter exercises with wily and elusive destroyers, wise in the hiding places around the Clyde, lurking in the shadow of the land so that their radar echoes were blurred and to human eyes they were difficult to distinguish.

The Gunnery Department then took the stage for Gun Trials, beginning with a spectacular overture off Ailsa Craig when all the guns were fired, frightening the gannets on the rocks, so that they rose in one vast white cloud from the nesting ledges, their squawking carrying across the water to us in a hideous cacophony. The 4.5 guns fired with an ear-splitting crack and a long tongue of flame from the barrels, and in the Director we had to wear our headphones in sponge rubber discs, looking like rugger forwards.

With all eight guns firing at once *Scylla* looked a terrifying sight, living up to her name in the list of Greek monsters, though the mythical Scylla was only armed with a bevy of fierce dogs which sprouted from her midriff and her eyes glared balefully while her hair streamed wildly behind her. Thus was she portrayed on the ship's official boat badge which was now being found on our boats, our quarterdeck and on the ship's stationery.

For Rupert Wainwright, Sub-Lieutenant Rowlands, the second Director officer and myself there now began a difficult period when the training of the Director, guns, and transmitting station crews commenced. Our first live firing at a drogue target was not auspicious as our shell bursts were ragged and off target, but as drogue after drogue fluttered across the sky behind the towing aircraft, it improved and there was grim satisfaction when my crew shot down the first drogue, and it went shuddering downward into the sea in a mess of crumpled canvas and wood. Almost immediately the other crews accounted for another drogue and so it continued with high drogue-mortality.

There was also practice with live shells on towed sea targets, with much the same results – a shaky start, followed by a gradual improvement, and the final satisfaction of seeing our shells tearing great chunks of wood out of the latticed framework of the target.

The pom-poms and Oerlikons had their share of exercise, as they fired at the high speed drogues towed by that wonderful biplane, the Gloster Gladiator, which would roar across the ship at its top speed which was not far short of that of a Hurricane, towing its much smaller drogue on a longer wire behind it. Then all hell would break loose from the pom-poms, the muzzles smoking and jerking, and the empty shellcases streaming backwards on to the deck. From the Oerlikons would come long arcs of seemingly languid tracer, because the proportion of tracer bullets was about one in five, while the gunners hung in their harnesses as the guns fired at a high angle, their boots scrabbling for purchase on the gridded decks and the empty shellcases shot sideways from the big, round magazines. Speed of firing improved greatly, and the 4.5s were firing a salvo of eight shells into the sky every four seconds, until the sky was dotted untidily with brown and black shell bursts.

So much time was being spent at sea that we only saw Greenock at weekends, spending the night either at sea or at the quiet little harbour of Lamlash in Arran, under the lee of Holy Island with Goat Fell looming above us. On some of these June evenings there were opportunities for walking in the hills, and on one occasion Maclean and I met the Captain riding a bicycle in a country lane. Punctiliously we saluted him and equally politely he returned our salute, but being more used to conning a ship than riding a bike, he lost control and swerved into the hedge, bounced off, recovered his balance and rode sedately away.

'Should you see me on a bike again, Hughes,' he said, later, 'please refrain from the usual salute. I shall be too pre-occupied to return it!'

Throughout June and July the working-up period continued with welcome breaks during which time I was able to see Charlotte. At other times we tramped across the island of Bute, penetrated inland from Lamlash, and made a delightful motorboat picnic to Arrochar at the head of Loch Long, and then tramped over the pass into Loch Lomond at Tarbert. This was a pleasant way of testing the motorboat's efficiency! Towards the end of July we were considered to be working at full efficiency and we anchored at the Tail of the Bank with a definite air of expectancy pervading the ship, as to what and where our first operation would be.

Then that strange naval phenomenon the 'Buzz' began to function. The buzz is a mixture of definite small facts, overheard conversations and imagination, sober, or wild. The Captain tells his steward to look over his tropical uniform, containers of lime-juice are broken out from a store, and this is enough evidence to circulate a buzz that we are bound for the Mediterranean. The strongest and most credible buzz in late July was that we were going on a Malta convoy. The June Malta convoy had been heavily attacked and only two merchant ships reached Malta, while there had been heavy losses in cruisers and destroyers at this time. Another convoy would obviously have to be formed, and a brand new cruiser was an obvious re-inforcement in the Mediterranean.

The supply ships began to load us up with many extras and there was a mysterious consignment of medical supplies. The sudden announcement came that we were to prepare for sea and a last leave ashore was given to one of the watches. Tension began to build, and then came anti-climax and sailing orders were cancelled. In the Wardroom later, the truth was revealed. We had indeed been ordered to Malta, and up to the moment when leave had been announced we were poised to proceed. Then the security leak was discovered. During the morning a coded signal had been received from the shore stating that, 'Medical supplies for Malta would arrive that afternoon'. The originator of this top secret message had omitted to give instructions for such a vital signal to be sent in cypher, thus to be dealt with by an officer; it had therefore been sent in code, and decoded by a coder of the very watch that was now on leave ashore! Without a doubt, a few careless words in a pub would reveal the preparations for a Malta convoy. There was only one way to cover up the slip, and that was to cancel *Scylla*'s sailing. So we hung around the Clyde for a few days more. The projected convoy sailing to Malta in August, was heavily attacked, and during the operation the tanker *Ohio* made her epic voyage to the island, bombed and burning, but still largely intact.

We heard this news in Scapa Flow for which we had sailed at the end of July. I had never been to Scapa Flow, the Home Fleet base, and was not impressed by the bleakness of the ring of islands that made the Flow into a small inland sea. The approach through the Pentland Firth was always a rough passage and the high cliffs of South Hoy, frowned down on you, with the giant, isolated high crag of the Old Man of Hoy like a grim sentinel, isolated from the main landmass. As we passed through the boom, the guillemots and puffins skittered along the water in front of us like aquatic clowns, and to port, over the low land we began to see the aristocratic outlines of the battleships and heavy cruisers of the Home Fleet, commanded by Admiral Sir John Tovey, in the battleship HMS *King George V*. Humbly we took our anchor berth, far over by the island of Flotta, nearer to the destroyers in Gutter Sound than to the aristocrats of the Home Fleet. This move was to prove prophetic and strategic.

After a few days Guns revealed to me in confidence that we were destined for a Russian convoy, a worse prospect than any Malta convoy, with the added dangers of the Arctic cold to contend with. In addition, the Home Fleet was still reeling under the impact of the destruction of the ill-fated PQ 17 convoy of the previous June. For such a romantic month, June 1942 had been cruel to the Royal Navy, the losses of major ships had been heavy and the German Luftwaffe had inflicted great losses on us.

'They're determined that this next convoy is going to get through!' confided Guns. 'We're going to be flagship of Rear Admiral Sir Robert Burnett, the Rear Admiral of the Home Fleet Destroyer flotillas; there's going to be a huge escort of destroyers and we'll also have one of the new small escort aircraft carriers with us, *HMS Avenger*.'

In the succeeding days, there was very little traffic from *Scylla* towards the Home Fleet, it was all directed towards the destroyers in Gutter Sound, where the crack L, M and O class destroyers lay at anchor, large, fast, hard hitting ships, commanded by famous Captains such as Beaky Armstrong and Sherbroke. Then one day, Admiral Burnett and his staff arrived on board, and the Saint George's Cross flag with two red balls in the two cantons nearest the staff was run up at the masthead of the mainmast, and I was ejected from my cabin to bunk-in with the Captain's Secretary!

Meetings on strategy, gunnery tactics, lay-out of the convoy and escort were continuous and there was a grim air overall. Admiral Burnett turned out to be a jovial, ruddy complexioned man, very fit-looking, as one would expect from an officer who had done a great deal of work in physical and recreational training for the Navy. He was a bluff, voluble man who laughed and smiled a lot, and was popularly known to us as Bullshit Bob! I saw no signs of these characteristics as we listened to his serious and factual account of the conditions and attacks we could expect.

In the latter half of August we sailed from Scapa Flow back to the Scottish mainland, and anchored in that great remote loch in Wester Ross – Loch Ewe. I had never been to such a remote place before, and a study of the chart and the use of dividers revealed that we were 40 miles from the nearest railway station and there was no town of any size nearer than Inverness on the east coast. Other facts I picked up were that the salmon fishing was excellent and that somewhere further up the Loch were some tropical gardens, made possible because the Gulf Stream warmed the whole area. Even in August it was a rainswept, eerie place.

When we arrived the huge loch was crowded with merchant ships, destroyers, supply ships, even a hospital ship and as such a self-contained force, no one set foot on the shore. I pondered on what the people of the scattered cottages made of this grim assemblage, intent on its own business, and supremely uninterested in what went on ashore. A few years ago I visited Loch Ewe again and it had changed very little, but there was not a ship to be seen, and only a lone gull perched morosely on the ring of a mooring buoy where *Scylla* had lain nearly 40 years before. The heavy gun batteries which had guarded the entrance then, were untidy heaps of concrete, where men of my own age, who had probably served in the Army then, wandered silently among the heaps, silently reminiscing.

It was now possible to study the make-up of the convoy at close quarters and it was immediately evident that this was a convoy of the sinews of war, vital military supplies for the Russian armies fighting the battle that was to be the turning point of the war on the Eastern Front – the Battle of Stalingrad. Every ship, except the tankers, carried a diversified cargo; that is, a cross-section of the sinews – weapons, ammunition, fuel, food and machinery. Every deck, even those of the tankers, carried tanks, motor vehicles, partly assembled aircraft, and huge packing cases of supplies.

The warships were the crack destroyers of the Home Fleet and the veteran destroyers and corvettes of the Atlantic escort groups, together with the escort aircraft carrier *Avenger*, three anti-aircraft ships, *Pozarica, Palomares* and *Alynbank* formerly merchant ships of the Macandrews and Bank Lines. Other vital elements were the Fleet minesweepers *Harrier, Sharpshooter* and *Leda* which would sweep ahead of the convoy to deal with any mines laid by aircraft. In addition there was a submarine which would be sailing discreetly in the centre of the convoy, ready to submerge when reconnaissance planes spotted us, with her main task always being to attack any heavy surface ships such as *Tirpitz, Scharnhorst* or *Gneisenua* which might break out of the Norwegian fiords to attack us. The whole convoy now being assembled, there were various conferences during which the Captains of the merchant ships were briefed.

Late one afternoon, steam began appearing on the fo'c'sles of the merchant men, and the rumble of anchor chains being weighed floated across the loch. One by one the ships began to manoeuvre, sirens boomed, funnels erupted smoke and triple expansion steam and diesel engines began to turn over their respective rhythms. The first ship sailed past *Scylla*, anchored near the entrance, engines faintly pounding, exhaust steam streaming from aft the funnel, lifeboats swung out ready and decks crowded with cargo. Admiral Burnett stood on the quarterdeck waving them God-speed and a deep boom echoed from the siren. Ship after ship glided past, British, American, Norwegian, Greek and Panamanian; ships from famous cargo lines, and others I had never heard of.

A ship flying what seemed to be the Red Ensign came past and then we noted that it was not the Union Jack in the corner but the crossed hammer and sickle of the Russian flag flown by the very aptly named freighter *Stalingrad*. A smaller merchant ship with a nice turn of speed turned out to be the convoy rescue ship, equipped to pick up survivors, and with a proper medical staff and facilities aboard, the former Egyptian merchant ship *Zamalek*.

It was obvious that no chances were being taken with this convoy and the escort was the strongest ever assembled, with a wide range of facilities, both aggressive and humane. The mistakes learned in June with Convoy PQ 17 were not going to be repeated with this one.

The first ships were now lifting to the Atlantic swell and beginning to form up in their columns. I felt a sense of excitement mingled with fear, for now we were committed; the convoy was at sea, and it must go on to Russia. I glanced idly at one of the last of the passing merchantmen, flying the Panamanian flag, and spoke to Maclean watching with me.

'Read her name!' I pointed to the nameboard on her bridge.

'Macbeth!' said Mac, who had a degree in English Literature.

'Not exactly propitious, eh?' I said grimly.

'I'd have preferred 'All's Well that Ends Well!' he answered.

Late that evening we sailed northward for Hvalfjord in south west Iceland, and the light kept pace with us, for now we were entering the northern regions of the midnight sun and the aurora borealis which lent an air of unreality to the whole operation. There was a short stay in Hvalfjord and we set course ever northward again to the remote fiord of Seydisfiord on the north-east coast with the grim Icelandic coast ever on our port side, with its snow-capped mountains, swirling mists and the dreaded katabatic winds which would descend without warning from the heights and turn the fiords into raging maelstroms. The grim word pictures of Icelandic sagas came to life before my eyes, and in my mind the wild, eerie tune of Sibelius's *Swan of Tuonela* rose and fell on the cor anglais . There was no spontaneous laughter in the ship, and even Able Seaman Andrews, the rangetaker in the Director and the life and soul of that small steel box, fell silent.

The ship was now constantly at Defence Stations, or Second Degree of Readiness, with all guns manned by the ordinary watch and only one degree less prepared than for full Action Stations. I lived with the Director crew which consisted of Leading Seaman Cornish, the Director layer whose telescope pinpointed the elevation of the target, Able Seaman Mead, the Director trainer whose telescope followed the target laterally, and Able Seaman Andrews, whose rangefinder/heightfinder further fixed the target.

I sat in the middle with my own special telescope, with Cornish below and to the right, Mead to the left and Andrews's head on a level with my feet, as he pored over the complicated images in his rangefinder, whose lidded eyes protruded on stalks from either side of the Director tower. Behind sat Able Seaman Freeman, the Communication Number, with a telephone headset similar to mine in contact with the guns, while my set was in contact with the bridge below us and the Transmitting Station far down in the bowels of the ship. From the top of the Director protruded the fishbone aerials of the Gunnery radar set, outwardly just a bristly antenna, but electronically a live member as it rose and fell with the telescopes, ever searching and recording.

Apart from the crow's nests we were the highest inhabited part of the ship, though the After, or Blue Director was much lower than the Red up forrard. Climbing the dreaded mast at *Ganges* now came into true perspective, as the last stages of entering the Director through the trapdoor underneath were the equivalent to climbing over the formerly dreaded Devil's Elbow or futtock shrouds. We performed this gymnastic feat in fair weather and in howling midnight gales and thought little of it.

Inside the Director, space was severely limited and a four-hour watch in cramped positions was very tiring. Socially there was a special relationship between us all – everything was shared, and cigarettes, sweets and other things were handed around without ceremony. We knew many facts about each other, about our homes, our wives and sweethearts, our likes and dislikes, our funny stories and our smutty songs.

'Be I 'Ampshire, be I, buggery, I be come from Fareham.'

'My old woman has 13 kids, and she knows 'ow to rare 'em!' Andrews would sing, while I would retaliate with,

> 'They're digging up uncle's grave to build a sewer,
>
> They're doing the job regardless of expense,
>
> They're digging up uncle's remains,
>
> To put in lavatory drains,
>
> For some Society twit's new residence. Gorblimey!'

Then suddenly the Target Indicator Bell would clang urgently, and we would swing into action.

'Train left!' The indicator needle would swing towards centre. 'Elevate a little!' The needle would edge to dead centre.

'Cut!' would come Andrews' voice from under my feet.

'Have plot, have height!' would report Band Corporal Hollier from the TS below.

'A Gun ready, B Gun ready, X and Y Guns ready!' would snap Cornish as the Gun Ready lamps lit up in sequence on the array before him, and I would see his knuckles tense on the pistol butt of the firing lever which would fire every gun in the ship by remote control on the tightening of his index finger. Radar would have joined in by now, supplementing our visual range.

'Radar and Visual plots coinciding. Range 7,000 yards!'

'Ready to open fire!' I would report to the bridge as the target begin to assume more definite recognition characteristics.

'Looks like a Catalina flying boat to me?'

'I think you're right, Sir.'

'Forebridge-Director? No panic. Aircraft identified as a Catalina, and she's showing IFF (Identification Friend or Foe) on radar. Resume normal watch!' The Director would resume its way of life.

'Not much different from driving a railway engine on the LNER is this Director!'

'How come, Meadie?'

'Well, you spin this ruddy training wheel in the same way as you take off the brake on one of those Gresley Pacifics, and I've done plenty of that.'

'Why don't you work on a proper railway like the Great Western?'

'Sir, please don't start that again!'

'Cigarette anyone?' Freeman, who was a solicitor, was always placatory.

We went ashore at Seydisfiord and I relished every step I took on dry land, as I pondered on the grim prospect before us on the very threshold of the operational area and close to the Arctic Circle. We passed a fish-oil factory outside the village, and then a bakehouse from which came the smell of freshly baked bread. The proprietor must have sensed our forebodings because he beckoned us in and handed us fresh scones and butter which we wolfed greedily, while gazing about at the giant landscape around us – the steep black mountains, with the eternal snow in the high gullies and ledges, and it was easy to imagine the trolls and giants of Grieg's music.

Nearer the fiord the grimness relented a little and there were rocky fields in which harvesters were gathering the summer hay and loading it into fishing boats, while women dug potatoes from the rich lava-soil deposits. The village was picturesque with its gaily painted wooden houses, surrounded by neatly painted fences, and some of them were turf roofed, the grass long and bright green in September. There were even a couple of shops and I bought some perfume and silk stockings with my stock of kroners. At the top of the fiord a huge waterfall gushed down, and below this Capt MacIntyre was calmly casting for trout!

That evening we weighed anchor in the sunset, a sunset that was as red as blood, and the anchor cable jammed. The anchor was firmly caught in the rocky fiord bottom, and had to be left there and marked by a buoy to be picked up on our return, if ever.

'Bloody good start!' growled one of the Cable Party. I silently agreed with him listing the cruisers already lost on the Russian run – *Edinburgh, Trinidad* and who knows? But our bows were pointed northwards towards the Arctic Circle and Spitzbergen, and we were fully committed. Somewhere abreast of us and to the east, the convoy was sailing on a great north-easterly arc which would take it up to the Arctic ice edge. *Scylla* had not entered the stage yet, as we needed fuel to complete the convoy and

105

the return convoy, and the slow steaming ate into our stocks, so we were making for Bell Sound, Spitzbergen to rendezvous with a Fleet oiler.

Northwards we drove past islands which heretofore had only been of academic interest – Jan Mayen, Bear Island and finally Spitzbergen, the last sizeable island in the Arctic Ocean before the North Pole. It was a nightmarish place, remote, stark and devoid of any life other than a huge gull perched on a rocky promontory. A glacier, glinting ice-blue was poised over the Sound, and at intervals, great pieces of ice detached themselves and plunged over the lip of the cliff with a thin scream and a gigantic splash, to become small icebergs which dotted the water. The Ranger class oiler of the Royal Fleet Auxiliary was faithfully waiting for us, having arrived there by means unknown to me, and with considerable danger.

Oiling was quickly completed and we headed east for the convoy, picking up en route the discouraging news that the convoy had been sighted and attacked by U-boats that had already sunk the *Stalingrad* which only a few days before had sailed bravely out of Loch Ewe. *Scylla*'s turbines whined as 64,000 horses drove our four screws through the water at well over 30 knots towards the Arctic battle which was now opening in the grey waters of the Barents Sea.

8 The blooding of *Scylla*

The great convoy already had a slightly beleaguered air about it as we came up astern. Though it plodded along in steady formation, there were smoke smudges in the air around it and now and again there was an orange flash from the guns of one of the escort. The awful wails of the Action Stations alarm howled through the ship and we streaked for our stations, pulling on anti-flash helmets and gloves, groping with lifebelts and adjusting steel helmets. I checked my Action bag, stuffed with torch, knife, chocolate bars, cigarettes and the flat yellow tin that contained the row of morphine ampoules which I prayed I would never have to use, and hauled myself into the Director.

Almost immediately we were in action as a Junkers 88 bomber dropped out of the clouds, giving us enough time to get three salvoes close to him before he climbed back into cloud cover, leaving two huge white towers of water in the convoy lane where his bombs had exploded wide of the mark, his aim deterred by our fire. As he climbed away a great weight lifted from my mind, as if we had broken a magic spell. We had fired our first shots in anger and a heartening sight it had been, as the eight muzzles spat their long spiteful tongues of flame skywards, and the multiple pom-poms pumped in a blue haze of burnt cordite, and the shell cases spewed around in a brazen vomit.

'Radar reports six aircraft around the convoy above the clouds, so keep a good look-out!' ordered the bridge. The afternoon wore on with the Luftwaffe playing hide-and-seek in the clouds, and our guns sneaking the odd salvoes at them.

'Come out and be shot at, you skulking bastards!' said Andrews, and I knew for others the spell was being broken and we were emerging from our chrysalis as a blooded and fighting unit.

'It's bloody cold!' said Mead, rubbing his mittened hands, 'and it's only September.' I wriggled my toes in my sea-boot stockings encased in ridiculous rubber sea-boots, and vowed that if I got back, I was going to order some fleece lined leather sea-boots from Gieves.

'For your information,' said Freeman, 'today happens to be Sunday, the 13th of September.' There was silence as we absorbed this fact, and I thought of far-off orderly Sundays in boyhood Wales, with church

107

services, visitors to tea, best crockery and Sunday clothes smelling of naphtha balls.

'Stand by, Director!' came the peremptory voice from the Air Defence Officer on the bridge. 'There's a 25-plus echo coming in!'

'25!' I breathed, aloud. 'It can't be.' The target bearing indicator clanged, handwheels whirled and the horizon swung into view in my binoculars, a horizon so unbelievable that for a moment it was beyond comprehension, for wherever the Director trained there were aircraft, wing-tip to wing-tip, coming up from the south, flying almost at wave height, black torpedo bombers. Every available plane from the German bases at Banak and Hammerfest in Norway must have been gathered for this attack. We waited fearfully, the ranges closing, and Freeman calmly counting.

'I make it 42, Sir.'

'Open fire when ready!' I detected a slight catch in the voice from the bridge.

'7,000 yards,' chanted a voice.

'Open fire!' I croaked, and started to pray in the frightened recesses of my mind, a simple primeval invocation for aid from a Supreme Being. Then all hell broke loose, an inferno of fire and destruction that no one man can ever describe. The guns roared again and again, and the cordite and smoke eddied around us. Then, through the binoculars, I saw our first shells burst in orange confusion right in front of the target aircraft which lurched sideways into the path of its partner. There was an instant of flame and explosion as the two Junkers 88s collided and crashed into the sea, leaving a funeral pyre of thick black smoke. I let out a stream of profanity.

'For God's sake, Hughie,' came Daddy Poore's voice from the TS. 'What's going on? Please tell us.'

'Two in bloody one!' I shouted back hysterically. 'There's 42 aircraft attacking us and we've just shot down one, and another one's crashed into it.'

'Well keep on speaking, Hughie, keep on swearing, as long as we have some idea of what's going on up there.'

'OK!' I replied, and so began my profane battle commentary which I always maintained. 'Here comes another lot!' The target indicator clanged, the Director swung, and the guns spoke and spat again, and then the torpedo bombers were amongst the convoy, like a pack of ravening wolves. The 4.5s were silent and the pom-poms and Oerlikons took over at close range. The whole convoy area was encased in gigantic parabolas of tracer shells, glowing red and purple, the sea was churned up by thousands of small explosions as the shells expended themselves, then into the convoy lanes between the ships, came the German torpedo bombers. One streaked down *Scylla*'s side, its engine noise drowned by the clatter of gunfire, its black-helmeted pilot clearly visible through the transparent nose, its torpedo unlaunched. A faint red glow appeared at the point of the nose, grew in intensity as the incendiary shells hit home and in moments the plane was a raging inferno, ploughing drunkenly into the sea.

At the same moment another Junkers 88 swept over our masts at right angles towards a merchant ship on our starboard side, with our close range gunners hanging in their harnesses to get shots into her exposed belly. No one saw her torpedo released but moments later her target dissolved in one of the most stupendous explosions I had ever heard and the hot shock-wave shuddered the Director Tower. Instinctively we crouched low, expecting huge fragments of disintegrated steel to squash us like flies for we were only a few cable-lengths from the explosion, but nothing came down on us, only great flakes of ash which we rubbed wonderingly on our fingers!

We found ourselves near the base of a huge mushroom cloud of smoke with, to its right, another oily cloud of smoke which must have been the aircraft which had driven into the explosion it had caused. The sea all around was mud-coloured and littered with smoking fragments.

'God!' I breathed into the headset to Daddy Poore, 'an American merchant ship has blown sky-high just on our starboard side. I think she's called *Mary Luckenbach*.'

Fire died down from the ships and three Hurricane fighters from the *Avenger* flew over the convoy. We had forgotten our fighter support whom we found out later had been wreaking havoc among the slower torpedo bombers. The Germans reformed to mount attack, and the guns roared into action again and again as the planes weaved and bobbed among the convoy. Suddenly Freeman grabbed the neck of my duffel coat and pointed to the starboard side.

'Look, Sir – a torpedo. Coming straight towards us!' I think we were all paralysed at the inevitability of a direct hit and waited like stricken rabbits for the weasel's killing stroke. But the ship seemed to leap forward from the ten knots we were doing, and the torpedo track drew aft, as full speed was put on the turbines. Like a greyhound released, *Scylla* shot forward, a huge mound of turbulent water at her stern. Into this solid mass crashed the torpedo to explode with a violence that shook the whole ship, bringing urgent enquiries from the gallant TS crew, far down below the waterline. The ship shook herself like a labrador retriever from the force of the explosion and the cascade of water, and sped on, undamaged. Firing became sporadic and then died away, while to the south of us, the remaining black shapes of the swarm of bombers which had attacked us, roared homeward to the German base at Banak.

From our position ahead of the convoy, we could now assess the damage inflicted in those vital minutes. The *Mary Luckenbach*'s funeral pyre was only just astern and around it lay the other stricken ships, some in their last agonies, sterns upwards, screws still revolving, others at ungainly angles as they poised for the last plunge into the depths, and everywhere there seemed to be the lighter coloured shapes of lifeboats and life-rafts.

Eight ships out of our 44 had been sunk, and it did not take much of a mathematician to work out that four more attacks like this could annihilate us. It was little comfort that the battle commentary announced that this attack was the greatest single enemy torpedo bomber attack of the war. Enemy losses had not been collated, but we had seen three shot down in our vicinity, and it was certain that of those we had seen high-tailing it for home, many would crash into the Barents Sea from their injuries. I took a vicarious pleasure in imagining the empty places in the Officers' Mess at Banak that evening, and in a book which I read many years later, written by a pilot of this group, Fluggruppen 18 of the Luftwaffe, my vision was very true.

As it seemed inconceivable that another attack of this magnitude could be mounted in the next hour or so, the Action Messing system got under way, and in the Director we ate a meal that I shall always remember – hot soup, great chunks of fresh bread and a beautifully cooked naval speciality, the Tiddley Oggy or Cornish Pasty, liberally spattered with brown sauce, the whole washed down with a strong brew of tea.

Hardly had we wiped the crumbs from our mouths with cordite grimed hands, than a group of nine bombers mounted an attack. This time they came in line astern, but the first one ran into such an intense cone of fire, that it glowed momentarily like a cigar then disintegrated, while the gunfire moved inexorably towards the second in line, which took avoiding action by climbing steeply up and away, followed by the other seven.

From the clouds dropped *Avenger*'s Hurricanes, picking their targets, and hounding them out of our sight. Out of the mêlée soared a Hurricane, expressing its joy in a victory roll, and bringing the score to at least two out of the nine. This attack was rather half hearted, but the next attack at dusk was to the enemy's advantage. They sneaked up astern, bagging another ship, but paying for it with a Heinkel bomber which was shot down by a Hurricane, the Heinkel being forced down on to the sea which it hit in a series of grotesque skids, sheets of water spraying away crazily, until it exploded on final impact.

As the short night fell we secured from Action Stations and reverted to Second Degree of Readiness, which was four hours on watch and four hours off. There was little sleep that night because now the U-boats took over and the night echoed to a long series of underwater explosions.

Between dozes we compared notes with Arthur Oakeshott, the newspaper correspondent from Reuters who was covering the convoy for his agency. The film cameraman had little luck, as he had been able to get few shots from his position on the Signal Deck, although I had previously pointed out that his best vantage point would be the Director. As a result, this tremendous attack was never filmed and what finally appeared was very sketchy, the bulk being made up of shots of our guns 'in action' at nothing but the sky on our way back to Scapa Flow! The short Arctic night was coming to its close as I climbed into the Director, and the guns immediately went to Stand-by as a destroyer attacked a U-boat, bringing wreckage and oil to the surface.

After breakfast a Blohm and Voss reconnaissance seaplane picked up the convoy and we stood by for another air-attack. Nothing materialised and we took advantage of the lull to transfer survivors to *Scylla*. These had been picked up by the minesweepers *Harrier* and *Sharpshooter* who, with superb seamanship, came alongside and secured themselves to us while still under way, so the survivors could clamber aboard. They were men from many of the Allied nations and of many colours – American negroes, thin Lascars from India, high-cheekboned Russians, some quite old and grizzled, others young and wide-eyed at the horrors they had witnessed. One Englishman was clutching a little puppy in his shirt, and one of the Negroes was the sole survivor from the *Mary Luckenbach*.

'One minute Ah'm walkin' along the deck with a cup of cawfee for the Captain, next minute Ah'm in the water, half a mile down the convoy!' he told me later.

The Wardroom was crowded with survivor-officers, one of whom stood out – silver, wavy hair, erect bearing, his uniform immaculate, medal ribbons a splash of colour on his jacket. A number of them were from the United Molasses Company's tanker *Atheltemplar*. The owners later presented us with a huge silver salver and a large donation for comforts for the crew in recognition of our hospitality; the salver is now a treasured possession of the present *Scylla* – a Leander class frigate.

In the afternoon the Luftwaffe attacked again, with a force of 22 bombers, an encouraging number denoting heavy losses, and it was yesterday afternoon on a slightly smaller scale, with the attack concentrated on the carrier *Avenger*, whose planes were proving a deadly menace to the enemy. Out on the flank of the convoy *Avenger* was giving a good account of herself, like an enraged mother hen, with her Hurricane chicks flying around her and her small calibre guns, blazing away and churning up the water around her low-flying attackers. 17 torpedoes were unsuccessfully launched at her, but her planes accounted for four aircraft with a further three probables. The merchant ships were unscathed, and none of the warships had been damaged in any way.

Our calculations of enemy losses seemed over-confident when the radar picked up a 25-plus echo, but these aircraft turned out to be high-level Heinkel bombers, taking advantage of cloud cover to sneak downwards for attacks which did no damage other than to dot the waters with harmless pillars of water. All our Scapa Flow conference resolutions about barrages had gone by the board, and the pattern of defence emerging was for *Scylla* and the other three anti-aircraft ships to engage at long-range, continuing up until the moment when the close range weapons of the escorts, the merchant ships and *Scylla* could take over. While they were thus engaged, the long range 4.5s took on the next distant target, while overhead the Hurricanes patrolled, ready to pounce.

During these first two days *Scylla*'s gun crews acquired an expertise in Gunnery which earned her the name in the Navy of 'The Toothless Terror' – toothless because of the apparent small calibre of her guns for a light cruiser, but a terror for her accuracy and amazing rate of fire. Having survived such a baptism of fire, my confidence was at a high level, and a sighting report brought an academic coolness to the task and a confident profanity of, 'Take that you skulking bastard!' as eight shells burst around the target, and 'there's another bloody load!' as the next salvo of eight followed it and the plane dived back for cloud cover, despatched with a derisory, 'shit scared, eh?' Daddy Poore informed me that these remarks, amplified on the loudspeaker in the TS were great morale boosters.

The second day ended with another 20-plus attack by torpedo-bombers, beaten off again, as we threw up our familiar pattern of dirty black shell-bursts on the darkening grey backcloth of the Barents Sea. The second night was cold and cheerless with little sleep, the usual dismal pinging of the Asdic set, and the rumble of depth-charge explosions on the outer destroyer screen as the U-boats tried to break through. They gained one success that night and the sky blazed momentarily as a torpedo struck home at a merchant ship. She did not sink immediately, and was sunk by our gunfire at dawn, after the survivors had been picked up. Like an animal being put out of its misery, she shuddered once, and slid under the grey, cheerless waters.

The third day dawned quietly, with only the occasional appearances of the Blohm and Voss reconnaissance plane, and some Focke-Wulf Condor minelaying planes. *Harrier, Sharpshooter* and *Leda* moved out ahead to start a sweep for any mines dropped. There was a feeling that perhaps the Luftwaffe had had enough, but this was dashed by the appearance of 25 high-level bombers which kept up an attack for three hours. Our confidence and skill was now such that we could conduct an almost copy-book attack through the clouds without seeing the aircraft, and the radar-plotting was developing a high degree of skill.

'Beautiful radar plot – steady as a rock!' reported the TS on numerous occasions, and the shells would streak through the clouds.

'Turned away! We've got the buggers guessing!'

Very suddenly, from nowhere apparently, a plane appeared on our

112

starboard bow, to be met immediately with a hellish concentration of Oerlikon and pom-pom fire, which stopped her dead in her tracks and she hit the sea with an ungainly slither. All around her, the sea was pitted with shell explosions as her crew ran out on the wings. The parabolas of fire lifted lazily towards them and they tumbled and crumbled like rag-dolls and flopped into the sea. This horrified me, and I bawled to no one in particular,

'Cut it out, for Christ's sake! Give them a chance! We could have done with a few prisoners!' I added defensively to the crew.

Though some bombs landed in the convoy lanes, the vast majority exploded on the far flanks, the Jerries confused by the accuracy of our fire, and thankfully, the attack petered out and the radar screens were cleared. The battle commentary from the bridge became facetious and relaxed, as we unconsciously realised that we were coming out on top. In the Wardroom, reports were being studied and experiences shared. There had been a still-born baby, born in the Russian ship *Stalingrad*, mute evidence to the presence of death in the convoy lanes of PQ 18. A flimsy piece of signal paper was handed to me on which was written:

> O Weak of Faith
> Now Yesterday is dead
> How dull was yesterday while it did live
> How sweet it was today
> For does not this day bring me nearer death.
> And now I wait in dread,
> For when I meet my judgement, can I thrive,
> Or shall I fade away.
>
> The ice reflects a thousand darts of light
> And still in fear I wait.
> Surely, death must come to me tonight!
> I lie with breathe abate
> Whilst Thor himself a'hammers at my breast
> I start. Relax again
> And think of the importance of my quest,
> Yet still I wait in vain.

This simple poem had been written by Alan Skinner, a young officer survivor of the *Atheltemplar* after the first awe-inspiring attack by the torpedo bombers.

On the second day, Admiral Burnett, had weighed up the odds against us with 13 ships lost. Should he turn the convoy back or fight on. His hand reached out involuntarily for his Bible, and he opened it at random at the Book of Isaiah. Certain words on the thin paper cried out for attention and he read:

'When thou passest through the waters, I will be with thee; and through the rivers, they shall not overflow thee; when thou walkest through the fire, thou shalt not be burned; neither shall the flame kindle upon thee. For I am the Lord Thy God.'

His mind was made up and we fought on, though we did not know of the Admiral's dilemma and its solution. From that moment we did not lose another ship.

The fourth day dawned, and it was announced that we were leaving the convoy and sailing northward to rendezvous with the homeward bound convoy which had left Murmansk. It was considered that our convoy was within short steaming time of Murmansk, and relatively out of danger. That we were so near Murmansk came as a great surprise to me, as I had been living in a gunnery vacuum, forgetting that through all the three preceeding days at eight knots we had covered well over 600 miles. It was as if the convoy had stayed without movement while we fought on.

So northward we sailed into rougher weather which we welcomed as a deterrent to the bombers. But we had counted without the U-boats, homed on to us by the reconnaissance planes which couldn't fail to pick up a convoy in the limited area between the Arctic ice edge and the Norwegian coast. Knowing that we would sail as close to the ice edge as practical, it was only necessary for them to patrol along the ice to find us. The weather grew worse and the smaller convoy, QP 17, consisting of the remnants of the ill-fated June convoy, PQ 17, rolled and plunged, for many were in ballast, though a few were loaded with timber deck cargoes. The wild weather suited the U-boats and snapping at the outskirts, they sank the gallant little minesweeper *Leda* but her survivors were picked up by the rescue ships. Then the weather moderated and the shadowing aircraft made their appearance.

One morning as I exercised on the quarterdeck, idly glancing now and again at the seemingly harmless shadower, I heard a booming of sirens in the convoy astern, and a great confusion as ship after ship inexplicably altered course. The continuous sounding of sirens was the signal for 'Torpedo in Sight' but the frantic course alterations denoted the fact that this torpedo was one of the Germans new refinements – the circling torpedo, fired into a convoy to cause alarm and confusion, and perhaps score a random hit.

Almost instantly, the ship directly astern of us, the *USS Silver Sword* lurched slightly sideways and a gout of what looked like steam rose at her side, followed instantly by a huge explosion. Her deck cargo of timber, rose up in the air, a grotesque fountain of whirling planks, with, in the centre, a hissing pillar of steam from her riven boilers. In minutes she had sunk, leaving a huge log jam of timber on the surface, among which her survivors bobbed in their life jackets. From then on, we ceased to treat shadowers with disdain, firing on them whenever they came within range, and giving them little chance to drop circling torpedos at close range. On recounting to the torpedo officer, the strange phenomenon of the gout of steam which preceded the explosion, he explained that I had seen a rare sight – the 'ghost' explosion of a torpedo, probably caused by the release of the compressed air from the driving chambers of the torpedo.

Another three days passed, but the Germans were not greatly interested in what our convoy was carrying from Russia which was indeed very little of value and attacks were on a small scale, mostly aimed at destroying shipping. *Scylla*, with over 200 survivors aboard, was the most valuable ship in the convoy and Admiral Burnett decided that we should forge ahead for Scapa Flow. Accordingly, the boat crane was brought into novel use, and he was swung across, strapped to a chair secured to the crane hook, and dropped gently on to the deck of the Fleet Destroyer *Milne*, commanded by the redoubtable Capt Beaky Armstrong. The whole manoeuvre was carried out with both ships travelling at 15 knots, only feet apart in a lively sea, Capt MacIntyre and Capt Armstrong chatting amiably to each other from their respective bridges, like two London cabbies in a traffic jam! Our Admiral's flag slithered down the halyard, and another one climbed quickly to the *Milne*'s mast as the transfer was completed.

A few hours later we made our departure from the convoy, forging ahead at high speed, while the Tribal Class destroyer *Somali* moved across to take our place on the screen. As we watched, she gave a visible shudder, and the boom of a torpedo explosion rolled across to us. She came to a stop, rolling sluggishly in the trough of the waves, one of the largest and hardest-hitting destroyers of the Fleet, mortally wounded. There was little doubt in our minds that *Somali*'s alteration of course had put her in a direct line with a torpedo meant for *Scylla*! Her Aldis lamp flickered and another destroyer creamed her way to her aid, while we stormed past her with our human cargo. After being in tow for three days she sank, but by this time we were in Akureyri, the most northerly town in Iceland, close to the Arctic circle.

The next day, I shed my role of Gunnery Control Officer and took up the mantle of Entertainments Officer, to produce a mid-ocean version of 'Shirkers' Gaytime' the Saturday variety show we had produced since commissioning whenever in harbour. The show was broadcast live over the internal loudspeaker system, using the Royal Marine Band as a nucleus, surrounded by the various talents of the crew – crooners, comedians, instrumentalists and the Officers' Mouth Organ Band which could only play one tune, *Cock of the North*! This was our official march, given to us by permission of the Gordon Highlanders whose home city was Aberdeen. Aberdeen had raised immense sums of money for *Scylla* in

Warship Weeks and there were close ties between the ship and the Granite City. With all our survivors we had a huge new reservoir of talent which included the negro steward from the *Mary Luckenbach* who sang the spiritual, *Water Boy*. That evening the Principal Medical Officer, our compère, opened the show with the words:

'Shirkers' Gaytime' shipmates. Coming to you at enormous expense from inside the Arctic circle, produced by that Welsh Wizard from the Rhondda, presenting talent from the United States Mercantile Marine and all the best shipping lines of Great Britain, and compèred by yours truly. We begin with *Honeysuckle Rose* rendered by Bill Breeze and His Boys, otherwise known as the Royal Marine Dance Band. Go to it, Bill!'

As I listened to the well-known jazz tune, through the headphones in the control tower, I gave thanks for our deliverance from the violence of the enemy, and for me my *Te Deum Laudamus* was *Honeysuckle Rose*. The next day we sailed into Akureyri which was situated in a fiord lined with conical mountains, dropped our one anchor and transferred the survivors to a transport ship awaiting them. We spent a rather wild evening in the Wardroom, with the first gins we had tasted for weeks, as we had an unwritten law among executive watchkeeping officers that we never drank at sea. It was a short journey from Akureyri to Seydisfiord to pick up our anchor which had been recovered for us.

'Never thought you'd come back for this!' said the Harbour Defence Officer, somewhat tactlessly. 'I hear you had rather a rough time!' We stared stonily at him, and said nothing.

Two days later we entered Scapa Flow with pride, and not with the humility of early August. We were salt-caked, cordite-stained, and the paint was blistered from the guns. As we passed the anchored vessels, the bugles sounded the 'Alert', the sailors lined the decks and gave us that greatest of naval accolades, – they cheered us in!

In the Wardroom later we read of our exploits in huge headlines in every national newspaper – 'Arctic Convoy Fought Four Day Assault' blazoned the *Daily Telegraph*, 'U-boats, Bombers and Minefield Defied', 'Worst Air Torpedo Attack of the War', 'Hurricanes Struck Back from Air-Carrier', Arthur Oakeshott from Reuters had done us proud.

'What price the "Toothless Terror", now, eh?' asked someone, with satisfaction.

A greater honour was to come when Mr Winston Churchill made a personal visit to the ship and inspected the Ship's Company. Dressed in his familiar yachting cap and short greatcoat he passed along our ranks, and wound up the inspection with a typically short, barking speech from the top of Y turret. I can only recall the words that mattered most to all of us.

'You heroes will have leave after your labours!'

116

We had leave alright – 24 hours of it, most of which Cdr Fisher and I spent waiting for a train connection to Glasgow on Inverkeithing Platform. Charlotte met me by arrangement at Buchanan Street Station in Glasgow. 'Never thought I'd see you again!' she said breathlessly. 'The rumour was that you'd been sunk!'

'Sunk?' I echoed. 'Everybody seems to think that. But we're heroes – Winston Churchill said so, and has given us 24 hours leave to prove it, so let's go somewhere for dinner, eh?'

9 The years of victory

A couple of weeks in Scapa Flow with football, fishing and rambling on the various islands, healed over mental wounds of PQ 18, and we knew that we would be on the move again. Meanwhile we had a preview of the film of the convoy, a derisory, patchy affair, a great disappointment and no gain to naval archives. The awards for the convoy were announced, and included three DSOs, several DSCs and DSMs for officers and men aboard. There was some disappointment that no RNVR officer figured in the awards, and Rowlands and I were quoted as worthy recipients.

With his usual forthrightness, Capt MacIntyre, who had got wind of the feelings expressed, summoned me to his cabin, and gave me the simple explanation that he had thought of the professionals first, an award to them being the equivalent of a degree in my profession. Sensing my lack of conviction of this explanation, he added that should I ever need his help in any way, he would willingly give it, and this promise he honoured after the war in a glowing testimonial.

Quite suddenly and without ceremony towards the end of October, we weighed anchor and sailed for Plymouth, that ancient naval port which we now entered with honour and a reputation. It was heartening to see the autumn tints of South Devon again, but we only glimpsed them fleetingly as we dropped anchor in the Hamoaze, and were boarded by a mysterious party from a little boat harbour on the Cornish side. I was Officer of the Watch at the time and as they came aboard the leader was instantly recognisable as Admiral Sir Andrew Cunningham and his Staff, accompanied by various experts, such as the naval historian, Capt Ritchie, who wrote under the pseudonym 'Bartimeus', and a French-speaking RNVR Lieutenant named Dampier whom I had met months previously when we were ratings in Liverpool. The whole operation was shrouded in mystery, deepened by the fact that the Admiral's flag was not hoisted, and that I, now the Wardroom Wine Caterer, was given charge of a number of crates of wine addressed to Vice Admiral Somerville at Gibraltar. To me, therefore our destination was evident, and indeed that evening we sailed southward to Gibraltar.

At Gibraltar our important passengers were whisked away as mysteriously as they had arrived. Undoubtedly, the presence of a fighting

Admiral such as Cunningham in Gibraltar, presaged some big operation, and though a few days shore leave in Gibraltar, with drinks at the Rock, afternoon tea in the Library Gardens, and hectic evenings in the Embassy Club were pleasant, there was an underlying tension. This was snapped when we sailed westward, and Capt MacIntyre broadcast to the ship's company that we were embarking on Operation Torch which would be the Invasion of North Africa, and we would soon sight the greatest convoy of troopships so far assembled.

Our area of operation would be the most easterly of the landings, and we would cover the Algiers operation. As he spoke I heard the name *Broke* being mentioned as the ship which would crash through the boom at Algiers, together with the destroyer *Malcolm*, and I immediately thought of 'Dinger' Bell and his fish and chip supper at Hvalfjord. I wished him a mental Good Luck!

The convoy was the most outstanding I had ever seen with the cream of the British passenger liners among them, from the P&O, Union Castle, Orient, and Royal Mail Lines with their decks packed with troops and equipment. Among the lesser ships were tankers, supply ships, tank-carrying ships, and the fast Commando carrying ex-Cross Channel steamers *Princess Juliana* and *Princess Josephine-Charlotte*. Though there was a natural apprehension over the success of a sea-borne invasion, there was an underlying exhilaration that, at last, we were going to hit back hard at the enemy, and that Operation Torch would be a great turning point in the war.

7 November was a sunny Mediterranean day and we sailed eastward, out of sight of the North African shore, undetected, and gradually edging south-eastward towards Algiers. As darkness fell, we could make out the shadowy heights of the Tell Atlas mountains to starboard, and the smell of pines and spices floated to us on the light offshore evening breeze. Though my thoughts were of our own safety during the invasion, I could not help thinking of the thousands of British and American troops aboard the transports for whom this would be their first experience of war; to us it had become a way of life. Only weeks ago we had been in the Barents Sea on the northern outposts of Europe, now we were preparing to fight on the northern fringe of Africa.

Towards midnight we were closing in on Algiers, the transports and landing craft, shadowy, waiting shapes in the darkness around us. The unblacked-out city seemed so defenceless, with the street lights glimmering along the waterfront, lights showing from distant windows and the odd car headlight cutting a swathe through the darkness as it came down from the high ground above the city. As the hands of my watch moved towards one o'clock, the zero-hour for the attack, lights began to go out gradually as the cafes closed, the student closed his textbook and the lovers sought the darkness.

My thoughts went to my old ship, the *Broke*, tensed and ready for its high speed dash for the boom, followed by the quick berthing alongside the Quai de Falaise to disembark the American Ranger detachment which would storm the fort at the tip of the Quai. At one o'clock, there was an imperceptible vibration in the air as engines came up to full power and all movement accelerated shoreward. A searchlight on shore stabbed seaward and began a nervous search, darting to and fro over the waters, and then suddenly the sky was filled with the coloured arcs of tracer, and the searchlight steadied on the harbour entrance as the *Broke* went in.

'TS?' I whispered, 'stand by! The show's begun!'

Contrary to our expectations, the night was uneventful for us, as we steamed back and forth, shepherding transports and landing craft towards the beaches and the harbour. As dawn lightened the sky, the Fleet Air Arm Albacore bombers with their unfamiliar American star markings on the wings, roared over the defences and bombed them into submission. For diplomatic reasons it had been felt that the French would take more kindly to aircraft with American markings, though the logic seemed questionable, as the British Army swarmed up the beaches and into the city!

Algiers Bay was full of transports, their davits and hoists empty now of the boats and landing craft which covered the water like beetles. Clearly revealed in the rising sun was the beautiful city of Algiers, dull gold now, but rapidly silvering and whitening as the sun grew in strength, picking out the minarets of the mosques in the native quarter or Casbah, and sweeping along the elegant arcaded front of the modern French city with block after block of imposing buildings, the Basilica church high on the hillside, and the E-shaped modern block of the government buildings, austere and modernistic.

We had only a short time to admire the sights before we began to head even further eastward, on learning that the city and the airfield had capitulated, and that the Army were pressing onward. With us we took the elderly aircraft carrier *Argus* and the dear old *Avenger* with whom we were now 'chummy' ships after our PQ 18 partnership, and we had exchanged a number of social visits. Escorting us was a group of Hunt Class destroyers, and a Black Swan class sloop *Ibis*. One of the destroyers was the *Wilton* now commanded by Lt Northey, my former Captain of *Scarborough*. Visiting *Scylla* in Gibraltar he had been surprised and gratified to see me and knowing that I was rapidly approaching my second, Lieutenant's stripe he said,

'You'll be breathing down my neck in the seniority list now!'

The morning and afternoon passed, and there was no sight of the enemy whose bases at Cagliari in Sardinia, in Sicily and on the Italian mainland were getting nearer and nearer to us.

'We'll be in Tunis, tomorrow!' joked Mead. 'Where's Jerry, then?'

'I don't like it one bit.' I returned, soberly. 'Only five months ago, in this very area, Jerry was knocking ten bells out of the Malta convoy. D'you realise we're 120 miles from Algiers already? Jerry's been caught with his pants down, but he'll be pulling them up, don't you worry!'

Then, just before dusk, the attack came and the forrard Red Director took over all the guns to attack a group of Junkers 88 torpedo bombers, streaking in low. We followed them in the Blue Director ready to take over, as they passed down our side. In my eyepiece was the now so familiar sight – the sea, the enemy aircraft and the shell bursts. Then Freeman grabbed my shoulder and pointed skyward to a swarm of black shapes in tight formation.

'Bridge!' I screamed into the headset. 'Give me the guns! There's a formation of pattern bombers coming overhead. We've got a synchronised attack!'

The target bearing indicator showed that we now had control of all guns, as the muzzles suddenly shot up at a steep angle from the low angle of the torpedo bombers. Andrews made his cut, and in seconds we had a clear-cut plot and the first salvo went up to 15,000 feet and kept at it, while all around us the smaller guns blazed at the torpedo bombers. The diamond formation of Heinkel 111 high level bombers forged on through the hail of shell from *Scylla* and the other ships, and then the convoy was momentarily obliterated from sight as they dropped their entire load on a signal from the leader.

Mountains of water rose all around us and above the gunfire, the whine of falling bombs could be clearly heard. Then the waters subsided and we looked around. At the stern of the *Argus* there was an oily black cloud of smoke with a red glow in the centre indicating a hit, but she was still sailing on. So the simultaneous attack from low and high level had failed because the high level bombers had been just those vital few seconds late on target, giving us time to greet them with an accurate hail of predicted fire which had spoiled their aim and shaken their morale.

The night was strangely quiet and the day following was like a Mediterranean cruise, but dusk brought the torpedo bombers out in strength. Gunfire was intense, as we had now been joined by the heavy cruiser *Sheffield*, a newcomer to this type of fighting. While the Director had disengaged from firing at a Junkers 88, allowing the close range to take over, *Scylla* was suddenly surrounded by a hail of shrapnel as shells from *Sheffield* began to burst around us, and the Director sides clanged as the fragments pounded us.

'You careless, wild bastards!' I yelled, uselessly. 'You're firing at us!'

Below the Director, Paymaster Lt Joisce in charge of the After

Oerlikons, was hit by a fragment which later led to the amputation of his leg, and there were various cuts amongst the gun crews. The Blue Director had protected us well and its steel sides were dented and scraped by splinters. It was a bitter thought that Joisce, after surviving the Russian convoys on the same deck, should have been seriously wounded by shells from one of our own ships.

There was no time to ponder on these lines, for the Junkers 88s pressed home another attack. We were firing at an aircraft heading for the sloop *Ibis* and the range was extreme, but we were confident that the well-armed sloop with her six four-inch guns could look after herself, so we ceased fire as *Ibis* took over and the tiny red flames of her distant guns glowed confidently in the gathering dusk. The plane banked away, but her torpedo had been well-aimed, as seconds after, *Ibis* was engulfed in a huge white flame as it struck home, and she heeled over and within minutes she had disappeared beneath the waves.

As the tropic darkness snapped on, we arrived at the spot where she sank, guided by the cries of the survivors, and the winking of a tiny pocket torch waved by her First Lieutenant who had only drawn it from the ship's stores that morning. Our boats were lowered and we chugged sluggishly through the oil-covered sea, dragging out choking, coughing survivors, slithering like wet, slimy fish over our gunwhales. Late that night the rescue was complete, but many fine men had died in the explosion and drowned in the horror of oil. One of our survivors had been her Captain, Commander Darrell-Brown, but he died soon after coming aboard. Operation Torch, which had began so easily, was beginning to take its toll as the enemy recovered from the surprise.

In the following days, the Inshore Squadron of which we were now a member, performed a variety of escort duties as the Army advanced down the coast towards Bone. Yet it was nearly a week before we set foot on the land for which we were fighting, when we put in to the French naval base of Mers-el-Kebir, near Oran. As the linguist, I was deputed to knock on the door of a villa to enquire the time of the autobus to Oran, whose delights we felt would be greater than the stark Mers-el-Kebir. An angry Frenchwoman answered the door.

'Pah!' she spat, 'marin Anglais! You bomb me in Cherbourg, you bomb us again this week, and you knock on my door. Pah!' I inwardly cursed the coincidence that had made us choose her villa above all the others, but I recovered, and decided to try Gallic charm and Welsh treachery.

'C'est la guerre, Madame!' I shrugged sympathetically and switched to treachery. 'Mais, Madame, je suis Gallois, les autres sont Anglais!' Somewhat mollified, she relented, and gave us the time of the bus, Maclean and Holifield were intrigued at the change in her attitude.

'Well,' I explained, 'she doesn't like English people, so I told her that I was Welsh, and if she came from Cherbourg she was likely to be Breton, and they are Celts like us, so I was practically her brother!'

'You crafty old bastard!' said Holifield, 'no wonder you Welsh get on!'

Oran proved to be a beautiful city and as the weeks passed I grew to love this part of Africa, with its elegant French colonial architecture, and the evidences of French culture and good taste everywhere. In the shops there were French cosmetics for my family and for Charlotte, and there was a lovely music shop where I browsed for hours, picking up music by Debussy, Ravel and Poulenc, unobtainable in wartime Britain. It was in North Africa that I first got to know Elgar's *Violin Concerto* really well, as we had found a recording of it by the youthful Yehudi Menuhin. I listened to it under strange circumstances, played on a portable gramophone set up underneath the Red Director while we were Anti-Aircraft Guardship waiting to open fire on any German aircraft attempting to bomb Algiers.

The First Army had now been halted at Mateur, 100 miles east of Bone, and re-inforcements were being sent in by sea to Bone each night, escorted by a force which rejoiced in the name of The Bomb Alley Taxicab Company. The Company would escort one or two troop transports, and would consist of one light cruiser chosen from *Scylla, Aurora, Argonaut* or *Sirius*, with a small force of Hunt Class Destroyers and the very fast Polish destroyer *Blyscawisca*. There was rarely a night on which we were not attacked by torpedo bombers at sea while on passage, or by Stuka dive-bombers while covering the disembarkation at Bone, and we looked forward to our off-duty nights when the other cruisers took over.

On one of our runs, the large transport *Cameronia* was struck by an aerial torpedo and began to heel over immediately as the soldiers rushed to the side on which she had been holed. *Scylla* drew up alongside and the authoritative voice of Capt MacIntyre over our loud hailers managed to restore confidence aboard the transport, to such an effect, that we were able to gently beach her on the shore near Bougie, and for each soldier to disembark without wetting his feet! Six months later I saw *Cameronia* in a convoy bound for Malta. An ironic fact had emerged from Naval Intelligence, that the torpedo bombers which we were now fighting were none other than our hard-hitting pilots from Fluggruppen 18 in the Arctic, now reformed, re-inforced and transferred to Sardinia!

Our off-duty days were very pleasant with visits to French friends we had made, and pleasant afternoons in the Hotel Aletti which was then the great rendezvous spot of the town, reputedly the haunt of beautiful Axis spies. I, however, made a hit with an Arab sheikh who presented me with a walking stick with an ivory goat's head handle which he said was almost a royal sceptre and would protect me from all Tuaregs, Bedouins and other Arab tribes. This I promptly lost on the way back to the ship during some tipsy horseplay so I was never able to test its magic powers!

The evenings were pleasant and relaxed and I used to give informal piano recitals to Capt MacIntyre on the rather inadequate Wardroom piano, stumbling through the purchases I had made in the music shop. Another evening task I remember from those days were my efforts to give a creditable translation to the Latin motto over Admiral Cunningham's fireplace in the villa he had made his headquarters: 'Nulla fluit cujus meminisse non juvet'. Admiral Cunningham, like Belshazzar at his feast, had commanded that a translation would be welcomed, and Capt MacIntyre had accepted the challenge for the honour, feeling that there was enough talent aboard *Scylla* to provide an adequate translation.

Life was not unduly unpleasant and we looked forward to Christmas, having made a fortunate foray among the merchant ships in Bone, descending on a Ropner Brothers tramp, the *SS Millpool* (which I had seen many years before in Port Talbot) and discovering that she had frozen turkeys, and all kinds of canned beer aboard. But our hopes were dashed, as Admiral Darlan was assassinated in Algiers on Christmas Eve, just as we entered harbour after another Bomb Alley Taxicab run, and all shore leave was stopped.

Instead we had a hectic shipboard Christmas, and a messdeck dance with various sailors dressed up in evening dresses intended for wives and sweethearts, and reeking of perfume destined for the same ladies. Busts were made of soup ladles and the general effect was astonishingly good as the Commander led the dance, squiring a willowy Eton-cropped blonde in a glittering green evening dress, who looked suspiciously like one of the crew of the Chicago pianos. At the height of the fun, the Germans raided the town with aircraft and we closed up to action stations in our party clothes.

'Where's your spirit of Christmas, Jerry?' called up someone into the heavens. 'Spoiling our fun!'

The raid was soon over, and we did not have to open fire. We made one more run to Bone, during which time I met, of all people, PO Hunt, the scourge of *Ganges* who was a Gunner's Mate in *Sirius*. We were lying alongside *Sirius* during an air-raid, and she recklessly opened fire across our bridge and Director, scorching us with the flames from her forrard 5.25s. In my wrath, I demanded that the Control Officer should come and see me, and who should arrive crestfallen on our bridge, but PO Hunt, who for some unknown reason had been in the Director at the time of the Air Raid Warning, and had opened fire. For old time's sake my censure was very slight!

On our return we received orders to proceed to the United Kingdom, our destination Greenock. Our joy knew no bounds, as there was promise of our first long leave since commissioning. So, high-heartedly we left Algiers, picked up passengers at Gib, and headed for the Clyde. On New

Year's morning, I turned out of my bunk, to find the deck vibrating to a vastly increased thrust of our screws. I dressed hurriedly and dashed up to the Wardroom to ascertain the situation.

'We're heading into the Bay of Biscay to intercept a German blockade-runner,' said Maclean. 'She sailed from Japan about three months ago, so Intelligence reckons, with a valuable cargo of rare metals like wolfram, tungsten etc. She was sighted by Coastal Command last evening. On the other hand she could be an armed raider.'

During my watch in the Director, I went through the drill for anti-ship firing which we had never done in earnest, and watching *Scylla* scythe through the heavy seas at 30 knots, taking the white water over the fo'c'sle, as she plunged her bows into the rollers. In the late afternoon we went to Action Stations, and soon after the surface radar picked up the blockade-runner, 20 miles ahead, while aircraft radar reported the presence of the shadowing Sunderland. I marvelled at the navigational skill shown by our navigator Lt Cdr Green, who had brought us dead on to the target, through bad weather and poor visibility with no chance of a sun sight in the drab January weather.

A look-out reported the masts and funnels of a ship and this was undoubtedly our target, unaware, as yet, of the sleek, deadly cruiser, overhauling her from astern at 20 knots. A sudden gout of smoke from her funnel indicated that she had sighted us and I felt an instant sympathy for her crew who had seen Death stealing up on them. The range shortened and B gun opened fire, and two columns of water spouted ahead of her. She turned broadside on to us, and there was no answering fire, as one would have expected from a commerce raider. We therefore began the unsavoury task of sinking her with gun fire and torpedoes, after allowing time for her crew to get clear in the lifeboats.

She was a difficult ship to sink with light calibre guns like 4.5s, and though we hit her with 50 or more shells, until she was afire from stem to stern, the coup-de-grâce had to be delivered by torpedoes, the first of which missed, probably driving straight under her as she lifted sluggishly in the heavy seas. The second struck home, and she heeled over quickly and sank. I sadly identified her for Capt MacIntyre, from the Merchant Ship Identity profiles as the Hamburg-Amerika cargo liner, *Rhakotis*, of 8,000 tons – a large prize.

We were now quite near Bordeaux and radar was getting edgy with reports of air and surface activity, so we turned away from the errand of mercy to the lifeboats, knowing that they would soon be picked up. Little did we know at the time, that in those boats were a number of British prisoners-of-war being returned from the Far East, who viewed our retreat with more than mixed feelings.

Homeward we sped into St George's Channel up the Irish Sea and into the Clyde, the news of our sinking going before us. We dropped anchor in the Clyde, to be greeted by batteries of cameras, and pencil-poised reporters. '*Scylla* does it again!' screamed the headlines. From the Clyde we sailed northabout to Newcastle for a refit which was ominous; we were going to be 'arcticised' for a winter Russian convoy, which meant that all gun-mountings would be supplied with steam heated pipes to prevent the oil lubrication freezing, and that steam would be led to various points on the Upper Deck so that steam hoses could be rigged from them to thaw out the ice that would form on the hull from spray and snow. The fortnight's leave which we were given was thus an uneasy one, counting the days to our return to Newcastle and the inevitable northward pointing of our bows as we left the Tyne.

At the end of January, 1943 we sailed down the Tyne, the arcticising complete, various refinements added to the radar, the guns overhauled, and the crew outfitted in Arctic clothing. In my case this consisted of a fine gaberdine parka with furlined hood, the inside lined with fearnought blanketting, trousers of the same materials, foul-smelling sealskin gloves, with another pair inside made of fearnought, to absorb any perspiration. These inner gloves were interchangeable, and a new, dry pair was put on every time you went on the upper deck. Should you put on a sweat-dampened pair in Arctic conditions, the glove would freeze to your hand.

I had treated myself to a pair of fleece lined sea-boots, which Cocks, my Marine bandsman servant, had impregnated with Russian tallow in his usual quiet, efficient way. Beneath this outer suit we would wear our usual uniform trousers, sweaters, seaboot stockings, finishing off with the grotesque 'Arctic Pants' – long-legged combination underwear of the thickness of a Fair Isle sweater! This rig was issued to Director personnel in cramped quarters who could not move about freely; gun crews and other upperdeck personnel were fitted out with a lined oilskin suit, Arctic Pants, etc, and a Russian type fur-trimmed cap.

As we sailed down the heavily polluted Tyne at South Shields, to meet the equally tea-coloured, murky North Sea with the rain slanting down and the white horses prancing to meet us, my thoughts were at a low ebb. Though I had become engaged to Charlotte during our leave, I had deep misgivings that the contract would never be fulfilled, with a Russian convoy before us, but the engagement was a form of psychological insurance and that its fulfilment was something to fight for.

The now familiar pattern unfolded itself – north to Scapa Flow for conferences, north again to Seydisfiord, but this time there was one great difference – the ferocity of the weather. It was some consolation that we and the Germans had a common enemy in the fury of the Arctic winter which curtailed the operation of their aircraft, their U-boats and their surface warships. However, the enemy were the more fortunate, as they could stay grounded or in harbour, while we faced the knifing winds and the mountainous seas.

As we neared Seydisfiord, we ran into seas which I had not believed could exist; seas which rolled forward like towering ridges, the howling north wind slicing off the top layer of water and sending it in freezing, screeching layers, far ahead of the wave top. In the troughs between the ridges, *Scylla* and the other warships looked like children's toys, as they clawed their way to the top, to tip over with a sickening slither into the next trough. The aircraft carrier *Dasher* which had taken over from *Avenger* which had been sunk just before Christmas with heavy losses, was a grotesque sight, as she pitched and rolled like a great packing case.

Entering Seydisfiord under these conditions required superb seamanship, but we managed to turn in the huge troughs and speed for the shelter of the fiord. Here *Dasher* reported that she had developed a large hole in the bows due to heavy seas and regretfully she was withdrawn from the escort, so we would have to make do without our air cover. Bad luck dogged *Dasher* for when she returned to the Clyde, the ultimate tragedy struck here, and she blew up while at anchor off Ardrossan with only 11 survivors out of 600 men.

Leaving Seydisfiord we made contact with the convoy and set our usual course, directly for the Arctic ice edge, via Jan Mayen Island, Bear Island and Hope Island. The convoy was code-named JW 53, a little smaller than PQ18, but the same make-up of vessels and cargoes, the same escort, of which *Scylla* was senior ship, though without an admiral this time. There were two changes in the Director Crew, Andrews having been replaced by Oliver, another humourous character, with the most distinctive headgear in the ship – his mother's red-fox fur made into a round cap, with the brush hanging down behind making him look like a marine Davy Crockett. Freeman had left and been replaced by another CW candidate.

Conditions in the Director were squalid in the extreme. It was impossible to leave normally on a visit to the Heads, and so we used a bucket which immediately froze over, and as in these cold conditions body fluids were urinated rather than perspired, it was in continuous and loathsome use.

'Pass the bucket!' would come the call, and the heavy stinking container would be manhandled across to its recipient.

'Like a lot of bloody tigers, you lot!' moaned Oliver, one day. 'Tigers are always cocking up their legs and pissing in zoos, you'll notice, and you lot are just the same.'

The heater was absolutely useless and whenever possible we huddled together for warmth, like sheep under the lee of an outcrop on a Welsh mountain. The weather overrode any distinctions of rank in the Arctic. Key upper deck officers slept in a noisome cubicle, under the bridge,

127

grandly called the Officers' Dormitory. No bunks were ever made; you kicked off your sea-boots, burrowing under the mound of blankets seeking the heat of your predecessor. When you awoke, you brushed off the hoar frost from around your face, and trusted that the icicles which had formed from your breath on the deck head above you, would not fall down and stab you! With the fantastic rolling, it was not unusual to be hurled out of the bunk, and Nobby Clark, the Warrant Electrician, incurred permanent injury to his back in one such fall, when he struck the edge of the empty 4.5 inch shell case we used as an ash-tray.

On the upper deck, spray coming inboard instantly froze on the guard-rails until they were the thickness of a man's arm, while the fo'c'sle was nothing but a cluster of indeterminate ice mounds encasing the capstans, cables and electric motors. This increased weight affected the stability of the ship, and the watches spent long periods thawing out the ice with steam hoses. To take off a glove and place a bare hand on any metallic surface in these conditions was to risk a burn, or to leave an expanse of skin on the metal to free your hand.

To the north of us, the inevitable ice-edge glowed malevolently and at times we were so close that the whole convoy was pushing its way through ice-floes, from which startled seals flopped into the water at our approach. There was music of a strange kind in the air, as the ice floes tinkled against the hull or collided with each other in a high pitched squeal. There was one great consolation however, better than ice music – that of knowing that the enemy would be unlikely to attack in such conditions.

As Murmansk drew steadily nearer, the weather moderated suddenly, and there was a magical transformation as the sun picked out the myriad facets of the ice-crystals, the sky was revealed as an intense Arctic blue, studded with great masses of fleecy white cloud. Conditions being ideal for attack we went to Action Stations, and radar plot was not long in reporting a large formation of aircraft approaching from astern. Taking the initiative we opened fire at 7,000 yards, surprising the pilots, who turned away irresolutely.

'Chicken-hearted lot!' said Cornish, contemptuously.

'I expect they're without the veterans of Fluggruppen 18' I added, 'and these lot are newly trained replacements. Though they're Junkers 88s, they're not torpedo bombers, thank God!'

Though the attack developed with hit and run dive-bombing from the cloud cover it was not pressed home with any confidence, and it was obvious that PQ 18 had mauled and sapped the spirit of the Luftwaffe. Our vastly improved radar was enabling us to plot the aircraft in the clouds, and we began to use our auto-barrage unit, sending salvos up into the clouds to burst around the surprised Jerries.

In the Director now, we had two radar screens for Mead and Cornish, and it was their task to keep the 'Blip' on their screens in a central position by training or elevating as needed, so that the radar office could track the plane, calculate its speed of approach, and aim off the guns far enough ahead to shake them with an accurate fixed barrage as they crossed the 6,000 yard limit. We had tried this gadget on the Bomb Alley Taxi run one night on two aircraft echoes which we could not see. After firing the barrage, one echo completely disappeared, while the other materialised into a shadowy Junkers 88 which sprayed the Blue Director with machine-gun bullets, bringing forth one of my most inane remarks:

'Who the bloody hell is chucking gravel up at the Director?' The chatter of the machine-guns which followed this remark gave the answer, but it was a small price to pay for an aircraft possibly destroyed by our new toy.

The short Arctic day was on our side, and as it was dusk soon after two o'clock, the planes sheered away after a completely unsuccessful attack with the bombs dropped miles away from the convoy centre. The next two days brought a number of such half-hearted attacks, and a great deal of shadowing by Focke-Wulfs, but by this time we were off the Murman coast and the promised air-cover from the Russians. This duly arrived in the shape of an antiquated sea-plane, in the nose cockpit of which stood a fur-helmeted gunner with a machine-gun on a traverse frame.

'Christ, look!' pointed Andrews, 'the bloody Wright brothers!'

We shepherded the convoy into Vaenga Bay where it proceeded to the unloading wharves and was then systematically bombed every few hours by German aircraft from Finnish Lapland where there was a little known battle front between the Germans and Russinas at Petsamo.

Murmansk was a grim place, set in a huge area of stunted pine trees, and it reminded me of the Alaska gold rush towns of the films, minus the noisy gaiety of the saloons. The Russians we met were sullen and uncommunicative, but quite ready to drink our whisky and accept with alacrity our chocolates and cigarettes. We were not impressed with the Communist way of life, and were very suspicious of some of the chained prisoners we saw through the powerful air-defence binoculars, as they filed through the distant pine trees towards clusters of low wooden huts in the clearings. We were getting an early view of the political prisoners who were described years later by Solzhenitsyn and other Soviet writers.

We were glad to weigh anchor and leave this cheerless place with the return convoy which consisted of timber laden ships and others in ballast. Our last sight of Russia were the barrack buildings of the old Tsarist naval base of Alexandrovsk, now Polyanoe, at the northern entrance to the Kola Inlet, and we turned to meet the common enemy – the Arctic weather.

The return voyage was an unending fight against the weather, freezing spray and blizzards of snow which was as fine as flour and which found its way into every part of the Director until we were like snowmen. One by one we began to succumb to bronchitis in the atrocious conditions where there was no muscular action to encourage circulation, and we began to drop into the fitful dozes which can be the first signs of death by exposure.

Day after day this continued with the winds howling down from the Pole and the seas mountain high. Under the strain, the US Liberty ship *JLM Curry* broke in two and foundered with an Admiralty trawler standing by to pick up survivors, and she was followed by the US ship *JH Latrobe* which showed signs of breaking up and was taken successfully in tow by the destroyer *Opportune* to Seydisfiord.

At this time, I collapsed from the cold, and woke up to find myself in my bunk at Seydisfiord, my trunk completely encased in great wads of Thermogene to bring up my body temperature. So ended Convoy JW 53 and its return convoy with all the casualties, the results of gigantic natural forces and not the violence of the enemy!

We had only been in Scapa Flow a matter of hours when we were told that we would be inspected by His Majesty, King George VI, then visiting the Home Fleet, so it was out with the paint brushes and paint pots, and everybody painted the ship, even down to the Chaplain.

I was Officer of the Watch to pipe the King aboard and so I had a front seat in the proceedings. My first impression was of how small and slim he was, and my second impression, as I held his knitted navy blue woollen scarf, was that Kings had scarves like mine, and as far as I could see, it was not as nicely knitted as the one my sister had knitted for me. My only worry was the state of his uniform which had acquired quite a number of stains from our only partly dried paint!

Officers of the Watch on State occasions are apt to be regarded as part of the furnishings, and not formally introduced, but on His Majesty's return from his tour to the quarterdeck, I just happened to be in the way and so an introduction was made. After an inspection of the many tokens of gratitude from grateful shipping companies, and presents from the City of Aberdeen, the King left, and that I imagined would be the end. But a few days later we were given the great honour of taking him back from Scapa Flow to the mainland of Scotland at Scrabster, near Thurso. I felt that, bearing in mind the mystery of the loss of the *Hampshire* in those same waters of the Pentland Firth with Lord Kitchener aboard in 1915, the Commander in Chief was taking no chances.

After passing proudly through the assembled Fleet we stormed across Pentland Firth with an escort of Fleet Destroyers, two motor torpedo boats and an air escort of Spitfires. The King was a sailor again and spent every minute of the passage on the bridge, while we looked down on him from the Director, as we swept around in our search of the skies.

As Boat Officer, Scrabster Pier and the First Motor Boat was my headache. Our First Motorboat as befitted a flagship was a thing of beauty, but far from being a joy for ever, she was the most temperamental and cussed of craft. In fact, Capt MacIntyre infinitely preferred a tiny speedboat for his journeys, a wasp-like craft which rejoiced in the name of *The Skimming Dish*. However, a Skimming Dish in Scrabster was out of the question, and I said a small prayer as we lowered the First Motor Boat into the water. Overawed by the occasion however, she only stuttered once and then her engines settled down to a limousine-like purr, and she proudly whisked away His Majesty to the waiting train.

For the next few days we breathed sighs of relief after the strain of a Russian convoy so closely followed by a Royal visit. There were the usual buzzes – a quick escort of minelayers to Norway, another Arctic convoy, and the only time we went to sea was on exercise. We found out how hazardous this could be when we acted as target ship for the cruiser *Bermuda*. This was to be an 'Aim-off' shoot, and quite harmless if done properly. The theory was that *Bermuda*'s Director instruments would be adjusted so that the telescopes would actually focus on *Scylla* but the guns would be lagging astern and the live shells should fall harmlessly behind us. I considered the matter a huge bore as I gazed out of the Director waiting for the shell splashes to erupt 3 or 400 hundred yards astern so that I could report the accuracy of the range.

'*Bermuda*'s guns have fired!' reported Cornish, pressing the 'fall of shot' which would activate a hooter when the shells arrived. The hooter duly sounded.

'I can't see a damned thing!' I growled, disgustedly and with infinite boredom.

'Bloody hell, no wonder, Sir!' yelled Mead. 'Look they're all alongside us.' Boredom banished, I turned my head, to see eight great columns of water around us.

'Holy smoking cats!' I spat out my favourite expletive. 'They've forgotten to adjust the bloody instruments for the aim off! Let's get to hell out of here!'

Capt MacIntyre agreed with me as *Scylla* heeled over in an emergency turn at full speed, fleeing from the inefficiency of *Bermuda*'s gunnery, while our signal lamp chattered our infinite displeasure.

'What a gunnery ship!' I snarled, with a curl of the lip. 'They want to see a bit of real action, not try to kill their own oppos!'

Quite unexpectedly one day, we weighed anchor and proceeded to the Clyde, and I wangled the Morning Watch on the bridge, so if there was any leave I could go ashore, collect the confidential books, and then do a quick dash to the Naval Officers' Club to see Charlotte. In this little operation Capt MacIntyre was a kindly participant with a Nelsonian eye. But there was no visit ashore for me, because after a stay of a couple of hours we were bound for the Atlantic to escort the great *Queen Mary* bearing Mr Winston Churchill to the Trident Conference in Washington.

Usually the *Queen Mary* sped across the Atlantic at 28 or more knots, unescorted, but with such an important passenger it was again decided to take no chances, and so we went along at 28 knots as her anti-aircraft protection. Such a speed for a huge giant such as the QM meant no discomfort, but for a 5,000 ton cruiser, lamming into the Atlantic rollers for hours at that speed, it was no picnic. For the two days we escorted her until *Bermuda* took over, we were continually half under the water, the decks awash with the ship rolling and plunging wildly and the turbines whining. A passenger in the QM at the time, later told me that we were the star attraction of the voyage.

'Let's go and see how that tiny cruiser is getting on, keeping up with the Atlantic Blue Riband holder!' was on everyone's lips. We took a more serious view.

'I hope to God she doesn't run us down like the *Curacoa*,' said Andrews, referring to a tragedy not publicised at the time, when owing to some confusion over a U-boat alarm, the *Curacoa* cut across the QM's bows to give chase to the suspected U-boat, and was immediately hit by the huge ship, which rolled her over and under her bows like a matchstick, sending her plunging to the bottom with only two survivors.

Our fuel running low, we were glad to sight *Bermuda* and hand over our charge for the final leg of the voyage. Returning to Scapa Flow there was an exercise with battleships and carriers in the Atlantic, as a dress rehearsal for such an occasion as the formidable *Tirpitz* breaking out of Trondheim Fiord. In this exercise, *Scylla* was cast in a sinister role – we were the German cruiser *Prinz Eugen* so we dodged away into the secret places of the North Atlantic, and skulked about, waiting to be found by the carrier *Furious*'s Swordfish aircraft.

In the atrocious weather the whole exercise went sour, and *Scylla-Prinz Eugen* finished up as rescue ship to three of the Swordfish aircraft which had lost their way when the radio beacon in *Furious* broke down, and they homed on our radio beacon. It was during this exercise, that we watched with interest a Swordfish, in the gale force wind, trying to land on *Furious* and making no headway at all, remaining astern like a puzzled albatross.

'Don't make her land on you!' I yelled, quite uselessly, to the vast delight of the Director and TS crews. 'Slide your ship back underneath her.' As far as we could see this is exactly what *Furious* eventually did.

'It's good to be back in the West Country again, eh?' I said to the new Gunnery Officer Lt Roy Yendell, one of the first RNVR full naval Gunnery Officers. 'If we have some leave you can go home to Exeter and

I'll nip up to Taunton.' Guns looked longingly at the gentle landscapes around Plymouth and sighed.

'I don't think so, Hughie. We're all set to begin these patrols in the Bay of Biscay, chasing after German destroyers escorting homecoming U-boats and protecting the convoys to Gib which are being routed much closer in now. We're the first two cruisers to use Plymouth since the war began, *Charybdis* and ourselves, and we'll probably be based partly here, and partly in Gib.'

'Well, that's not so bad,' I persisted, optimistically. 'We're in spring now and the summer's coming on.'

So began a very hectic period in our career. As a prelude we engaged in a long stern chase after five Narvik class destroyers which had ventured out from Bordeaux to escort some U-boats safely to their base. Our force was an extremely scratch one, consisting of ourselves The Toothless Terror, the fairly modern destroyer *Havelock* and three elderly V and W Class Destroyers of World War I, *Vimy, Viscount* and *Volunteer*, converted to convoy escorts and with hardly any armament for a surface action. Against us I counted the 25, five-inch guns with which the German destroyers were armed, and I did not give much for our chances. However, we gave chase and were soon within 24 miles of our quarry. One of the V and Ws chose this moment to stop dead with boiler trouble, so she and another one dropped out.

'Five little nigger boys' parodied someone in the Director, 'chasing after Jerries, two dropped out with pains in their bellies. Three little nigger boys' he continued.

'Ah, nark it!' said another voice, the tension building.

'How far are we from Bordeaux, Sir?' enquired Cornish.

'About 110 miles.'

'Cor, at this rate, we'll be giving shore leave there this evening', laughed the irrepressible Oliver. Then mercifully, as the aircraft echoes ahead began to build up over the destroyers and there was a chance of us being attacked by aircraft, the Admiralty ordered us to give up the chase, and we turned thankfully back to Plymouth.

However, there were picturesque sights to be seen in the Bay – the Spanish fishing fleet of gaily painted stern-fishing trawlers, popularly supposed to be passing information to the Germans, and one beautiful blue, cloud-studded day, we sighted the three-masted Irish schooner, *Mary B Mitchell* scudding along with all sails set and glowing, bound from my home in South Wales, Port Talbot to Bordeaux. Ironically, this famous ship, now a neutral, had been one of the most famous Q-ships of World War I with a couple of U-boats to her credit.

As spring gave way to summer, there were the more pleasant aspects of life to be enjoyed – to see the wartime holidaymakers on Plymouth Hoe, the men's faces pale from long hours in the factories snatching a few days rest from the assembly line. We joined them too with afternoon trips across to Cornwall and sedate afternoon teas in Looe, which were apt to degenerate into long distance pub crawls from Looe, via Liskeard, via the Officers' Club in Lockyer Street, and finally to *Scylla*'s wardroom, as she lay at No 5 Jetty in the Hamoaze. At the other end of our operational area, Gibraltar in summer had its delights, with bathing in Sandy Bay or Rosea Bay and the clamour and fun of the night clubs in the evening. Then we began to notice that we were escorting convoys which were routed much nearer to the enemy than ever before and there was an expectancy in the air that something was afoot.

The new routes put the convoys within easier striking distance of the Focke-Wulf Condor airbase at Champagne-Merignac, near Bordeaux. These planes were now going on the offensive, casting aside their old shadowing and sneak attack tactics and bombing convoys in groups of six. *Scylla*'s protection was therefore in great demand and in June and July we were constantly at sea, escorting convoys from the UK which consisted mainly of large troopships, and at the end of July the purpose of all this close inshore routing was made clear when the Allies invaded Sicily. With homeward bound convoys there was a similar urgency to give the ships a quick turn round and send them out again to build up the bridgehead in Sicily.

The Germans were naturally anxious to disrupt these convoys as much as possible and the Focke-Wulf attacks increased in intensity. At the same time our methods had reached a high degree of sophistication, and besides improved radar – especially the new Plan and Position Indicator with its circular screen and scanning beam of light – now such a commonplace, we regularly embarked a listening team of German-speaking Dutch sailors in charge of a Lt Stephenson, RNVR. These experts could tune-in to the radio-telephones of the Focke-Wulf Condor and listen to the pilots with such a knowledge of German regional accents that they could identify fairly accurately the region from which the pilot originated. They were directly connected to my headset and were a great help.

'Hughie, there's a lot of worried Jerries up there, scared stiff of the flak you're sending up. Keep at it!' Stephenson's voice would interpose. 'Chap talking now is a Wesphalian by his accent . . . Oh, oh! They're turning away . . .' 15,000 feet up a Condor would bank and turn away.

'There's a chap going to come in from the sun . . . Watch out for it!' The Director would turn into the sun, the radar aerials scanning and fixing, and the guns would roar. 'Oh, beautiful . . . He's moaning like hell about the flak and he's not going to press it home.'

So the days would go on, and then back in Gib. would come the compliments, like the American captain in the Rock Hotel.

134

'Jeeze, Lootenant, that *Scylla* is the most awe-inspiring sight I have ever seen when she goes out in front of the convoy to take on those Focke-Wulfs. She's a continual blaze of gunfire from end to end, and she beats off those Jerries every time, and, boy, does she give us merchantmen some confidence.'

At the beginning of August the enemy mounted a massive attack on one of our convoys, having mustered 18 Focke-Wulfs at Merignac. Our intelligence sources there, the famous Col Remy and his Resistance helpers had informed us that only six were operational, but from another source in Portugal, we had a report of the actual sighting of 18 aircraft heading our way.

At 3.45 in the afternoon we went to action stations and soon after a large number of aircraft were detected by radar, and the promised 18 arrived. With their long range, they could stay for hours over the target area, and so, on a lovely summer's evening began our longest and most intense period of firing, greater than that on PQ 18. Yet there was not the urgency about it of the Arctic, these aircraft came in always at 15,000 feet, flying steadily, each one taking it in turn to make solo runs. To us, it became an academic exercise as this height was our best operating height and we methodically beat off every attack, our salvoes bursting with monotonous regularity, around and in front of the aircraft, and the Condor, just as monotonously, turned away before bombing range could be reached.

'Shift target . . . One coming in from the sun!' The process would be repeated, and the hours passed by.

'X and Y Turret request permission to throw empty shell cases over the zareba . . . the place is littered with them.'

'Alright, carry on, but make it snappy, we'll be firing again soon.'

During a lull I climbed out on to the outside of the Director to see the decks crammed with empty shell-cases from the superstructure to the guard-rails. Then perhaps our guard was down and a Condor sneaked in from the sun. The Director telescopes shot upwards and Cornish impaled the Condor in the sights.

'Christ!' he shouted, 'she's in bombing range of us. Telescope angles are reading 50°.'

'Barrage, 3,000 yards! Barrage 3,000 yards. All guns, all guns!' I screamed.

'God!' breathed Mead, 'she's dropped her load. You can see 'em Sir!' Three black dots were clearly visible falling from the Condor – 6,000 pounds of high explosive aimed directly at us. The barrage roared upwards and roared again and again, but I had no ears for it.

'Damn and blast it!' I thought. 'We're going to get it on a beautiful summer's evening.' *Scylla* shook to three gigantic explosions, and the sea rose up around us in huge mountains, higher than the mastheads, and poured into the Director like a cloudburst.

'Have we been hit?' enquired the TS, breathlessly. 'We've had a hell of a shaking down here.'

Out from under the bomb splashes we surged, on a completely even keel, the wake stretching true behind us.

'He's bloody well missed us!' I exulted to the TS. 'Well, I'm damned. I thought we'd bought it then!'

At ten o'clock that night, the attack over, I slid out of the Director and sat for a moment, utterly exhausted, my back against the steel of the Director mounting. I glanced up to see Capt MacIntyre regarding me.

'Well done, Hughes!' he smiled, and, as I scrambled to my feet. 'Don't bother to stand up, just stay there. You must be tired out.' I nodded, wordlessly, and breathed the six hours of tension out of my body in a great sigh as he walked away.

In the Wardroom, the theorists were explaining our escape.

'I think the bombs landed in the water on the starboard side, and from that great height, they must have dived down underneath us and exploded somewhere on the port side', said one of them, reasonably.

On the next convoy, there was a small attack and after B gun opened up there was a peculiar whistling noise and the shell dropped harmlessly into the sea. This was repeated again and we realised that the rifling of the guns was wearing out and what was happening in B gun which had a little more use than most, was very soon to happen in the other turrets. So in late August we sailed to Algiers where new riflings were fitted to the guns, and we enjoyed the fleshpots again.

In just over 14 months *Scylla* had completely worn out her guns, a phenomenon I had never come across before and a witness to our many actions. Luckily, for posterity the whole of that convoy had been recorded by the camera of the veteran *Picture Post* cameraman, Heywood Magee, who had been a popular and welcome guest of the Wardroom for three weeks. Practically the whole issue of *Picture Post* for 11 September 1943, was devoted to his magnificent pictures of *Scylla* in action, in boiler and engine rooms, at the turrets on the bridge, even to Prayers for our deliverance being broadcast over the internal communication system by the Chaplain, Rev David Muir.

On the afternoon of 8 September 1943 Force Five was passing through the Straits of Messina between Italy and Sicily. We were a brave sight, the escort carriers *Hunter*, *Stalker*, *Attacker*, *Battler*, the small Fleet carrier *Unicorn*, ten Hunt Class destroyers, including the Polish *Slazak* and *Krakowiak* ever ready to serve, and last but not least, by some classical coincidence, *Scylla* and *Charybdis*.

It was in this area according to Greek mythology that the monsters Scylla and Charybdis had preyed on seafarers; Scylla darting out from her cave on the cliffs to snatch the sailors, while below her dwelt Charybdis who three times a day swallowed the sea, and spewed it out to form a whirlpool from which no ship could escape.

Our intentions were strictly strategic, being quite simply to provide aircover from our total of 120 Seafire fighters, while the Army established a bridgehead at Salerno and secured the great airfield at Monetcorvino from which the RAF could then operate and relieve the Fleet Air Arm. This was the beginning of the Italian campaign, the establishment of a foothold on the mainland of Europe, and *Scylla* for the second time was one of those on the front of the stage.

During the afternoon, the BBC announced that the Italian Forces had surrendered, but over the tannoy, Capt MacIntyre was insistent that the Germans had not surrendered and that there should be no relaxation of vigilance or intent. So, as the afternoon, evening and night passed, we stole past the volcano of Etna to port in Sicily, through the Straits, past the volcano of Stromboli near the Lipari Islands, gradually edging inshore towards Naples, and our destination to the south – the beach at Salerno. I pondered on what volcanic welcome awaited us there at zero hour, 5am on 9 September.

There was a volcano there alright – in the presence of the crack German Divisions of the 15th Panzers, and the 65th Panzer Grenadiers. Capt MacIntyre had been right and so began a grinding week of losses. At the end of this time we had only 24 aircraft left out of the original 120, and Montecorvino airfield was still not completely secured. We accordingly returned to Palermo for replacements, and once again the Fleet Air Arm, that much under-publicised and magnificent body, was providing the aircover, and taking the brunt of the fighting as it had done in Algiers, the previous November.

There was always an undercurrent of bitterness against the RAF in *Scylla*, for in so many operations in which it was scheduled to play a part, its performances were far short of expectations, but its publicity department was superb, managing to tack on, for instance, to the end of the PQ18 official communique, the empty words 'throughout the whole of the operations Coastal Command of the Royal Air Force provided invaluable air patrols and reconnaissance under the most arduous flying conditions.' I never saw an RAF plane within hundreds of miles of the real PQ18 action – but I saw many planes from the gallant *Avenger*.

Salerno pointed the shape of things to come, for one afternoon we saw one of the first successful attacks on a battleship by a guided missile, the HS 293, launched from a Dornier Flying Pencil skulking in the shadow of the Lombardy poplars on the Salerno shore, while we engaged a decoy

Dornier flying near the battleship *Warspite*. Cornish drew my attention to the missile with an urgent, pointed finger.

'Look at that little tiny plane, coming from those trees. It's got a sort of light at the back of it, just as you told us!' The guns swung away from the decoy and ranged on the missile, but we were too late, even for the close range weapons. Suddenly the tiny plane dived straight at the *Warspite* hitting her amidships in a fountain of flame and smoke, putting her out of action for months and killing many in her boiler room. We made straight for her to take her in tow, but were unsuccessful, and she was eventually taken in tow by an American minesweeper, and we escorted the sad convoy to Messina. It was 16 September, and in a way we envied *Warspite* her forthcoming period in dock.

'Have you heard any more about the mysterious tremor in the engines, Sir?' probed Mead, hopefully. I shook my head, but wished I knew more. During a voyage to Tripoli earlier in the week we had increased speed to 30 knots, as the troops we were going to bring from Tripoli, together with *Charybdis*, were an urgently needed 1,500 for the beach-head. As we touched this speed, the ship began to tremble violently, and when it was reduced the tremor ceased, but an increase to 30 knots seemed to be the critical point, and the whole ship would shake again, and the turbines would whine in mechanical agony.

'I bet it's those bombs that missed us,' ventured someone else. 'Buggered the turbines, I expect.'

In a few days we found ourselves headed for Bizerta for a rest, then we took off for Malta, full now of sleek, surrendered Italian cruisers with long names like *Emanuele Filiberto*, *Duca d'Aosta*, and ravishing Wrens in white tropical uniform, a far cry from the beleaguered island of only a year ago.

Mysterious and important-looking engineers were seen to descend to the engine-room, looking wise but non-committal. So we passed on to Gibraltar and more engineers with grim looks. The buzzes proliferated, and then the truth came out. *Scylla*'s turbine seatings had indeed been severely cracked by the bombing and we were going to Devonport. As we surged homeward over our recent battlefield, I decided to get married, and to keep Capt MacIntyre to his promise. He consented to send a signal from sea requesting special leave for Charlotte from the WRNS to enable us to get married.

Familiar, dear old Plymouth soon appeared over our bow, and I began to make wedding arrangements. The engineers were quick to make a decision, but inconvenient to me. We were to sail to Chatham, north-about to Scotland and down through the North Sea, and I chafed at the delay and tossed restlessly in my bunk as we ploughed south through the cold-tea waters of the North Sea, but brightened perceptibly as we sailed up the Thames estuary past the gaunt steel forts, and turned up the winding Medway to Chatham.

I was off the *Scylla* like a missile after we docked, best uniform pressed and immaculate in my suitcase. At Cannon Street Station I dashed into the hairdressers' before making for Paddington and Pembrokeshire.

'The full treatment!' I ordered the barber, 'I'm getting married.' The barber looked at my hair, murdered over the years by stokers, able-seamen and sailmakers, and sucked his teeth lugubriously.

On 20 October 1943 Charlotte and I were married in the little twelfth-century church of the village of Hubberston, near Milford Haven, and the wheel turned full circle when we spent our honeymoon at Newton Ferrers, our haven of refuge from Heybrook Camp where so long ago, it seemed, I had started to fire guns in earnest, yet it was only 18 months, thousands of shells and eight worn-out guns later!

The Indian or Saint Luke's summer was glorious during those days, and we forgot about the war until tragically reminded of it by the news that *Charybdis* had been sunk quite near to us, on a night sortie to the coast of France close to the Channel Islands.

I had not long returned to *Scylla* at Chatham when the expected appointment came – as a Watchkeeping Officer to the escort carrier *Slinger* commanded by Capt ANC Bingley, RN, and so Capt MacIntyre had kept his promise to me that he would find me an appointment where I could complete my qualification period for a full naval watchkeeping certificate. In *Scylla* I had been able only to keep a pitiful number of watches, because we were always in action wherever we went, and I had spent most of my life in the Director.

Capt MacIntyre had left *Scylla* at Sheerness as we came up the Medway, and it had been a great honour for me to be chosen as one of the Officers' Boat's Crew which had paid him the highest compliment possible – that of rowing him ashore on his last boat trip from the ship.

For a few weeks there was a gentleman's agreement between *Scylla* and Capt Bingley that I could help out in *Scylla* which had now reduced to two thirds complement. This was easy because *Slinger* had now arrived in Chatham to have English equipment fitted, and was moored in the next basin to us. One of my last duties was to meet *Scylla*'s new Captain, Capt TM Brownrigg at Chatham Station and bring him back to his new command.

One morning a tall, fair-haired Captain walked up *Scylla*'s gangplank.

'I'm looking for an officer called Hughes!' he said to me.

'I'm Hughes, Sir', I offered.

'I'm Capt Bingley, young man, and I want you back aboard *Slinger* at once. Please take me to Capt Brownrigg, and you'd better get packed, eh!'

139

10 A new sea weapon...the escort carrier *HMS Slinger*

'My God, you're an ugly bitch!' I muttered to myself, as I walked towards *Slinger* in the next basin. Though in the past weeks I had looked at her often, I could see no redeeming feature to her, with the graceful, eager-looking *Scylla* just over my shoulder. To me she was a huge, towering vessel of 12,000 tons, the American standard C2 merchant ship hull very evident when you took away the flight deck to reveal the bluff high fo'c'sle, and the rounded cruiser stern. On either side of the hull were four protuberances called sponsons, the aftermost two on either side carried mountings for the two five-inch guns, while the remaining three on either side carried gun platforms for 20mm Oerlikons, boat decks, and gangway access.

Huge girders carried the flight deck from very near the stern to close up to the bows and the port and starboard sides were boxed in with steel plates to form the closed hangar deck. On either side of the flight deck was a long catwalk, just below the deck level, and this bristled with quite an array of 40mm and 20mm cannon, with their ready-use magazines. The bridge was a flimsy-looking box on the starboard side, looking too delicate to carry the huge radar aerials of American pattern which reminded me of flying bedsteads! She had only been completed recently at the Willamette Iron and Steel Company's yard at Portland, Oregon, and sailed across the Atlantic by a small crew for final organisation and fitting out in the United Kingdom.

Appearances are not everything – the people are the ones who count, and I took an immediate liking to Cdr WH Roberts, RN, her Executive Officer. He was a naval officer of the old school who had been at Osborne when World War I broke out, had served in the Battle Fleet at Jutland as a Midshipman, and after the war had completed his education at Caius College, Cambridge, before returning to the Navy. Academically, as I was to find, he was an extremely well-educated naval officer, extremely intelligent and a forceful leader, yet by that strange system that the Navy had between the wars, he had been passed over for promotion, eventually retired, and then recalled to service as an Acting Commander.

He belonged to the same breed as the famous U-boat killer ace of the Battle of the Atlantic, Capt Walker, similarly passed over, his value not realised until the war. Cdr Roberts had served all over the world, and his

140

abiding love was the China Station and the river gunboats on the Yangstze River. What he didn't know about seamanship could be written on the back of a postage stamp, with ample room left for the Lord's Prayer!

Cdr Roberts was tall and extremely well built, with an appreciable paunch, a ruddy complexion and battered features. When speaking, he adopted the Beatty attitude, hands cramped into his reefer jacket pockets, thumbs outside; gold laced cap at a jaunty angle, and he rocked continually on his heels, as the countless waves he must have crossed passed through his consciousness, while his small humourous blue eyes twinkled under his huge eyebrows which jutted out like old thatch!

'You see, Hughes,' he rasped in his loud voice, 'you've been sent here to stiffen this lot up, what? Nearly two years in a crack cruiser, so you know a bit about routine, eh? Couple more like you will be arriving soon and we're going to chase this bloody lot, officers and men, from arsehole to breakfast time! Sun's over the yardarm, so let's have a drink, what?' He gave his characteristic sniff which seemed to express his disdain of everything and stumped off with me in train.

'Got a lot of T124X wallahs aboard,' he boomed, over his pink gin, 'the senior ones are alright, like the Chief Engineer and the Paymaster who all come from the big liners like the P & O, Royal Mail, and their deputies are good too, but some of these young engineers – damn their eyes! Know what they do, eh – come out of their apprenticeship at some shipyard, dash over to the Shipping Federation, join the Merchant Navy, get a brand new discharge book, and then make a bee-line for the Naval Recruiting Office, present the discharge book, ask for Form T124, fill it in, and lo and behold, they're seventh engineers or some such thing! See that young feller over there, what? He's the one with some ridiculous thin gold stripe with a kink in it. He's fifth engineer or some such thing.'

'Well' explained the Commander, pausing to take a long pull at his gin, 'when war breaks out and the Admiralty takes over a merchant ship, they say to the crew, "If you want to join the Navy, we'll take you on, pay you your Merchant Service rates of pay, plus your danger money but you must accept Naval discipline. If you like the idea then fill up and sign the Agreement Form T124X, and if you don't like the idea, well back you go to the Merchant Navy."' He sniffed, leered, and spoke confidentially in my ear.

'And that's where we've got some of these young 'uns – naval discipline. So don't take any messing from any of them, just keep chasing 'em, what? Tell you one thing, though,' he said rubbing his hands and smacking his lips, 'these stewards and cooks are absolutely first-class. They mostly come from these Furness Withy *Queen of Bermuda* ships on the millionaires' run from the States. Let's sample their hamburger steaks, and pommes de terre Lyonnais.'

141

'Really, Sir?' I asked, and he nodded as he steered a course to his seat at the head of the table.

'Crockery and cutlery's bloody awful,' rasped the Commander, reaching for his napkin, 'all US Navy stuff . . . seen better in Plymouth market!'

'Soup, Sir?' There was an immaculate white-coated steward at his elbow.

'See what I mean?' asked the Commander, as the steward catfooted away. Undoubtedly *Slinger* had advantages. The food was marvellous, chicken Maryland was commonplace, there was a beautiful processed cheese new to me, and there was imagination in the dishes, while the savouries were a joy. My cabin was large and well furnished and my desk even sported a combination safe. The bunk was very stylish and well provided with blankets. All curtains were glass-fibre, and the Commander chuckled throatily as he put a match to them without any effect.

'The great danger in these ships' he said, 'is fire. We carry a few hundred tons of high octane petrol for the aircraft when we're operational and that's kept in tanks under our cabins. As it's used, the space is filled with an inert gas, but the real danger is in the vapour left in the pipe-system after all the petrol drains back to the tanks. This is where the 'No Smoking' discipline must be rammed home to these people.'

'We worked with *Dasher* and *Avenger*' I added, 'and they went in a flash!'

As I had done Forecastle Divisional work, I became the Forecastle Divisional Officer with half the seamen under my care. As Cable Officer I found the fo'c'sle very different from a cruiser's, with two electric windlasses or winches instead of capstans, anchor cables of different lengths and an entirely different pattern of anchor. Everywhere there were new standards to get used to, light switches went up instead of down, American spellings were standard, and American gadgets such as ice-water dispensers intrigued me.

As Gunnery Officer I had myriads of small guns, including 27 20mm Oerlikons, eight twin barrelled 40mm Bofors, and the two American 5-inch guns at the stern which were new to me. There was the usual array of small arms of British manufacture ranging from a strange small machine-gun called a Lanchester carbine down through the Lee Enfields to four beautiful Richards shot guns for clay-pigeon shooting to keep the fighter pilots' eyes in! Added to this was the astronomical amount of ammunition which went with it, but thankfully, this was looked after by the grizzled, veteran Warrant Gunner, Mr Anderson.

The Gunnery Office was palatial, with typewriters which appeared and disappeared into steel desk tops, filing cabinets, duplicators, stationery, propelling pencils and even the refills for them, all furnished by the US

Navy. Every article of furniture was made of steel and every bit of it was stamped McCutcheons of New York – a contract worth having, I mused. There was no inflammable timber anywhere, and all the boats were steel except the two 32 feet motor cutters, added to British traditional specification.

The Chief Engineer was an old Lieutenant Commander RNR, with an engaging manner, and a delightful lisp. His life revolved around the creation of some mysterious condition in the boiler room called a 'Wacum' which I eventually deciphered as a vacuum. He was very proud of the Allis Chalmers turbines, though I had always associated this name with tractors and agricultural implements in America. They could push *Slinger* through the sea on a single large screw at 20.5 knots which British engineers told me was propulsion, years ahead of its time. The labelling of the stores which littered the ship was confusing. Kelvinator did not mean a fridge, I found, but a spare Pratt and Witney aircraft engine!

Weeks were passing like magic, as I absorbed these details. The Wardroom was filling up with new officers, including Bob Meyer, the Senior Lieutenant and Quarterdeck Divisional Officer. There were a confusing number of Hughes's and we adopted the Welsh custom – Hughes the Guns, Hughes the Navigation, and Hughes the Pay. As I was the only Welshman I changed my name again and became Taff, mostly at the instigation of the Commander, an ex-Devonport Services rugby player who had toured Wales many times, and to whom every Welshman was Taff, while on a wider scale every Maltese was Giuseppe, every Arab was Abdul, and every Chinese was Ho Ming. His theory was, that wherever you happened to be, you bawled the appropriate name at the top of your voice, and someone was bound to answer you.

I soon found another of the Commander's idiosyncrasies – plain stealing – for the good of the ship of course!

'I'm a picker up of unconsidered trifles', he said, one evening, leaning over the guard-rail. 'Have you noticed that coil of steel wire rope over there, eh? Come in useful that would! Reckon you can pinch it, Taff?'

'Could be arranged, Sir', I replied, eyeing the terrain. Shortly after, it was acquired, 600 feet of rather useless wire, to which we added over the commission, many tins of paint, boat anchors, and the pride of all the steals – several sections of ball-bearing roller path which made ammunitioning ship much easier!

The Wardroom was beginning to fill up with the addition of Lt Jake Norwell the Torpedo Officer, Lt Roy Ireland the Fighter Direction Officer, Lt Cdr Bud Abbot the Operations Officer, our two Doctors, Lt Cdr Elliott and Lt Vaughan, plus a Dentist Lt Duprez, and last but not least our Chaplain, the Rev WC Morgan. The Senior Chaplain at Chatham, the Rev Rowland Evans, had asked me to look after Rev

Morgan who had been a reluctant recruit to the Chaplain's service, having served as an Able Seaman on minesweepers for a long period, though fully ordained. Morgan, a typical wild Welshman, was erudite, personable, but entirely unpredictable. One day he approached me, ingratiatingly.

'Taff?' he asked in his Cambridge accent with Welsh overtones, 'I should like to join your Cable Party as an AB, so could I have oilskins and sea-boots please?'

'You'll cramp our style, Bishop!' I protested. 'For a start we won't be able to swear, and there's a lot of that on any fo'c'sle!'

'Don't I know it. Very likely I'll join in, so can I have those sea-boots, eh?'

So we became the only ship that I heard of, with a Chaplain-cum-Able Seaman, and this was typical of the little differences which were beginning to put a stamp of individuality on the crew. Frank Kermode the Paymaster invited me to his cabin. For a man with a degree in English his book case was rather meagre. A shortish row of books, all in the same binding, and all by the same writer – the novels of Marcel Proust under the general title of *A la recherche du temps perdu*. I arched my eyebrows.

'That's all I need' he grinned, 'and, yes, I've also got a violin copy of a sonata by Dvorak which you and I will play one day, eh?'

Capt Alexander Bingley, popularly known in the Navy as Baron Bingley was entirely different from Capt MacIntyre. He was of course much younger, and this was his first wartime command. He was tall, fair-haired, rather handsome, extremely shy when ladies were present and as a result, a bachelor. But above all, he was an intellectual. To dine with him was always an interesting occasion – his conversation was wide-ranging, his manner easy, his hospitality excellent, and his cooking of savouries and sauces which he always made himself on such occasions, was impeccable. I soon found that there was one snag. Having wined you and dined you, he was apt to say.

'Now, Hughes, with regard to those answers you sent in to my questionnaire on the progress of the war, the economic state etc, how can you justify the statement you made on the situation in the Western Approaches in six months time . . . hold on, I have it here . . .'

It then behoved you to shake the alcoholic mists from around your brain and start to think. I found it rather challenging, just as Capt MacIntyre's challenge to be truthful had been in *Scylla*.

On 5 February 1944, all modifications having been fitted, the ship's complement complete, we were towed down the Medway by tugs, to Sheerness where only a short time before we had rowed Capt MacIntyre ashore. The following day we were to sail for the Clyde and the familiar exercise area for the working-up period. Leave was given and I went

144

ashore with the Chaplain, Doctor Davies who had replaced Vaughan, Jake Norwell and Paddy Ireland, all seasoned beer drinkers.

'I say,' said the Bishop, pointing to a long row of quart pewter pots over the bar, 'look at that! Quart pots! Can we use them?' he asked the barman, who nodded. 'Six quarts, then!' he ordered, grandly, 'drink up, men!' This we did indeed and I don't know how long we stayed there, but on the way back in the motor-cutter, the Doctor fell off the thwart into the bilges, and arose therefrom, full of Welsh Methodist guilt.

'The wrath of God will fall upon us, for what we have done this night!' he intoned. 'Men who should know better, men of the cloth, men who teach the young, men who heal the sick . . .' So saying he fell off the thwart again.

'Drunken bugger!' said someone in the darkness. 'Sorry Bishop!'

At eight o'clock the following morning, I was on the fo'c'sle weighing anchor and feeling none the worse for the orgy, but looking forward to my first sea-watch in this ship. The anchor aweigh, we set our course for the North Sea, and round about for the Clyde. During the morning we fired all our guns, and a clamourous occasion it proved to be with the vast array of small arms we carried. The noise affected one young seaman so badly that he went berserk, and started to run in erratic circles all over the flight deck.

'Catch that man!' I bawled into the microphone, connected to loudspeakers at all the guns, our primitive method of Gunnery Control, and the figure of a Gunner's Mate appeared on the Flight Deck, evidently a rugger player, for he brought down the young man with a beautiful tackle and promptly sat on him. This adverse reaction to gunnery noise was the first I had seen, and it haunted me.

The gunnery practice over, I went up on to the bridge where Bob Meyer was on watch, and observed for my afternoon watch, how this unlovely looking ship behaved under her helm and at varying speeds. Glancing at my watch I saw that I should be having my lunch to be on time for 12.30 on the bridge. The Commander was already seated and pointed to a place beside him. We began with soup, and I went on to shepherd's pie, while the Commander decided to have a second helping of soup. As I raised the last forkful to my mouth, the world blew up, in a shattering explosion.

There was blackness everywhere and I seemed to be suspended in a black, silent world.

'If this is Death,' I thought, 'I don't like it, and besides, now I've lost my Zeiss Ikon camera.' Then there was the noise of crockery falling, breaking the ghastly silence and the black void disappeared and I realised we were alive, though still in some unknown darkness.

'Christ, we're alive!' shouted an incredulous voice.

'Let's get the hell out of here!' shouted someone else, and there was a rush of bodies towards the general direction of the door. It was like a rugby ruck at the door and as I shot free, I went through the plan of the ship.

'Turn right,' I thought, 'go a little way, steel ladder on the left, up to the Hangar.' The air was hot, and there was the smell of oily steam, and from the Engine Room behind me, I could hear the roar of escaping steam. The steel ladder scraped my shins and I was scrambling up it, into the Hangar. In the Hangar there was daylight and I looked back to the hatch up through which I had just climbed, and steam was pouring from it. I rushed to a door leading to one of the sponsons, and looked over the side. The ship was still under way, with the water sliding past, and then I glanced at a figure, standing silently beside a suitcase – one of the T124X people.

'Where the hell, d'you think you're going?' I snarled, pointing to the case.

'Waiting to abandon ship!' he answered, coolly. 'I've done it before in the Merchant Navy.'

'This is the Royal Navy!' I spat. 'Now get to your proper Action Station!'

The thought struck me that I had no lifebelt, so I returned to the Hangar, scuttled down into the steamy darkness and felt my way to my cabin, where I knew a torch hung by a lanyard from the light switch. My fingers found it, and by a miracle the torch was still there. Its beam revealed utter chaos in my cabin, with the steel furniture uprooted and thrown everywhere. I hastily snatched my oilskin, my lifebelt, some chocolate bars and a packet of biscuits, and began the return journey. Where this coolness came from I do not know, but as I passed the Officers' Toilets, I decided to ease myself of a little liquid. As my torch beam passed over the deck, it caught an oblong of white cardboard. I bent to pick it up, and as I urinated, I read it in the torchlight. It was a postcard with a short poem, illuminated and coloured like a monastic text.

'God holds your hand, Where'ere you be' it said, and I put it wonderingly in my oilskin pocket, and went out. In the alleyway I met Ferguson, a diminutive Scots stoker.

'The turbines have gone sky-high,' he reported, 'and the engine room's filling up wi' watter. The rudder's jammed up into the stern, and we canna' steer!'

I dashed for the fo'c'sle, where the Cable Party was beginning to assemble under the direction of CPO Foley, a tall gaunt Irishman.

'There's no power on the windlass', he said shortly.

'Anyway!' I ordered, 'standby to be taken in tow. Get those ten-inch manillas flaked out, and get the light coir rope to float out to the destroyer which was escorting us. She'll be around soon.'

Then suddenly from the edge of the Flight Deck above us came a huge bellow. There stood Cdr Roberts, but with a face I couldn't recognise and which horrified me for a moment. It was a grey, scabby mess which I first

146

took for scalding, but which I realised was the slowly congealing remains of his second helping of soup, hurled up at his face by the explosion. From the mask, his blue eyes glared and his lips writhed.

'Well don't stand there gaping!' he yelled, 'you're to drop the starboard anchor under foot to stop us swinging.'

'Aye, aye, Sir!' I acknowledged. 'Get the windlass disconnected for the starboard anchor. Hold her on one slip. We'll check her at two shackles, and she should be swinging underfoot in this depth of water.'

'Ready to let go!' said the Chief, dubiously.

'Let go!' I shouted, but the Chief hesitated to knock off the slip. 'What the hell's the matter with you, Chief. I gave an order. Now let the bloody thing go!' With a roar and a cloud of dust the cable links shot across the deck, one kink of links shooting up and hitting me on the thigh, to send me sprawling. I picked myself up in time to stop the windlass as the second shackle with its special marking whipped past.

Slinger's swinging eased and she began to slow down. Over the bows now, the stern of the Hunt Class destroyer *Garth* was edging up to us, screws slowly turning, her wake bubbling as she prepared to take us in tow. Our heaving lines snaked downward, followed by the light coir rope which would float on the surface and keep the huge eye of the ten-inch circumference manilla towing rope from sinking. The tow was secured, and *Garth* began to take the strain.

It was only then that I noticed that the deck angle was altering and we were beginning to list. I went into the eyes of the ship, in the angle of the bows, and looked aft to the bridge. It was a scene of confusion; the huge 'Flying Bedstead' radar aerials had collapsed on the bridge, the surface warning aerials were bent back like an inverted 'U' while the direction finding aerial had fallen on one of the twin Bofors gun mountings, bending the barrels downwards. An inspection of the well-deck showed that much of the British welding of various stowage racks had ruptured and the deck was littered with fire-hoses, wire ropes and large cans of paint from the paint store. The list seemed to be increasing and I remembered that I had not inflated my lifebelt. As I did so, I saw Chief Foley regarding me with sombre eyes.

'You'll be needing that, Sir!' he said. 'Things don't look so good.' The Chief's foreboding irritated me.

'Incidentally, I said icily, 'what came over you, Chief, when I told you to drop that anchor?'

'You know where you were dropping it, didn't you Sir?' he asked. I shook my head.

'Into our own minefield!' he said. 'That's where we'd drifted – right out of the swept channel!' Momentarily shocked, I recovered quickly and groped in my oilskin pocket for the card I'd found.

147

'We'll be alright, Chief,' I smiled. 'Just read what I picked up on the floor of the Officers' Toilets after the explosion.'

'God holds your hand' he read, looked up at me, and crossed himself.

'You see?' I continued reassuringly, 'now who feels like a bit of chocolate.' As we gathered round for my little snack and a quick smoke, there was unanimous assent that we had struck a mine of some sort, probably an acoustic one, as no look-out had reported any objects on the surface.

'I expect it was a teller mine', I explained. 'A very refined gadget which takes about six vessels passing over it to arm it in various stages, until the seventh vessel passes, and up she goes!'

The afternoon passed quickly and it was soon quite dark. Dimly we could make out the shapes of the two commercial tugs of the Cock Towing Company, coming towards us with the characteristic bone in their teeth, as they plunged on at full speed. Just before the final darkness overtook us, we secured *Slinger* to them, and *Garth* cast off the tow, and took up a position ahead, to protect us.

Weak lights had appeared below decks, as the emergency diesel generators were brought into action, and some tea was brought up to the fo'c'sle, made by injecting hot steam into buckets of water. Though a noisome brew, more reminiscent of washing-up water, it was eagerly gulped down. I was relieved from the fo'c'sle to stand-by watch on the bridge, a sinecure in effect with the ship a dead listing thing in the water. There was time up here to cogitate, and I felt the utter ignominy of the whole situation. After all I had been through in Russia, the Atlantic, and the Mediterranean this was a whimpering way to go – ten miles off Harwich, where I had started as an Ordinary Seaman! Messages were coming up from the engine-room, reporting that the water was slowly gaining and the auxiliary pumps were losing ground.

'At Sheerness some lighters with electrically operated pumps should be waiting for us,' said Capt Bingley grimly in the darkness of the bridge. 'We must hold out until then.' He moved to the aft end of the bridge, and bent over something. I thought I detected the smell of cooking. 'Care for some soup?' asked the Captain, proferring a mug which steamed deliciously.

'Well I'll be . . .' I burst out and stopped. 'Sorry, Sir, and thank you very much.'

'Got a little Silex coffee maker plugged into an auxiliary circuit down aft there,' he said proudly. 'Adapted to soup-making. I've had nothing since breakfast.' I sipped gratefully.

The Wardroom was tense when I went down for a makeshift meal.

'We keep watching these lights,' said Jake Norwell. 'If they begin to dim we know the generator's failing, then the lights will go, and the pumps will stop and then you know what'll happen.' I gazed hypnotically at the lights, my heart jumping as they dimmed, and far down we heard the diesels stutter and recover. We spent the whole night thus, going up on deck as we slowly approached Sheerness in the murky Thames estuary dawn.

Slowly we came to our anchor berth, listing dangerously. The anchor went down, the tugs fussed around us and the lighters with the electric pumps were secured alongside. There was no lack of willing hands to haul aboard the huge flexible pipes and to lower them down into the oil-slimy, waterfilled engine room. The powerful diesels in the lighters coughed, spluttered and began to roar, and the first gouts of dirty water from the engine room began to spew over the side. We heaved a collective sigh of relief and began to make the ship a living thing again.

After a few days, the list was corrected and we began the journey up the Thames to Harland and Wolff's Dry Dock at Albert Dock, Silvertown. We spent the first night of the long tow at Tilbury, tying up in the middle of an air-raid, one bomb of which landed on a pub near the landing stage, staggering us on the fo'c'sle as we tried to get ropes across, and shell fragments from the anti-aircraft guns pattered all around us. Finally we got a rope ashore, largely due to the guts of an elderly Thames waterman in his little boat, who carried on when all the others had fled.

The next morning, the procession continued, and in the afternoon we edged our way into the dry dock, thus gaining the doubtful distinction of being the first aircraft carrier to enter the London Docks since the war began. So began one of the most inactive periods of my naval career, as workmen swarmed over *Slinger* to bring her back into shape again. As the last of the water drained from the dry dock, we were scrambling down the slimy steps to get underneath the ship to see the damage. Two great holes had been punched in the bottom as if by a gigantic tin opener, while the rudder had been pushed upwards by a giant hand into the steelwork of the rounded stern, and the huge propeller was badly bent.

'We'll be here for months!' said the Chief Engineer. 'Plenty of leave for newly-married men, eh?' He winked knowingly at me.

There was leave alright, and courses to attend on Damage Control, the Western Approaches War Game, but D-Day in June 1944 passed us by, and I almost envied the soldiers crowding the transports in the Dock, waiting their turn for Normandy. From one of them a young Army officer approached me.

'Excuse me, Sir,' he asked, shyly, pointing at the medal ribbons on my jacket, 'I can see that you've been in some campaigns. What's it really like when you go into action. I suppose you were in this carrier when she was mined?' I nodded.

'I honestly can't tell you,' I replied slowly. 'You think of it, and then it happens, and you do what you've been trained to do . . . I pray, too!'

'Thank you, Sir', he murmured and offered his hand which I took.

'Good luck!' I muttered, and passed on.

One evening in June the air-raid sirens sounded and as Passive Defence Officer, or glorified Air Raid Warden, I took my position on the bridge, to be joined after a few moments by Capt Bingley. This was the period of the Germans 'Hit and Run' raids on London, employing the very fast Messerschmitt 210s. Our conversation was desultory until the barrage opened up and an aircraft streaked across the sky, flames pouring from its tail.

'They've got him alright!' said the Captain grimly, and then, as the aircraft crashed in a mighty explosion which lit up the area, he added, 'My God, the poor blighters!'

The next day we learned that what we had actually seen was the first VI, Pilotless Plane or Buzz Bomb sent over by the Germans to test its range. All German air activity that night had been halted but for the VI, and when the official communique announced that there had been 'some enemy air activity over London' they knew that the VI had arrived. So from June until October, we lived with the VI and its deadlier succcessor, the V2 rocket, described by one of the dockyard workers as like 'a bloody great telegraph pole'. The attacks slowed the work on the ship, and there was tragedy as one Buzz Bomb landed in the water near us, killing the Captain of a passing tug, and toppling cranes into the dock. Parts landed on *Slinger*'s deck, gouging the wooden flight deck deeply. On another occasion there was humour, as Graham Bence, the new Navigator and I walked down the Dock Road, and on hearing the bomb's engine cut out we began to run in the opposite direction. We were most surprised to see the Doctor and the Chaplain who had been ahead of us, running at us.

'Turn round, you fools!' gasped the Doc, 'something's wrong with the bomb – you're running with it!' Sure enough the bomb was overtaking us in its final glide, and we all fell in a heap behind the high dock wall as it exploded on some warehouses.

In October, everything was complete, my 27 20mms had doubled to 54, as we now had twin, power operated mountings with very accurate gyroscopic sights, the engines, rudder and hull were repaired and we set sail down the English Channel, now safe for shipping, and altered course at Lands End for the Clyde. Here we came under the aegis of the Flag Officer Carrier Training at Largs, and began our working-up period, with aircraft of all types flying on and off – Swordfish, Seafires, Grumman Avengers, Barracudas, Albacores – in fact anything and everything that wanted to land on us.

Some of the pilots were hardened veterans, others were landing for the first time on a carrier, and so we had crashes of all kinds – into the barrier, into the sea, and one even managed to get under the round-down at the stern and crash on one of my 5-inch guns! We became used to the danger of fuelling and de-fuelling, but we were never contemptuous, and I think we all breathed easier when the loudspeakers announced, 'Fuelling complete, carry on smoking!'

An Officer of the Watch on a carrier is no sinecure, because not only has a course to be kept and a position maintained, but at any moment, aircraft may fly on or fly off. This means that a quick calculation of the true wind must be made and the ship brought into the wind so that it is 5° on the port bow. As all piston-engined aircraft by reason of the propellers' rotation, tend to swing to port, the wind at this slight angle of 5° to the centre line, counteracts the swing. It is also for this reason that carrier bridges are always on the starboard or safer side. The position of the bridge too, is awkward when manoeuvring and you have to allow for the fact that the bow is actually to port of you.

After flying on or off, course has to be resumed, and after a few weeks of this, day and night, I could navigate my way around the Firth almost blindfold. After this type of experience and my former work in *Scylla* in an entirely different world of high-speed manoeuvres with destroyers, Capt Barry Moore, who had succeeded Capt Bingley, gave me my full Naval Watch-Keeping Certificate which I had been chasing for over two years. At last I was a full Lieutenant with none of the slight stigma of 'Acting Lieutenant'. The time in the Clyde was pleasant also for the fact that Charlotte was now working in Troon, and we were able to see a lot of each other.

All good things come to an end and in the New Year of 1945 we set sail for the Far East in company with the escort carrier *Speaker* and a half flotilla of the new V class destroyers. Our squadron, Number 1845 was now completely settled in, with their dark-blue, gull-winged American Chance Corsair fighters, great bulky aircraft but fast and superbly flown by the American trained British pilots. It was a new experience to live with these 'birdmen' whose attitudes were entirely different from ours, besides being much younger and brasher than our now rather elderly selves. However, a rapport was soon established and I began to make friends among the pilots, though with one I fell from grace, for after having sat in his Corsair in an unsympathetic mood, he had a barrier crash which he jokingly blamed on me for having jinxed his aircraft!

After leaving Malta it was new ground for me, and Cdr Roberts, or Big Willie, as he was secretly called, became my tutor. At Alexandria and in the Suez Canal he was the bane of the lives of every Arab who came aboard, treating them imperiously, and rapaciously. From one seller of leather articles he extorted his best and highest-priced article, an ornate blotter adorned with all the sights of Egypt, with the words:

'This my baksheesh for letting you sell aboard my ship!' Ignoring the pleas and imprecations of the Arab, he turned to me. 'That's how you do it Taff! This'll come in useful for my old aunt in Mannamead.' It was he who urged me always to read the testimonials tendered to us by Arabs with the words:

'Thees very good pipper from beeg naval officers, effendi. You read, eh?' On the paper would be written . . .

'I would not trust this black bastard farther than I could throw the Pyramids. Signed. Nonsuch, Lt Cdr.'

At Ismailia, the Commander joined me on the fo'c'sle and pointed to a curved embankment at the canal side.

'Wonder if old Abdul's still about?' he mused.

'Who's Abdul?' I asked.

'Feller who stands there, dancing like a Fuzzy Wuzzy waving his John Thomas about at passing ships. Blokes throw him money!' He sniffed. 'By God, there he is!' he shouted suddenly, pointing to a half-naked figure who was indeed capering around and as the ship drew nearer it was evident that he was displaying his distinguishing sex organ at us! 'What d'you think of that one, eh?' leered Big Willie as we drew abreast. 'These Arabs never have any toys to play with when they're young' he said, judiciously.

The Red Sea was like a furnace, with the thermometer in the 120s, and Aden was no better, though I always remember one afternoon, so hot that the tar was bubbling in the wooden deck seams, the ship was silent, and then I heard a plaintive eastern air played by a Somali, floating past in a dug-out canoe.

As we turned south-eastwards after passing Socotra we came across an Arab ocean-going dhow, the craft of the people who had taught us astral navigation, mathematical notation and algebra. The heat was less now as we sailed towards Colombo where we spent a few days, before continuing to Fremantle. Here we took on oil fuel after the long leg and then crossed the Great Australian Bight, one of the roughest sea passages in the Southern Hemisphere, where the winds from the Antarctic meet the Australian landmass and begin to pile up in huge rollers in which the albatrosses ceaselessly plane. One of our pilots spent all his time, flat on his stomach at the end of the flight deck, studying the aerodynamics of the flight of these huge birds, who could control movement by the flick of a wing-tip feather.

We came through Sydney Heads leading to the wonderful harbour on a Sunday morning in early February. The harbour was dotted with yachts and speedboats, and as we stood on the fo'c'sle ready to come to anchor, a speedboat with a ravishing cargo of Australian bathing beauties, shot across our bows and we leaned over, mouths agape, not because of the manoeuvre, but on account of the cargo!

'Can't you Pommies smile?' shouted up one of the sirens, breaking the spell cast on us by wartime restriction. There was a rush to the guardrails, and a chorus of wolf whistles which I reluctantly had to quell!

As one of the first units of the newly-formed British Pacific Fleet to arrive in Sydney we were given a huge welcome, as no British naval ships had visited Sydney for years. We lived widely on the huge range of fruit so easily available – peaches, nectarines, guavas, paw-paws, passion-fruit, melons, and a horrible looking thing called *monsteria deliciosa* with a heavenly taste. There were visits to the local vineyards, farms, and homes and I was beginning to enjoy the Pacific 'war'.

We were then ordered northward to the Admiralty Islands, 2° south of the equator where the American Navy had an important base at Lorengau. The navigation through the Coral Sea, through the Jomard Passage in the D'Entrecasteaux Islands, and then along the north-east coast of New Guinea, past New Britain and New Ireland, was most interesting. Not only was the scenery of great interest, with coral atolls, waving palms and huge mountains, but we were passing through areas where the Japanese were still in nominal control, but totally unable to mount any offensive action against us because of the overwhelming American mastery of the air. We passed Rabaul, a sizeable town in New Britain garrisoned by the Japanese, with the utmost contempt and headed north towards the Admiralties.

These islands had only been recently conquered, and it was said that the Japs used to slip into the film shows in the garrison cinema and melt back into the jungle when the film was over! The charts of the area were interesting, in that so many of the prominent points had German names; the great lagoon of Manus was called Seeadler (Sea Eagle) harbour, these being relics of the time before 1914 when these islands were part of Germany's Pacific possessions. In one part of the island which had only been first crossed in 1927, there was still a German Lutheran Mission House.

On Ponam Atoll we were re-united with Capt Bingley who was in command of the Mobile Naval Air Base there, which he had cleverly named after himself as *HMS Nabbaron* that is Naval Air Base Baron. Unfortunately he had contracted some tropical skin disease while making a garden around his hut. This was typical of the discomforts of the area which seethed with microbes of the fungoid type, besides those of malaria and bush typhus, and we all began to look like Chinamen, caused by taking Mepacrine, the yellow substitute for quinine which tints the skin yellow. Excessive perspiration caused heavy losses of salt, so we had to take salt tablets at each meal.

In January the Americans had invaded the Philippines and the British Pacific Fleet, with all its carriers, both the large Fleet carriers and the

Thirtieth Aircraft Carrier Squadron to which the escort carriers belonged set course for Leyte Gulf.

The new Japanese weapon current at this time was the Kamikaze (Divine Wind) Suicide bomber, aero fighter crammed with bombs, piloted by a Japanese in full ceremonial kimono and sash, who aimed himself at an aircraft carrier as a human bomb. American aircraft carriers had suffered badly from these attacks, as they had light wooden unarmoured decks like *Slinger*, and the bombers exploded into the hangars below causing great damage. The British carriers with their armoured flight decks suffered lightly. While operating with the Fleet, a Kamikaze made straight for the carrier *Indomitable*. There was a huge flash of flame and smoke as it hit the armoured deck, and the *Indom* was visibly shaken, and suffered a number of casualties, but within 40 minutes the fires had been put out and she was operational again.

Kamikazes were the only dangers we had to face, as the Japanese Navy rarely made any appearances, and the Japanese Air Force, apart from the Kamikazes was non-existent. The planes of 1845 Squadron ranged far and wide as the Philippines was gradually conquered, and Manila fell to the Americans in March.

A new word had come into use in the Navy-Logistics and Logistic Supply, and our first visit to the Fleet Train was an ample illustration. We made a rendezvous off the Philippines with the Fleet Train, a large assemblage of ships of all kinds – oil-tankers, petrol tankers, refrigerated meat ships, refrigerated vegetable and fruit ships, repair vessels with spare parts, even with spare aircraft. It was like a huge sea-going hypermarket and we made the rounds, oiling astern from one tanker for our engines, and from another for high octane petrol for the Corsairs, while the motor cutter journeyed a-marketing for food, vegetables, mail, and copies of the Fleet Newspaper *Pacific Post*.

Plans were actually being made for a floating Brewery Ship to join the Fleet Train, but they never materialised, and we had to wait for our leave and the pleasures of the strong Australian beer ashore! This system enabled us to keep at sea for two months without touching land, and after this period had elapsed there was a month's leave. At this time we were pioneering oiling at sea, transference of supplies at sea, etc – skills which are now a normal part of naval life, but which grew out of the Pacific War where ports with facilities were few and far between.

One afternoon I took over the Watch on the bridge and noted that at 1430 we would increase speed to 72 revolutions, which was about 20 knots. At the appointed time, I spoke down the voice-pipe.

'72 revolutions'. The order was repeated and the ship began to surge forward and then as full speed was reached the whole structure began to shake like a man with malaria. Everywhere heads looked up from the flight deck and the engine room telephone began to ring.

'Permission to reduce speed,' gasped the Engineer Officer of the Watch, 'the engines look as if they're going to take off through the deck!'

'Six-oh revolutions' I ordered, reverting to the former speed. The Captain appeared at my side.

'What in God's name is happening?' he demanded, and I gave a quick explanation, noting that meanwhile the tremors had subsided. There were urgent conversations between the Captain and the Chief Engineer, and it was decided to slowly come up to maximum speed again with the same result – the ship began to shake from stem to stern. It was evident from their conversation that the trouble seemed to be coming from the main reduction gearing of the turbine, a huge gear wheel, which engaged in a smaller pinion from the turbine, thus reducing the high revolutions of the turbine rotors.

Down in the radio offices, the messages began to go out, and the VHF speaker on the bridge was full of instructions from the Commander-in-Chief, the gist of which was that we must detach ourselves and make for the newly opened Cairncross Dry Dock in Brisbane. So back through the Islands we crawled at 12 knots, and entered the Dry Dock – another unfortunate 'First' – the first carrier ever to use it, just as we had been the first carrier in London. There certainly seemed to be a jinx on *Slinger*. Now we were nothing, for 1845 Squadron had left us, being divided up amongst the carriers of the Fleet who needed replacements.

The huge gear wheel was taken out through the hangar deck and it was found that many teeth had been stripped from it, but none the whole width of the wheel, so the broken pieces were lathed off, leaving a complete set all around the circumference but only about two-thirds of their original width. While this was going on, we spent many pleasant days at the cattle station of Wyaralong, near Beaudesert as guests of the Philp family, one of the original pioneering families of Australia.

Here were horses to ride, billies to be boiled alongside billabongs under the blazing Southern Cross at night, other stations to be visited though as next-door neighbours they could be anything up to 50 miles away. Graham Bence, Bud Abbott and I fell in love with Australian outback life, and had we not been married it would not have been difficult to have fallen in love with any of the three charming Philp daughters, Barbara, May and Heather, who were always ready to help the poor old Pommies to adjust to their way of life.

Rather too soon *Slinger* was ready, and we were towed out of Dry Dock after what the *Brisbane Courier Mail* called a painting operation! It was the first time I had ever heard of an RN ship being painted by others – it was generally a Do-It-Yourself operation – but it was a good security cover. As the engineers had prescribed a period of convalescence for the engines, or perhaps even, a permanent disablement, we could now only do 12 knots. We therefore became a Ferry Carrier, transporting aircraft from Australia to the Forward Areas as needed.

Capt Moore left for another appointment suited to his senior rank, and Cdr JG Hopkins RN, an ex-submariner was appointed our new Captain. As my life had been dogged by too many Christian names, and too many nicknames, and as a reader of Damon Runyon's short stories, abounding in memorable names, I christened him Black Jack, from his saturnine looks, just as I had bestowed Big Willie with his nickname! On introducing him to the Philp girls, one of them brightly exclaimed:

'Ah you must be the one they call Black Jack!'

Big Willie too, left us, to our great regret, and was given a hilarious send-off party. *Slinger* was now, with the exception of the Captain a completely RNVR ship in the Executive Department, a fact of which we were rather proud.

'We might as well be in the bloody Merchant Navy!' I moaned in the Wardroom.

'Anything for a quiet life,' said a philosopher, 'so shut up and come and help us on the *Times* crossword that's just come in.'

During July and August we tramped up and down between Sydney and the Philippines, every inch of the Hangar and Flight Deck crammed with aircraft of every sort, our largest cargo being 120, because the build-up was beginning for the last operation – the Invasion of Japan itself, now that Okinawa had been taken.

In Manila Harbour when we entered it, past the famous Corregidor Island and the Bataan Peninsula where the Americans had fought in 1941, there hardly seemed a berth available for us. A vast armada had been assembled there for the invasion of 1,200 ships.

On 6 August we were in an Officers' Club in Manus when the news of the Hiroshima bomb came over the radio, to be greeted with an awed silence.

'The war'll be over soon,' exulted one of our American friends, 'and you Limeys can go back home!'

I made a quick calculation on my birthday.

'My birthday's on the 13th, and I'm going to either postpone it or bring it forward to celebrate the end of the war. I'm going to get as drunk as a bloody handcart!' I proposed.

The Nagasaki bomb was dropped, but 13 August did not bring peace, but the next day did, and I went on a bender which started after lunch and continued into the early hours of the next morning, with frequent changes of clothes and shower baths in the humidity of the Wardroom which was about 98 per cent.

'What with the alcohol and the humidity' I remember declaiming. 'I'm afraid to light a fag in case I either blow myself up from the fumes, or cause a tropical rainstorm from the humidity!'

Shortly after VJ Day we sailed south to Sydney to load food supplies for Hong Kong and it was strange, after wartime security, to be able to know our destination openly without having recourse to friends in the Cypher Office or remarks dropped by the Captain. It was a quick turn around in Sydney as we loaded with food supplies of every kind, from staples such as rice and sugar to luxuries like tinned peaches. Such a cargo was a great temptation and there was a certain amount of pilfering on which we clamped down very severely, and everything was recovered from the hiding places, a favourite one being the Ready Use ammunition lockers in the catwalks.

We were one of the first ships into Hong Kong and my ambition to see China was fulfilled. The Japanese had left everything in a dreadful state. The Victoria barracks drains had been clogged for months, the Peninsular Hotel, then the largest hotel in the East had been gutted of European furniture in the rooms, and replaced with a sleeping platform and a vase in each. Unopened crates of crane parts from Stothert and Pitt, Bath, dated 1941 stood on Holt's Wharf Kowloon, and there was very little sign of what the Japanese had called their South East Asia Co-Prosperity Sphere!

The Chinese however soon appeared with silk and other goods which they had stored away and a brisk barter began. The standard unit was a packet of 20 cigarettes, for which for instance, Sze Zoo, 'Cloths Mended Woman' as her visiting card proclaimed, repaired the cuffs of my uniform trousers, lining them inside with soft leather against further chafing.

Japanese prisoners-of-war provided an abundant labour force when we began unloading, and I was struck by their intelligence. Our prisoners were Japanese Navy men, and before attempting a task they always requested time for a small tactics meeting to appraise the method. Having decided upon it they would ask for various tools, blocks and tackles, and in no time the job was done. Once again however, the roller paths that Big Willie and I had pinched were a great boon.

On the jetty there were always crowds of most attractive Chinese children, waiting to snatch up the merest grains of rice falling from a split sack, and I know that many a surreptitious cut was made by a sympathetic sailor in a sugar or flour sack. Then the children would lose all their innocent appeal as they fought like tigers to scoop up the sugar in their little cups. Sampans haunted the ship's side, waiting for the galley refuse to be tipped overboard. Potato and other vegetable peelings were eagerly snatched up, re-peeled carefully, and dropped into the cauldron constantly bubbling over the charcoal fire in the bottom of the sampan.

One morning I saw a Chinaman edging towards a stale loaf on top of the galley refuse bin. Before he could reach it a cook tipped a potful of tea-leaves over it, but in his hunger the Chinaman was not deterred. He snatched it up, stuffing the soggy mass into his mouth in great pieces. Ashore, hungry people, made raids on the go-downs stored with our food, and in the nights machine-guns chattered fitfully to keep off looters.

We managed to acquire a Ford Prefect car, and in it we made trips into the New Territories on the Kowloon side, penetrating into what is now Communist China, but in those days no-one cared. The ricefields, the pretty tile-roofed villages and the constant procession of folk along the road never ceased to intrigue me, and we often shared our picnic meals with anyone brave enough to approach the White Devils!

During our visit the weather became more and more humid and little whirlwinds would appear in open spaces near the ship, composed of litter and leaves, rising to a height of 20 feet or more. There was talk of a typhoon and this was confirmed when the harbour began to empty of junks and sampans as they made for 'Typhoon Bay' their traditional refuge. Shortly after, the whole of the British Fleet in Hong Kong weighed anchor and sailed into the China Sea to ride out the typhoon which developed into one of the most violent of recent times, devastating Okinawa Island already heavily damaged in the hard-fought Okinawa Campaign which had only just finished.

The wave heights and violent winds were reminiscent of the North Cape, though not as cold, but the night was awe-inspiring, with continuous lightning all around the horizon. Somewhere in the typhoon centre, to the north of us, an American destroyer was fighting for her life, as she fought her way out of the deadly centre, a terrifying ship-swallowing maw, in which very few ships survive. By a miracle she managed it and limped into harbour with her decks stripped almost level.

After a couple of days, the typhoon moved far enough away from us to return to Hong Kong and begin the embarkation of the civilian prisoners of war from the Stanley Road Prison Camp. They were a very mixed lot of civil servants, shipping company officials, servicemen and their wives and families, and a large number of Eurasians. All these people had spent their lives out East plus their children who had been born in Hong Kong, such as young Butch, a five-year-old boy who had the run of the ship.

We also took aboard three prisoners who had been accused by their fellow prisoners of collaborating with the Japanese – Maj Boon, the Camp Commandant, an elderly Army Lieutenant and a Sergeant. Feeling against them was so high that I had to arrange a guard along both sides of the flight deck when they were exercised, to keep the other ex-prisoners back, and to stop our prisoners from making a dash for the side and ending it all. For the first two days of our voyage to Sydney exercise times saw big crowds on the flight deck, but as the days passed the crowds dwindled to nothing.

158

'D'you know, Sir?' said a young Eurasian boy to me, one morning, 'now that we're free, things are so different. Perhaps Maj Boon wasn't such a bad chap after all. I'm beginning to think he shouldn't be a prisoner at all!'

'Well, it was you people who denounced him,' I snapped. 'If you feel like that, you people ought to do something about it, and support him at his trial.'

From this time I began to study Maj Boon. He was tall, bespectacled, and as thin as any person from Belsen. He was suffering from Beri-beri and almost too weak to walk, and I felt a growing sympathy for him. On our arrival at Sydney he was to be transhipped to the cruiser *Devonshire* to be taken home for trial, and at the time I had little chance to talk to him.

During the voyage Cdr Hopkins asked various officers with specialised knowledge of theatres of war to give the ex-prisoners short talks to bring them up to date with the four years of war they had missed. So forewarned by Graham Bence about emerging class distinctions, I gave my lecture and afterwards when the group broke up and I was asked to stay for a drink, I found, as had Graham, that there was such a division among the people, that the gin and whisky belonged to the upper classes and the softer liquour went to the rankers and the Eurasians. Ironically, the complete stock of liquour had been donated by the members of the Wardroom Mess.

I was also carrying under my care, various documents about the Camp for Naval Intelligence, the most interesting being a large number of photographs of the Japanese camp personnel, taken by an Indian photographer, with a useful dossier scribbled on the back of each. This Indian had had the forethought to print an extra copy of each photograph which he had taken for the Japs, and then hidden them away against the day of our victory!

During the voyage we produced a pantomime, as Christmas was drawing near, in which all the ex-prisoners took part, and for which purpose we hauled the Wardroom piano into the hangar. During some rough weather this instrument broke loose and had to be chased all over the hangar, to a tinkling of notes or a crash of disordant chords. I have since seen this ploy used in film cartoons, but I and some others can claim to have had the actual physical experience of a runaway piano. In particular my friend, Lt Bob Whiting RANVR, a cool customer, was trapped by the foot by this rabid instrument, but only reacted mildly, saying very politely:

'Would some of you gentlemen kindly remove this piano from off my foot?'

News of *Slinger*'s impending arrival had been broadcast over the Australian radio, so that when we came alongside the wharf at Pyrmont, in

159

Sydney Docks, there was a great crowd of joyful relatives awaiting the return of their loved ones, newspaper reporters, cameramen and radio commentators. We stood aside to watch these personal and moving scenes. There was also a lonely Australian soldier who stood aside, waiting for his wife to arrive. After a couple of hours he walked sadly away and an hour or so later his wife arrived in a flashy American car, elegantly dressed and arrogant.

'Where is my husband?' she demanded of me.

'He waited for you for nearly two hours, madam,' I replied. 'Then about an hour ago he decided to go home. He was the last to go.'

'Damn,' she spat. 'He would arrive at an inconvenient time. I was at a party!'

'Yes,' I said shortly. 'Now if you'll please excuse me.' I walked away with an urgent desire to spit.

Through the Australian summer's end we worked on various tasks, one of which was to take a nondescript cargo of scrap aircraft to Brisbane, and then sailed north to Manus for what was to be our last voyage in the Pacific. We lay off the atoll of Ponam, a long natural airstrip fringed with palms, and began to load aboard the elements of Capt Bingley's command, the Mobile Naval Airbase, *HMS Nabbaron*.

This consisted of a wide variety of transport vehicles equipped as electric generators, radio offices, air control vehicles – in fact everything that an airbase would need, mounted on motor vehicles and trailers. We worked with a will, because there was only one destination possible for all this equipment and that was the United Kingdom.

During this time there were amazing scenes of destruction of war material in Manus where the Americans were ditching barge loads of aircraft into the Pacific, some still in their crates. One of these crates we took aboard was the personal property of a naval officer who had exchanged it with the Americans for a case of Scotch! It was a complete Stinson Reliant light reconnaissance aircraft, rather like the Auster, its British counterpart.

We arrived in Sydney in early November and began taking on passengers, and we heard that there was great competition ashore to secure a place in *Slinger* which we felt spoke well of our reputation. Among our passengers was once again Maj Boon, who had been taken seriously ill a few days after I had taken him over to *Devonshire* so he had been sent ashore to hospital.

I had taken him over to *Devonshire* in our motor cutter with two sailors armed with American policeman's night-sticks, and I had a US Navy Colt automatic, unobtrusively in the pocket of my white shorts. On *Devonshire's* quarterdeck, there was a Marine guard with rifles awaiting him.

'You're running a risk, aren't you?' asked the Executive Officer.

160

'You're not even armed!' I patted my pocket.

'Look down in the boat, please, Sir?' I asked. 'He's a very sick man, and 'he'll give no trouble to anyone.' The Commander took a quick understanding look at the frail bespectacled figure, huddled in the stern sheets.

'Fall out the Marine Guard', he ordered.

'Thank you very much, Sir', I said and called down to the sailors: 'Help Maj Boon up the gangway, please.'

Now he was with us again, still very thin and pale, in his worn-out uniform, and his sole possessions in a battered fibre suitcase together with a small portable typewriter.

At eleven o'clock on Saturday morning, 10 November 1945, we slipped our moorings at Great Sirius Cove, Sydney, and set course for Sydney Heads and home, our long white commissioning pendant trailing from the masthead to the end of the flight deck, its length indicating how long we had been in commission.

We had lobbied the Captain to allow us to sail northward along the Barrier Reef, then across the Timor Sea to Singapore and thence to Colombo, confident as we were in our radar, and our navigational experience in the Pacific Islands, but the Commander-in-Chief counselled caution, so we sailed south from Sydney Heads, setting our course for Fremantle and then north-west to Colombo, Suez and home!

As we left, the radio chattered its signals to us with an appreciative one from the Commodore of the Thirtieth Aircraft Carrier Squadron which read:

'*Slinger*'s readiness to perform cheerfully and efficiently the many and varied tasks thrust upon her has made her a most valuable member of the 30th AC and she will be missed on her departure. I wish you all good luck and peace and prosperity in the future and a well-deserved rest.'

This was followed by one from Admiral Sir Bruce Fraser, the Commander-in-Chief, British Pacific Fleet:

'I wish you all a good trip home.'

We even made the front page of the *Sunday Times* with a short paragraph, headed: 'Naval Christmas Leave'.

'The British Escort Carrier *HMS Slinger* left Sydney yesterday for England where she is due to arrive in mid-December in time to give most of her crew and her 600 naval "passengers" leave for Christmas. The passengers include the entire personnel of the base established on Ponam Island in the Admiralty Group.'

'There you are!' I said, trying to vindicate a former statement. 'We're a merchant navy passenger liner – we've even got women aboard!' This was a reference to the nursing personnel we were carrying home, but by Suez and Port Said we had increased our female passengers by the addition of some Wren officers.

I had always thought that liner officers had a wonderful time, wining, dining and dancing with the gorgeous female passengers, but as we only had three watchkeeping officers, with irregular mealtimes we saw little of our passengers, though I had met some of them in past years, one, even in *Scylla*, and it was warming to chat with old shipmates again. There was no lack of volunteers to help us on the bridge, but none of them had watchkeeping certificates and so they could only assist in the lowliest of capacities. I would only take on an assistant if he kept watch with me in fair weather or foul and this cut the volunteers down! Some however were very faithful and as we approached Ceylon one of them asked for instructions.

'I want you to look dead ahead for a mountain in Ceylon called Westminster Abbey on the chart. It's shaped rather like the Abbey with a tower and nave. You should see it in about half an hour, so keep looking.'

'The confidence of you fellows amazes me' he laughed. 'After 6,000 miles, you expect this mountain to be up ahead there.'

'Definitely,' I smiled. Half an hour later he gave an exclamation.

'My God,' he whispered, 'you're right. There is a mountain up ahead, like that. Will you check it?' I checked, nodded and chuckled.

'That's navigation,' I boasted. 'Our Graham Bence's the best in the game!'

Graham Bence and I had a habit of singing to ourselves while on watch to pass the time away. He reckoned, as a former amateur operatic enthusiast that a complete sing-through of *Lilac Domino* would last a four hour watch. My repertoire was more varied and I sang anything that came to mind. As I was carolling merrily one evening, there was a passenger visiting the bridge.

'I see that you are a watch-singer too?' he said, and I nodded in mid-song.

'Good habit . . . passes the time . . . yes, Forebridge here . . . thank you.'

'I was singing too, on the bridge of the *Curacoa* when the *Queen Mary* went over the top of her,' he said sadly.

'Good God!' I said wonderingly, 'you're one of the survivors.'

We dropped anchor in Gibraltar Roads and a very short leave was given. The Captain and Navigator went ashore, leaving Bob Meyer, now the First Lieutenant, Jake Norwell and myself as the only watchkeepers aboard. Having been to Gibraltar so many times we were cynics who preferred a couple of gins and a quiet lunch before we sailed in the late afternoon.

'The Portsmouth girls will be hauling on the tow rope as soon as we get through the Straits, and it'll be England, Home and Beauty', I remarked,

162

smacking my lips over the first gin since Port Said, for we never drank at sea. Sub-Lt Cox dashed urgently into the Wardroom.

'Number One,' he said to Bob Meyer, 'the wind's getting up to gale force and I think she's beginning to drag.' We left the Wardroom as we were and dashed for the bridge. I had had the experience of *Scylla* dragging under me on two occasions, once when a catabatic wind hit us in Seydisfiord and I knew the drill. I dashed for the gyro compass and took a bearing. I gave a moan of anguish as I saw the bearing alter.

'She's dragging alright', I shouted to Bob. 'And if we don't look lively we're going to crash stern on to the North Mole!' Number One had alerted the Engine Room, and he spoke into the tannoy microphone.

'Duty Watch muster on the fo'c'sle at the double, together with any members of the Cable Party . . . the ship is dragging her anchor.'

'Taff,' said Number One, but I was already halfway down the bridge ladder heading for the fo'c'sle. There was a mixed bag of talent awaiting me, even including Fleet Air Arm personnel.

'Right,' I snapped, 'if you lads want to see England soon, get that bloody anchor up, or we're going to crash into the North Mole. And you, lad, lean over the side and watch those bubbles. They're coming towards the bows now because we're drifting astern. When you see them begin to go aft, then that means the engines are beginning to push us forward. Heave away as fast as you can, Chief.'

They were the best Cable Party I ever had, working like maniacs to save the ship running aground, seeing England slip from their grasp after all the thousands of miles, if we hit the Mole. I held my breath staring aft, the great random blocks of concrete which guarded the Mole coming so close I could almost see the mussels and winkles on their encrusted surfaces, while the links of the cable clanked agonisingly slowly on to the deck as they came inboard. I think we all prayed hard.

'Anchor's aweigh!' shouted the Chief, and I breathed a little lighter.

'Bubbles have changed direction,' bawled my watcher. 'They're drawing aft.'

'Now come on Old Lady,' I invoked the ship, 'let's see what you can do.'

'Bubbles are going much faster now.' I looked at the random blocks and they seemed just a little farther away.

'I think we're going to do it', I said cautiously and then the ship lunged forward as she overcame the inertia of her weight and a little wavelet appeared at the bows, growing stronger and frothier every second, until we had an appreciable bow wave. 'Carry on here, Chief and stow the anchor. We'll have to ride out this storm in the open sea, so I'm going back to the bridge.'

On the bridge, Bob Meyer and Jake Norwell were setting course for the open seas of the Western Mediterranean. We passed the signal station at Europa Point, our signal lamp chattering our intentions, feeling rather proud of ourselves – a Lieutenant Commander and two Lieutenants of the RNVR taking a 12,000 ton aircraft carrier out to sea! In the Inner Harbour we could see that there was chaos as a huge floating crane broke her moorings and went crashing into the troopship *Duchess of Bedford* moored at the North Mole.

'I say, Bob,' I laughed as we pored over charts on the bridge, 'I wish I could see old Black Jack now, I bet he's cursing and blinding something awful!' We laughed like three naughty schoolboys who had pinched an aircraft carrier.

The weather moderated somewhat and at nine o'clock that wild December evening we approached Gibraltar Roads again, hungry and wet from our long hours on the bridge and my scratch Cable Party dropped anchor. Cdr Hopkins and the libertymen jumped aboard from the liberty boat.

'Thanks, gentlemen,' he said, 'you've done a wonderful job. Now let's get the hell out of here and home!'

December 1945 saw some of the worst weather at sea for years and we rolled through the Atlantic, the Bay of Biscay and plunged our way up-Channel to Portsmouth, where I saw the amazing sight of waves and spray going over the top of the Eddystone lighthouse.

Portsmouth was calm and sheltered and I saw few of the passengers disembark as I had to superintend the unloading of the vast amount of mail we were carrying for the Post Office as a Royal Mail ship. I stood morosely on a huge pile of mailbags in the hold, helping to load the slings.

'Signal for you, Sir', said a Signalman, leaning over the hatch coaming.

'Not interested,' I growled. 'Too busy. Call again.'

'I think you'll like this one, Sir' he chuckled. 'I'll drop it down.'

'Lt RFC Hughes,' it read, 'has been nominated for Block Release in Class B as a teacher. Request you report if officer is willing, and whether relief required.'

'Yippee!' I yelled, jumping up and down on someone's parcels. 'I've done my time. Let's get these parcels out of the way and I'll buy you all a drink.'

That evening we sailed down Spithead, past Saint Catherine's Point and I took over my last watch in the Royal Navy in a force ten Channel gale. During the course of the Watch, I sighted two large merchant ships, in some distress, flying the international signals, but they declined assistance and we bucketed onward. I felt that I was leaving the Royal Navy on a Wagnerian note, to say the least, and exulted in the fact I would have preferred it this way, rather than a calm and placid sea.

The weather was so rough that we were unable to pass through the breakwater at Plymouth and anchored instead in Cawsand Bay, on the afternoon of Christmas Eve.

'There's a tug coming alongside tomorrow morning with the Customs' said the Captain. 'So I'll give leave to natives only. The rest will have to wait until we go alongside in Plymouth.'

'Good show,' I said, 'that'll mean me.'

'How d'you work that out, Taff?' enquired Black Jack.

'We've got a house in Keyham, and my wife's there at this moment, Sir.' By a fortunate coincidence, Charlotte's uncle and aunt were in Pembrokeshire and had given her the key of their house when they heard she was bound for Plymouth to meet me.

'You downy bird,' laughed Black Jack. 'Alright, you'll take charge of the party and see you're back here on Boxing Day morning.'

I walked up to the little house in Keyham, feeling like Father Christmas and Ulysses rolled into one. I knocked on the door and Charlotte stood there with eyes wide and I took her into my arms.

'You'll be alright, then, Sir!' said the Master-at-Arms, with a smile and a wink, having guided me to the house. 'So I'll be off then.'

'Happy Christmas Charlotte,' I breathed as we held each other. 'By the way, I want you to try a pair of shoes on. They're Joyce of California, wedge-heeled but in American size.'

'Is that all you can think of?' she asked.

'Oh, yes, I've got gin, whisky, brandy and all the makings. The Customs men were full of goodwill. Let's have a drink, eh?'

'There's nothing much for Christmas dinner, only a little bit of beef.'

'Blow Christmas dinner. Here, take a look at all these nice undies I bought you in Sydney.' I whipped open my case like a travelling salesman. 'How about this evening jacket from Hong Kong? All the embroidery done by little girls in Canton who go blind when they're 14.'

'It says "Made in England" inside these undies!'

'Well I'm damned. Anyway they're the most travelled undies in Plymouth – 12,000 miles out, and I've brought them 12,000 miles back. Look, an ivory elephant from Ceylon, and here's some Chanel perfume and oceans of silk stockings. I say, let's have another drink.'

The weather was so rough that we didn't manage to board the ship until 27 December, just in time for me to take part in a short journey I had done many times in *Scylla* to sail up the harbour, past Drake's Island, up the Hamoaze and secure alongside at No 5 Jetty.

The following morning the Army sent their escort to take Maj Boon to Exeter Prison – ten tough-looking Commandos and a smart Commando Major, while for some reason HM Customs felt that his battered typewriter and worn fibre suitcase should be cleared through Customs. As his custodian I had a few explanatory words with the welcoming committee, and the Commandos withdrew to a discreet distance and the Customs Officer made a quick inspection, smiling wryly at the meagre contents of the case.

Maj Boon came up the hatchway into the Hangar, still thin and haggard, his travel-stained Army greatcoat hanging from his shoulders and his eyes sad behind the spectacles. I thought back to the many things he had told me during the voyage – of the rifle-butt blows in his back by the Jap guards, the arrogance and cruelty of the Camp Commandant, and the indignities he had borne as Senior British Officer at Stanley Road Camp. The formalities were soon over and then the Major turned to me:

'Goodbye, Sir,' he said with extreme respect. 'You have all been very kind and understanding and I hope that you will convey my thanks to the Captain.' Summoning his strength he came to attention and saluted smartly. I returned the salute and then held out my hand which he grasped weakly.

'The best of luck', I murmured, and then he was taken away. Months later he was tried on 11 capital charges and acquitted. The credibility of so many prisoner-of-war stories is always suspect, in my mind, after my experiences with Maj Boon.

The usual routine of a ship in Dock was a great anti-climax, and my heart was only half in my work as I waited for my demobilisation date. A few days later the Captain sent for me.

'Your date's come through,' he announced. 'You leave on 31st December. Think about what I'm going to say to you. Stay with me and take the old ship back to the States. You're just over 30 now and I'll get you your half-stripe to take across to the States. A Lieutenant Commander RNVR, Taff – with a full naval watchkeeping certificate. There are not many about you know . . . How about it?'

'Sorry, Sir,' I shook my head. 'I think I've done more than my share. I've been in ships solid since May 1942, over three and a half years, in Russia, in the Med, in the Atlantic, two invasions on the first day' – I was ticking them off on my fingers, 'and then the Pacific . . .'

'You should stay in the Navy,' he persisted. 'You love the Service.'

'Capt Moore wanted me to stay in too,' I replied, 'but I've got an awful feeling that I'd "put up a black" somewhere along the line and end up as a passed over two and a half. I do love this Service, but I think I'm a better wartime officer than a peacetime officer. Once again, thank you for your support, but the answer's "No" Sir.'

'You stubborn Welshman,' he laughed. 'We'll give you a good send off.'

The jeep stopped at the Dockyard gates while the Admiralty policeman looked it over.

'Morning, Sir', he greeted and then stared. 'Well if it isn't the Doc!'

'Cox'n of the *Scarborough*' I whistled, 'after all these years. When you come off duty come and have a drink. The aircraft carrier, right? Got to make some arrangements for my demob.'

'When you leaving?' he asked. 'Got any rabbits?' (Naval slang for presents etc).

'Cases of them', I confessed.

'Leave it to me and bring 'em out when I'm on duty. See you later, Doc.'

On the morning of the 31st Charlotte and I were alone on the platform at Plymouth North Road Station waiting for the train to South Wales, when there was a commotion at the ticket barrier, and a group of officers dashed towards us, Black Jack in the lead, with Bob Meyer, Jake Norwell, Graham Bence in the van along with others.

'Come to wish you goodbye and good luck, Taff and Charlotte', he said, and then to my amazement, he and the others saluted us smartly and I returned their compliment shyly, near to tears, and wishing perhaps that I should have taken his advice and stayed in the Royal Navy with these and other great-hearted men with whom I had served in all my ships.

I stood at the compartment window, as the train drew away, with them getting smaller in sight, but never dimming in my memory . . . and in my mind others joined the group from the past years.

> 'Here is my journey's end, here is my butt,
> And very sea-mark of my utmost sail'

Wartime seamen talk over day of drama

By Frank Fuller

Two men who took part in an unforgettable experience at sea during World War Two have met for the first time in Shropshire.

Mr Robert Hughes, of Whitchurch, a former mayor of the town and a retired headmaster, was the gunnery officer on the anti-aircraft cruiser HMS Scylla during the war.

At the end of 1942, when the cruiser was returning to Britain after the North African landings, she sank the German blockade-runner Rhakotis.

Several allied merchant seamen were prisoners on the German ship, including Mr John Edmead (75), of Longlands Lane, Market Drayton.

Yesterday when they met for the first time, they reminisced about the engagement in which the cruiser sank the 10,000-ton German ship with a torpedo.

Mr Edmead was a steward and writer on the Ellerman liner City of Cairo, which was sunk by a U-boat in the South Atlantic in November 1942.

Signal

He was in a lifeboat with 52 other people, three of them women, which drifted for about 40 days. Finally, just three of them — two men and a girl — were saved by the German ship. The girl soon died and Mr Edmead's male colleague was also to die.

Mr Hughes said they had received a signal from RAF Coastal Command that a German vessel was trying to slip into Bordeaux. But they realised that the German ship would probably have a U-boat escort.

The Scylla, with its anti-aircraft guns, opened fire on the Rhakotis.

"We hit the vessel with direct hits 54 times, but the shells from our guns were not heavy enough to sink her.

"At the time the sea was rough and," said Mr Hughes, "Scylla fired a torpedo, but it went under the German ship.

"The next one hit her fair and square, and up she went — and down she went."

Mr Hughes, of Meadow View Road, Whitchurch, describes the incident in his book Flagship to Murmansk, an account of his wartime experiences in the navy. The book has now been issued in a paperback edition and he handed an autographed copy to Mr Edmead.

Mr Edmead (left) and Mr Hughes meet at last.

Mr Edmead said that with the arrival of the Scylla and the start of the shelling, the German captain allowed the prisoners to go up on deck and into the lifeboats. Up to then they had been shut in a hold.

He joined a lifeboat with 17 German seamen and arrived at Corunna in northern Spain after five days. Eventually, after spending time in a Spanish jail, he was able to make his way to Gibraltar and then home.

"You had a prevailing wind and could have sailed for Bordeaux. We thought that you would be all right," said Mr Hughes, who added that the crew of the Scylla did not know then that allied seamen were prisoners on the German ship.

Accurate

"The Germans treated us well on the Rhakotis, but we were not treated well by the Spanish in the jail," said Mr Edmead.

Congratulating Mr Hughes on the Scylla's gunnery, Mr Edmead went on: "It was far too accurate to be comfortable."

"I never would have thought that I would ever meet anyone off the Rhakotis," said Mr Hughes.

"And I never thought that I would ever meet anyone off the Scylla," said Mr Edmead.

With that, they went on to talk about their other wartime experiences and promised that they would keep in touch with one another.